The 'Knowledge Age' is the one we are living in – one where increasingly rapid technological innovation and diffusion are occurring. Yet, as this book convincingly demonstrates from its accounts of the spread of a wide range of new technologies, we know surprisingly little about the social and human processes involved. Why have some spread so successfully while, for example, so many agricultural engineering innovations in the Third World have been lamentable failures? What are the consequences of top-down diffusion strategies? Are there downsides to leaving the whole process to the private sector, and in particular to giant hi-tech corporations like Microsoft or Monsanto? Should the prevailing orthodoxy that the public sector should not play a significant role be re-examined? Indeed, should we look again at the disadvantages of instant patents and corporate-controlled intellectual property rights? And if users are democratically involved in technological adaptation and adoption, will not the result often be both better technologies and their more rapid adoption?

These are some of the hugely important questions explored in this engrossing account of some of the disaster, and success, stories around technological development and diffusion. The author's examples come from both industrial and developing countries. He tells the story of widely divergent technologies – agricultural appliances, wind turbines, Green Revolution high-yielding seeds, the Linux computer operating system, and Local Economic Trading Systems. And from them he constructs a highly significant 'how to do it' guide to innovation management that runs counter to many of the top-down, 'big is good', 'private sector is best' assumptions of our age.

A book that is likely to change our thinking about technology diffusion.

ABOUT THE AUTHOR

Boru Douthwaite is an agricultural engineer educated at the University of Warwick and at Silsoe College in the UK, following which he took his doctorate in agriculture at the University of Reading. His first job was with the Department for International Development (DfID). He subsequently worked in a research capacity at the International Rice Research Institute (IRRI) in the Philippines. While there, he contributed the main intellectual and design input to a project which developed and fostered the adoption of a small-farm stripper harvester (two patents pending) aimed at meeting farmers' needs for appropriate labour-saving technology. In 1999 he moved to the International Institute of Tropical Agriculture (IITA) in Ibadan, Nigeria. He is the author of a considerable number of scholarly journal articles and papers.

ENABLING INNOVATION

A Practical Guide to Understanding
and Fostering Technological Change

Boru Douthwaite

ZED BOOKS
London & New York

IN ASSOCIATION WITH

CAMBIA
Canberra

Enabling Innovation was first published in 2002 by
Zed Books Ltd, 7 Cynthia Street, London N1 9JF, UK,
and Room 400, 175 Fifth Avenue, New York, NY 10010, USA,
in association with
CAMBIA (Center for the Application of Molecular Biology to International
Agriculture), GPO Box 3200, Canberra ACT 2601, Australia

Distributed in the USA exclusively by Palgrave, a division of St Martin's Press,
LLC, 175 Fifth Avenue, New York, NY 10010, USA

Designed and typeset in Monotype Garamond by Illuminati, Grosmont
Cover designed by Andrew Corbett
Cover photo: Cristina de Leon
Printed and bound in the United Kingdom by Biddles Ltd,
Guildford and King's Lynn

A catalogue record for this book is available from the British Library

Library of Congress Cataloging-in-Publication Data applied for

ISBN 1 85649 971 5 (Hb)
ISBN 1 85649 972 3 (Pb)

To Cristina and Cian,
Mary and Richard

Contents

List of figures, tables and boxes

Acknowledgements

Writing this book was fun, but I could never have finished it without the help of the many people who took the time and trouble to explain things to me, to supply information or to comment on drafts. I am profoundly grateful to everyone who helped. Most of their names are listed here, but a few have unfortunately been lost or forgotten.

I want particularly to thank Martin Gummert, who helped me develop many of the book's ideas during the period we worked together at IRRI, the International Rice Research Institute in the Philippines. Martin, together with Bengt Bohnstedt, then his line manager at the German agency GTZ, helped me successfully apply for GTZ funding to write this book. Thanks must also go to Ken Fischer, the former Deputy Director General at IRRI, for finding some money to co-fund the writing effort. The book would not have been possible without this financial support.

I must also thank my two Ph.D. supervisors at the University of Reading, Professor Dyno Keatinge and Dr Julian Park. I developed and honed many of the ideas in the book under their tutelage. In fact if this were a journal article rather than a book then Dyno and Julian would be co-authors as well as Martin, Ken and Bengt. Another name that would appear would be that of my father, Richard Douthwaite, who edited the book for me, helped make it more interesting to read, and was both a source of ideas and a wonderful sounding board. My wife Cristina de Leon's name would also appear.

She accompanied me on many of my surveying trips, videoed interviews, translated the ones in Tagalog, and, most importantly, contributed intellectually the ideas about experiential learning cycles that became the basis of learning selection. Together my wife and father helped make writing the book an enjoyable experience.

The other group of people who contributed significantly were the reviewers of all or part of the book. These were Janis Jiggins, Robert Molteno, Gelia Castillo, Per Dannemand Andersen, Paul Smulders, Jill Sefang, Richard Markham and Brigitte Courtois.

As the funding arrangements might suggest, this book was originally envisaged as an IRRI publication. When it was completed, however, it became apparent that what I had written about failed agricultural machinery programmes in Burma and the Philippines would be a considerable embarrassment to the Institute. Rather than suppress my views, however, IRRI generously agreed to waive its copyright claim on my text so that it could be published elsewhere. Frances McDonald, Dyno Keatinge, Cristina de Leon, Bob Booth, Lukas Brader, Robert Molteno, Carol Nottenburg and Bengt Bohnstedt all provided invaluable advice and moral support. In fact the book would never have been published in the way I had intended without the support of Robert Molteno, Zed Books and Anne Moorhead who began the collaboration. It is a pity that neither IRRI's nor GTZ's logo appears on the cover to reflect their investment in this book.

I carried out the research on the adoption of agricultural machinery while working at IRRI and in collaboration with the Philippine Rice Research Institute (PhilRice) and the University of Agriculture and Forestry (UAF) in Vietnam. The success of this collaboration depended on the goodwill and support of Mark Bell at IRRI, Nyugen Quang Loc and Phan Hieu Hien at UAF, and Eulito Bautista and Sergio Francisco at PhilRice. I spent a lot of time surveying in both countries. For this I relied on a number of people to drive, guide and translate for me. In Vietnam Vo Van Thua, Le Van Bahn and Phan Hieu Hien took me on a number of trips that meant days away from home. In the Philippines I was accompanied by Elmer Bautista, Zaldy Aldas, Sergio Francisco, Artimio Vasallo from PhilRice, Pat Borlagdan and Philip Cedillo from IRRI, and engineers Gomolo and Platon from the regional Department of Agriculture offices. Special thanks must go to the machine owners, manufacturers, dealers and other key people who selflessly gave their time for interview.

Those involved with the wind chapter are Flemming Trænæs, Peter Karnøe, Per Dannemand Andersen, Eize de Vries, Gerrit Jacobs, Paul Smulders, Lars Gunnersen and Maria Olofsdotter. People who helped with the LETS chapter were Michael Linton, Richard Kay, Jill Seyfang and Liz Shephard, while Richard Jefferson, Paul Keese, Christian Witt and Brigitte Courtois contributed to the seeds chapter. My grateful thanks to them all.

Foreword

Niels Röling

The word 'praxeology' might have its drawbacks. But, to my knowledge, there is no other word that so well conveys the idea that practitioners do what they do on the basis of theories, praxeologies; and that it is better to make those praxeologies explicit and discursive than to leave them implicit or tacit. To paraphrase John Maynard Keynes: when I meet someone who claims to be too practical to bother about theory, he is likely to be operating on the theories of yesteryear.

If there is one theatre of action that is afflicted by sclerosis in its praxeology, it is the management of innovation. In ministries, companies, organisation development consultancy firms, farmers' organisations, international and national agricultural research organisations, extension services and universities, professionals whose job it is to promote innovation tend to conspire in agreement that innovation occurs according to the three big theories of yesteryear, all of which were spawned in the post-Second World War Mid-West US Land Grant Universities:

1. *The Agricultural Treadmill* (Cochrane, 1958), according to which productivity-increasing or cost-cutting innovations allow early adopters to gain windfall profits, propel later adopters to innovate to prevent their incomes from falling, and eventually force the non-innovative, small, poor, sick and old out of business.
2. *The Diffusion of Innovations* model, the popular version of which says that an innovation diffuses as the result of adoption decisions

by individuals who differ in terms of innovativeness and other attributes (Rogers, 1995).

3. *Transfer of Technology* as the best strategy for enhancing innovation. This is best expressed in terms of what I understand to be the translation of the word 'extension' into Chinese: push and shove.

Thinking about innovation tends to be very non-innovative. Usually there are good reasons for sticking to the big three of yesteryear. Scientists like to see themselves as sources of innovation, research stations like to claim funds for developing cutting-edge innovations that are going to change the world, and the powerful farmers who control farmers' organisations love the agricultural treadmill. But these reasons do not make the big three of yesteryear relevant or true. Sometimes they are merely ideologies.

For someone like me, who has spent more years than he cares to admit on trying to argue other praxeologies, it is a pleasure indeed to read Boru Douthwaite's book. His refreshing approach focuses on the innovation process as a complex adaptive multi-agent system. Innovation emerges out of the adaptations that occur as different agents learn and select improvements. It is not the experts who generate knowledge and technology for others to use: users themselves improve upon promising ideas. Based on a compelling use of examples from agriculture, industry, economy and IT, the book argues that successful innovation, as a rule, is based on diversity, on opportunity grasping, and especially on mobilising creativity among people who are willing to run with a brilliant idea, even if it is still flawed and underdeveloped. The fact that it is underdeveloped is a boon, so long as the various agents in the system are invited to improve upon it.

The very fact that the examples come from such diverse areas as wind turbines, LETS, and the Linux operating system, as well as agricultural engineering, shows that this way of looking at the world of innovation is applicable beyond the immediate field of agricultural research which is the author's original area of expertise.

Different times and places call for new theories of innovation. What works in one situation and set of conditions does not in others. One wave of innovation spawns another that works on the basis of different principles. The Green Revolution in rice in Indonesia, with its emphasis on a single crop, uniform fertiliser recommendations and high use of pesticides, necessitated a new wave of innovation, Community IPM, based on a totally new dynamic. Instead of extension agents, backed up by local governments, pushing uniform in-kind loan packages to the ultimate users, IPM Farmer Field Schools are based on the principle that farmers are experts in managing their fields as agro-ecosystems. Their impact relies on farmers applying their creativity to capture and manage diversity, and on empowering farmers to organise and create their own opportunities.

In my own country, the Netherlands, the reliance on expertise for water quantity and quality control is rapidly giving way to the realisation that the new uncertainties caused by, for example, climate change and the country's slow submergence into the sea require a totally different approach that includes creating space for water and interactive management of intractable and complex institutional and equity problems. Selecting options as part of an ongoing process is at the core of good adaptive management.

These two examples show that Boru Douthwaite's message is one that addresses us all. The uncertainties with respect to issues with high stakes which we humans have created by becoming a major force of nature compel us to move away from puzzle-solving science and reliance on experts (Funtowicz and Ravetz, 1993), and towards a form of innovation management that utilises a multi-actor learn-and-select approach. I believe that Boru Douthwaite has developed the kind of brilliant incipient innovative praxeology that innovation managers will run with, learning and selecting as they go.

Wageningen University, 2001

I

Introduction
Why innovation approaches matter

In 1995 Colonel Khun Sa[1] had a serious problem. The military junta running Burma at the time, the feared State Law and Order Restoration Council (SLORC), had decided that, to boost production, the country's rice farmers should grow two crops of rice each year instead of one. There was no question about this. The junta didn't tolerate dissent and the farmers would be made to do what SLORC said.

There was a good reason why most Burmese rice farmers grew only one crop, however: growing two meant harvesting the second in the middle of the monsoon; without very fast harvesting and drying, the grain would go mouldy and be fit only for duck food. The traditional single crop meant that the grain could be dried in the field after the rainy season and that there was far less rush. SLORC realised this, of course, and had asked Colonel Khun Sa, who was director of the Agricultural Mechanisation Department (AMD), to come up with a rice harvester that could save the second crop by working in wet conditions.

Up until this point AMD had done very little work on harvesters, choosing, sensibly, to concentrate on mechanical threshers, which are cheaper and simpler to build in relation to the time and labour they save farmers. This is because, unlike harvesters, they work in one position and do not have to move around the field. Colonel Khun Sa knew, however, that the only rice harvester in widespread use, a mechanical reaper developed in China in the 1970s, would not be suitable for wet season operation because it could not work in fields where the ground was covered by water. He had to find an alternative quickly because the farmers were to plant the first wet season crop in May 1995. Hundreds of harvesters had therefore to be manufactured and in farmers' fields by that September.

By July 1995, when AMD's search for a suitable machine had become frantic, drawings of a rice harvester landed on the colonel's desk. These drawings were the fruit of five years of research and development carried out with a team[2] I had led at the International Rice Research Institute (IRRI) in the Philippines, and with help from local manufacturers and the Philippine Rice Research Institute (Phil Rice). IRRI, of course, is the organisation that helped spearhead the Green Revolution by introducing new, high-yielding rice varieties to South and Southeast Asia. These helped rice production there to rise by 120 per cent over thirty years.[3] Engineer Thet Way, to whom the Colonel had delegated the search, had seen my team's machine working at IRRI when he was there studying for an M.Sc.

The harvester my team had designed and built is known as a stripper-gatherer because, rather than cutting the rice so that it can be carried elsewhere for threshing to extract the grain, it moves through the field gathering the grain by stripping it from the standing stalks. Desperate for a solution, Thet Way and Khun Sa set about building one immediately from IRRI's drawings. Their construction time shattered all previous records and a machine was ready to test in just two weeks. When it seemed to work they videotaped it in action and the colonel showed the footage to the Minister of Agriculture and then to the whole of SLORC. Four weeks after the drawings arrived, and without anyone using the machine more than twice, SLORC decided to build two thousand units, one thousand of which were to be ready within three months.

This was a tough target. The stripper-gatherer is very simple as engine-powered harvesters go but complicated in comparison with the threshers and hand tractors that AMD had previously manufactured. In particular, its construction needed much more attention to detail. The harvesting end of the machine (see Figure 1.1) consists of a huge rubber-toothed comb mounted on a rotor. This spins through the crop, combing off the grain and some straw and throwing it into the collection container behind. When the container is full, two labourers swap it for an empty one and tip the contents onto a large mat at the edge of the field to be cleaned. As this

Figure 1.1 The stripper-gatherer (SG) harvester

exchange can take place up to a hundred times a day, the containers have to be made so that they slot into place easily, leaving no gaps where grain can leak out. Another detail to watch is that the machine is made strongly enough not to bend when it sinks – as it inevitably will – into a wallowing hole left by a water buffalo, and four strong men have to heave it out. However, if the harvester is too heavily made, its twin wheels will bog down in soft, muddy soil. Building a frame that is both light and strong requires good welding and the use of high-quality materials.

Neither I nor anyone else at IRRI knew about SLORC's decision to build the stripper-gatherer until August 1995 when Graeme Quick, a former head of the agricultural engineering division at IRRI, visited AMD and faxed me the news. I was really excited because, until then, only about a hundred stripper-gatherers had been built altogether and Burma promised an adoption rate and impact that would delight GTZ, the German government aid organisation which was funding our work. My excitement was tinged with misgivings, however, as Graeme had urged me to visit Burma as quickly as possible to help solve some quality and design problems he had spotted.

I flew to Rangoon as soon as I could get a visa and arrived to find that the order for two thousand machines had been divided equally between AMD and the Ministry of Heavy Industry (MHI). AMD had to have its thousand machines completed by 15 September and had turned Base Workshop 1, which normally repaired four-wheel tractors, over completely to their production. About a hundred workers, most of them tractor drivers and mechanics rather than welders or machinists, were rushing to build a quota of twelve machines a day. They were already behind schedule: by 15 September only fifteen machines had been sent out to the government-run tractor stations which were to hire them out to farmers at a highly subsidised rate, just as they did with tractors for land preparation.

Graeme's warnings about quality did not prepare me for what I found when I inspected forty machines waiting for despatch. None would work. The list of faults was long but among the highlights were things like:

- a critical torsion shaft had been made from mild-steel pipe, which would immediately bend in operation;
- the removable collection containers did not fit, and were not locked in place;
- many of the rotating shafts were not straight, and the 'V'-belt pulleys were not centred properly;
- most of the stripper rotors were badly out of balance; this meant that the machine would quickly vibrate itself to pieces;
- as the 'V'-belt drives could not be tightened properly, the belts would slip, overheat and catch fire.

Although I discussed these problems with the factory manager, the forty machines were shipped out the next day – Base Workshop 1 had its quota to meet and little else mattered. The manager, who was very afraid that any hold-ups or negative reports from him to his superiors would cost him his job, conceded that the plant had no quality control inspectors because finding and fixing faults slowed down production. Later he told me he was embarrassed to go out to the tractor stations because he knew the problems the machines were causing there as people struggled to make them work. He was relying on the tractor station managers keeping quiet about the machines' problems. It quickly became apparent that this was the way things were done in Burma. I returned to IRRI after six frustrating days, leaving Colonel Khun Sa with an eleven-point list of remedial measures.

More than six hundred machines had been built by the time I revisited Burma three months later, but there had been little improvement in quality: only three of the eleven remedial measures I had suggested had been taken up. To make matters worse, I found out that the men assigned to operate the stripper-gatherers at the tractor stations were almost completely untrained. AMD had told a few of them how to use the machine but hadn't given them any hands-on practice, possibly because it could not get any of its products to run long enough before breaking down. It was like teaching people to drive without letting them inside a car.

Another serious problem was that the only criterion for deciding how many stripper-gatherers to supply to a tractor station was the area of rice being grown in its district. No tractor station manager, let alone any farmer, had been asked if they wanted the technology. That decision had been made on their behalf by SLORC. In the conversations I had with farmers and tractor station managers it became clear that most farmers would not use the stripper-gatherer even if it worked and they knew how to use it, because they wanted the rice straw for animal feed. Stripper harvesting leaves the straw standing in the fields, unlike other harvesting methods.

This time, my recommendation to the colonel was that, if AMD wanted to salvage anything from the stripper-gatherer programme, it should identify the parts of the country where the technology was likely to be accepted by farmers. It should concentrate its efforts in these and send teams to correct the faults in the machines shipped to tractor stations and to train the operators. I left Burma feeling very depressed about the prospects for the technology.

I returned to Burma eleven months later because AMD had told me that one tractor station was using its stripper-gatherers very successfully. I had just registered at the University of Reading to do a Ph.D. on factors affecting the successful adoption of new technology and, in view of the multitude of problems I knew that any tractor station would face in making AMD's machines work, I felt that a visit to the successful station might provide me with much to learn.

For the first time in Burma I was assigned an armed guard – two policemen with automatic weapons – to accompany me on my visit. They were present during my interview with the tractor station manager, who told me that over a hundred hectares of rice had been harvested by the strippers. However, when I asked to see the machines to find out how they had been modified, I was told they were still in farmers' fields too far away to visit. All the experienced operators were mysteriously unavailable, too.

My suspicions about whether the tractor station had harvested even one tenth of what it claimed were strengthened when another of the station's stripper-gatherers was demonstrated for my benefit. This was a disaster. As the tractor station had not fixed the problem with tensioning the 'V' belts, it took three people to push the machine forward. The 'V' belt driving the stripper rotor was also slipping and this caused a high proportion of the grain to be lost because it was not being flicked into the collection container with sufficient impetus. Mercifully, the demonstration was stopped before we wrecked too much of the farmer's field.

Later, away from the armed guard, my translator told me that it was not uncommon for tractor stations to give optimistic reports about the performance of the equipment dumped on them because positive feedback was better received. Several months later I met the tractor station manager at an international workshop, where he had been sent as a reward for being successful.

Some months later SLORC realised that growing two crops a year was not going to work and abandoned the policy, together with all interest in the stripper-gatherer. Only one thousand machines would go to waste, however, because, fortunately, MHI never got round to building its quota.

I could, perhaps, have drawn some comfort from the debacle if AMD and the Burmese Ministry of Agriculture had learned something about machinery adaptation and extension as a result. However, all the evidence suggests that they did not. Indeed, far from being a one-off mistake, the stripper-gatherer was part of a long series of attempted innovations that AMD had shipped out to tractor stations. At several stations I saw stripper-gatherers quietly rusting away next to two types of pedal threshers and several rice-hull-fired cooking stoves, all AMD projects before the stripper-gatherer (see Figure 1.2).

In 1996, AMD's next product was to be seven thousand mechanical reapers. These also harvest rice and have the advantage of allowing farmers to save their straw. However, they are harder to build and

Figure 1.2 At least twenty stripper-gatherers rusting unused at a tractor station in Burma

more complicated than the stripper-gatherer because, instead of using a single moving part to harvest the grain, they have a series of powered scissor-like blades called a cutterbar to cut the rice stalks near the ground. This must be made to a very high degree of accuracy from the right type of steel. An added complication is that the cut plants must be moved sideways out of the path of the machine by a conveyor belt, as Figure 1.3 shows. I therefore rated the chances of an AMD reaper working as even less than its stripper-gatherer.

At least $1.5 million of public money was squandered on the stripper-gatherer fiasco on top of the untold frustration the machines caused at the tractor stations and the grain lost in farmers' fields. Burma is a poor country and cannot afford such waste, particularly if it learns nothing from it. It would be easy to explain the incident as the inevitable outcome of a top-down system in which soldiers, out of touch with farmers' needs, made bad decisions and never learned of their mistakes because those affected, fearing dismissal from their jobs, generated false data and said everything was wonderful. This, however, would be a mistake, because the only way this

Figure 1.3 A mechanical reaper harvesting rice plants
and laying them out in a windrow

story differs from many I came across in the nine years I worked in
Asia is that it is more extreme and its lessons are consequently clearer
to see. The fact is that similar centrally made decisions about what
is 'good' for farmers have led to even greater wastage of resources
in other countries. In one of the case studies we will look at later,
three thousand dryers worth a total of $10.5 million were given to
co-operatives in the Philippines and then hardly ever used.

Even so, the Burmese experience made me wonder if I, as the
main researcher and designer of the stripper-harvester, had somehow
been responsible for what had happened. I began to ask myself about
the obligations that innovators should feel to those who take up
their ideas. Colleagues at IRRI with whom I discussed the matter
were clear: it was the responsibility of those working in the various
national agricultural research and extension systems (NARES) in the
countries which IRRI served to pick up our work and deliver it to
the farmers. Our role was to do 'upstream' research, not extension.

The closest we could get was to do pilot testing of new technologies and commission research to find out how our technologies were faring in the field, but then we had to be careful not to use the word 'extension' and not to be seen to be 'poaching' on NARES territory 'downstream'. Moreover, we didn't have the budget to adapt our technologies to make them work. This was because IRRI and the fifteen other international agricultural research centres that make up the World Bank-based Consultative Group on International Agricultural Research (CGIAR) had a combined annual budget of only 5 per cent of that of the NARES. We consequently had to assume that the NARES would feed problems back to us and keep us responsive to farmers' needs.

But Burma had shown that this top-down approach didn't work with new types of agricultural machinery, and a literature search suggested that it wasn't successful in other areas either. James C. Scott in his book *Seeing Like a State: How Certain Schemes to Improve the Human Condition have Failed* analyses government-controlled top-down development projects in poorer Third World nations and Eastern Europe. He says:

> 'Fiasco' is a too light-hearted a word for the disasters I have in mind. The Great Leap Forward in China, collectivisation in Russia, and compulsory villagisation in Tanzania, Mozambique, and Ethiopia are among the great human tragedies of the twentieth century, in terms of both lives lost and lives irretrievably disrupted. At a less dramatic but far more common level, the history of Third World development is littered with the debris of huge agricultural schemes.[4]

The only agricultural example I could find of top-down methods working was the production of new seeds for farmers in areas where the growing conditions could be controlled by the use of irrigation, fertilisers and pesticide sprays.[5]

Nevertheless, IRRI and its sister centres had used the top-down approach to introduce all types of technology for many years,[6] although from at least 1982 some people within the system[7] had been arguing for ways of working that integrated 'upstream' research with 'downstream' extension. Despite this, the basic organisational set-up, in which CGIAR centres are mandated to feed into, and build up, NARES hadn't changed much since the 1970s, so many of us were still forced to leave the hard part – the conversion of research findings into technologies that farmers actually use – to others. We wrote about our new technologies in optimistic terms to encourage others to take them up and rarely considered that politicians and planners would want to believe that the potential benefits could be achieved by widespread promotion and policy change alone. Government support and farmer enthusiasm might be enough to get a modern rice variety adopted but it failed for almost everything else.

Another literature search produced the surprising result that very little research had been carried out into the ways different types of technology had evolved from prototypes to useful products. However, the search did turn up a seminal book, *Diffusion of Innovations* by Everett M. Rogers, which explained why. After looking at around six thousand accounts of how technologies fared during attempts to put them into use, Rogers concluded that very few studies had been carried out which would have allowed a proper understanding of the complex human processes involved over the long periods of time they usually took to run their course.

The wrong type of studies had been done because most researchers belonged to an 'invisible college' which laid down the 'correct' research methodology. This methodology involved carrying out a single survey to measure the factors likely to affect the rate of technology adoption at a single point in time rather than doing a series of surveys over a long period to see how those factors changed. Consequently, most of the resulting papers provided a great many statistics but little insight into the human interactions involved. Studies that did trace the interactions were dismissed by the 'college' as 'soft science' or 'no science at all'. A good example of the battle between hard and soft science is given by Jared Diamond in his essay 'Soft Sciences are Often Harder than Hard Sciences', which describes a 'dogfight' in the American National Academy of Sciences over the nomination of Samuel Huntington, then a professor of government at Harvard, to its governing board. Diamond writes: 'This particular dogfight is an important one. Beneath the name calling, it has to do with a central question in science: Do the so-called soft sciences, like political science and psychology, really constitute science at all?'[8] Fighting Huntington's nomination in the hard science corner was Serge Lang, professor of mathematics at Yale, who called Huntington's work 'utter nonsense'. 'How does Huntington measure things like social frustration? Does he have a social-frustration meter?'[9] he asked. Huntington was not nominated.

The numbers bias had occurred in the agricultural technology diffusion literature because most of the researchers were technologists themselves and thus came from a 'hard' science background. The 'hard' sciences such as physics, chemistry and astronomy are based on the realist–positivist paradigm which assumes that reality is objective – and thus independent of the person who sees it and the context in which it happens. Moreover, reality is governed by natural laws which can be understood by taking measurements. 'Soft' scientists, by contrast, people from disciplines like social anthropology and sociology, see the world quite differently through the constructivist paradigm. This assumes that reality is not objective, but is socially constructed by groups of people who 'through discourse, develop an inter-subjective system of concepts, beliefs, theory and practices that they consider to be reality'.[10] In other words, people construct reality in different ways even if they live in the same environment, and can change what they see as reality to adjust to changing circumstances. Constructivists, therefore, want to understand the processes which bring about change whereas realist–positivists want to take snapshots in time and put numbers on things. In short, as most research into technology adoption had been carried out by realist–positivists, there was little understanding of how technology adoption actually took place, of how adoption processes were influenced by culture, context and the characteristics of the technology itself, and of how adoption could be better managed. The result was millions of dollars wasted developing and promoting technologies that were never used properly.

When, after my last visit to Burma in 1996, I began my doctoral research project to understand how postharvest equipment was developed and adopted in the Philippines and Vietnam, a very interesting conclusion began to emerge. It was that agricultural equipment was more likely to be beneficial to more people if the people who benefited could understand it and adapt it to their local needs. Moreover, the agricultural technologies that were most widely adopted were exactly the ones that had been most adapted. This link between adoption and adaptation had some far-reaching implications. In particular, it showed that contrary to the standard view that agricultural extension is the job of 'spreading the message to achieve diffusion and adoption of the innovation by as many small holders as possible,'[11] it is largely about helping farmers to understand and innovate. Moreover, if the rate at which an agricultural technology was adopted and its eventual impact were linked to how well the people who stood to benefit from it were able to adapt it to their needs, was this true for other types of technology too? And, if so, which technologies and why? Was innovation by the potential beneficiaries only relevant to 'simple' agricultural technologies in 'developing' countries or was it equally important with non-agricultural technologies in the industrialised world?

I was unable to give these questions adequate attention while working on my Ph.D., although I felt that they might be useful to people beyond my own discipline. Two years after leaving Burma, however, I was encouraged to think about them again by the worst moment in the oral examination – the viva – for my degree. I thought I was coasting along well until, after about an hour, the external examiner, Professor Norman Clark, an economist and chair of the Postgraduate School of Ecology at the University of Strathclyde, asked if I had read any of von Hippel's work. I hadn't because most of the books I had been reading had been from the 'development studies' stable and these made little reference to von Hippel's 'business management' approach. The ultimate nightmare of Ph.D. candidates loomed before me – finding out that the work to which you have devoted three years of your life in the belief that you were making an original contribution has been done before. Fortunately this was not the case and Norman Clark quickly put me out of my misery.

Nevertheless, I ordered von Hippel's book, *The Sources of Innovation,* the following day and discovered that he had come to very similar conclusions about the importance of innovation by potential beneficiaries in high-tech manufacturing in the USA as I had drawn from my research in rural Philippines and Vietnam. In other words, while technologies might be as far apart as semi-conductors and agricultural equipment, and the contexts as different as Silicon Valley in the USA and a muddy field in the Mekong Delta, the underlying adoption processes could be very similar. There might, therefore, be much that agricultural engineers could learn from other 'invisible colleges'. An analysis of the development and adoption of agricultural engineering technologies might teach other disciplines a few things too.

Indeed, agricultural engineering might provide one of the best fields to study technology adoption because of its 'fossil record'. Just as our understanding of biological development has been immeasurably helped by the discovery of fossil remains, simple agricultural equipment can contain a 'fossil' record. This is because, if someone with a welder and angle grinder modifies a piece of equipment, the changes they make are easy to spot and last until the machine is scrapped or someone cuts the modification off. Identifying these modifications and then finding out who made them, when, why, how and with what effect gives the researcher a snapshot of the innovation process. Many of these snapshots can then be linked together to produce a 'motion picture' of the technology's adoption. Technologies where modifications are not visible, or do not last, such as a change to a fertiliser recommendation that only persists in a farmer's memory, are not open to this approach.

I therefore urge readers who want to manage innovation better but who aren't agricultural engineers to wade patiently through the details of the farm machinery they will encounter in the next two chapters. We need the facts presented in Chapters 2 and 3 to understand the interaction between the people who develop and promote technology and those who build it and use it. Be assured: once we have built a model to help our understanding we will go on to look at other technologies of more general interest and see whether the fossil records from Asian rice fields can shine a light on more general truths. In Chapter 4, for example, we look at how a small country like Denmark beat the USA by building a wind turbine industry with a 55 per cent share of a billion-dollar-a-year world market. Chapter 5 looks at the evolution of a computer operating system built by volunteers that is causing serious concern at Microsoft. Chapter 6 considers the birth and early adoption of Local Economic Trading Systems (LETS) that allow people to generate their own money. In Chapter 7 we return to agriculture and look at the archetypal top-down innovation success story – the development and transfer of the high-yielding rice varieties that produced the Green Revolution – to help establish the circumstances in which our model is likely to be useful. Finally, in Chapter 8, I bring the strands together by incorporating our findings of Chapters 4 to 7 into a practical guide to managing the innovation process that I hope will prove useful not just to agricultural engineers in overalls and muddy wellingtons but also to business executives in smart suits and highly polished shoes.

2

The palaeontology of innovation

Lessons on success and failure
from the paddy fields of Asia

After seeing hundreds of the machine I had designed rusting away
on Burmese tractor stations, it was excellent therapy to begin research
for my Ph.D. on why some technologies sink and others swim. My
plan was to follow the fortunes of all the rice-harvesting and rice-
drying technologies introduced to the Philippines and Vietnam after
1975.

Both types of harvester we discussed in the last chapter – my
team's own stripper-gatherer and the mechanical reaper – met the
arbitrary criterion I established for an introduced technology: that
there had to be at least a hundred examples of the technology being
used in the country for it to count. Four types of dryer were also
eligible. These are illustrated in Figure 2.1. They ranged in capacity
and cost from the locally made SRR dryer – SRR means 'very low
cost' in Vietnamese – which can be bought for $100 and dries one
tonne of rice in two to four days, to recirculating dryers imported
from Taiwan which cost 150 times more but can dry six tonnes in
eight to ten hours.

The SRR dryer was invented by a Vietnamese university lecturer,
Le Van Bahn, who got the idea from the way that unhusked rice-
paddy is traditionally stored in Vietnam in a cylinder made from a
rolled-up bamboo mat tied with rope or wire. Bahn realised that if
you blew hot air through a similar, smaller cylinder at the centre of
a grain store, and both ends of the cylinder were sealed, the hot air
would percolate through the walls of the cylinder into the rice and

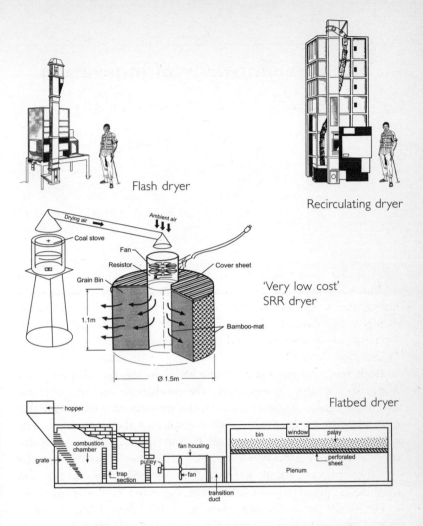

Flash dryer

Recirculating dryer

'Very low cost'
SRR dryer

Flatbed dryer

Figure 2.1 The four types of paddy (unhusked rice) dryer considered in the study

dry it. Obviously, the rice to dry first would be close to the cylinder and then the 'drying front' would move outwards in the direction of the airflow, but if air temperatures were low enough the grain near the cylinder would not have been damaged by the time the grain on the outside was dry.

Table 2.1 The case study technologies

Technology	Description	Adoption status	Cost ($)
Stripper-gatherer (SG) harvester	Walk-behind harvester	140 units sold in 5 years (Philippines)	2,000
Mechanical reaper	Walk-behind harvester	1,071 units sold in 8 years (Philippines)	3,000
SRR dryer	Low temperature dryer	700 units sold in 3 years (Vietnam)	100
Flatbed dryer	Heated air dryer with manual mixing	1,000 units sold in 17 years (Vietnam)	2,000
Flash dryer	High temperature dryer	2,000 units donated in 4 years (Philippines)	3,500
Recirculating dryer	Heated air dryer with mechanical mixing	1,500 units sold in 6 years (Philippines)	15,000

The SRR dryer is not for people with a lot of grain to dry in a hurry. A recirculating dryer is much better for such a job despite its large price tag. This also passes hot air through the wet rice but uses higher temperatures and avoids the problem of overheating the grain that dries first by continuously conveying its entire load to the top of the dryer and then letting it drop down through the air blowing in the opposite direction. Very little labouring work is involved because the same conveying system is also used for loading and unloading.

The third type of dryer I looked at is the poor person's alternative to the recirculating dryer, the flatbed dryer. This uses similar air temperatures and, if anything, can dry faster than the recirculating dryer but the mixing has to be done by labourers working inside the 'flatbed' drying bin. This is a very hot, dusty and unpopular job! Another drawback is that it lacks any sensing equipment to measure the moisture content of the paddy; the workers have to determine when the grain is sufficiently dry by checking its hardness with their teeth. Consequently, the quality of the grain produced by flatbed dryers depends on the skill and dedication of the operators.

Table 2.2   The case study technologies

Technology	Source of innovation	Introduced Philippines	Introduced Vietnam
Harvesting			
SG	Public	• •	•
Reaper	Public	•	•
	Private	•	
Drying			
SRR	Public	•	•
Flatbed	Public	• •	•
Flash	Public	• •	
Recirculating	Private	•	

The fourth type of dryer I included in my survey was the flash dryer, so-called because it uses much higher air temperatures than flatbed or recirculating dryers and thus dries grain in a 'flash'. Unfortunately, these high temperatures damage the rice when it is nearly dry. As a result, although flash drying is ideal for driving off the bulk of the moisture from dripping wet grain harvested in the middle of the rainy season, a second, lower-temperature drying stage is needed to bring the grain from 'skin dry' to dry.

As Table 2.2 shows, not all the technologies were introduced to both countries, and, in some cases, two introduction attempts had had to be made. In all, I found that I had thirteen innovation histories to follow, two of which were initiated by commercial interests and eleven by the public sector. There was a lot to learn from the two commercial introductions but, as this chapter concentrates on the public-sector experience, we will discuss them in the next chapter.

Judging from the results, it seemed that most of the people who had planned and implemented the eleven public sector technology introduction attempts I investigated had been to the SLORC school of top-down innovation management. The Burmese story of inadequately developed technologies being rushed into large-scale production had been repeated time and again. Only in communist

Vietnam, where one might have expected a great deal of central control, had the process been managed more fruitfully.

Earlier studies of agricultural innovation had shown that it took, on average, ten years for a technology to move from the basic research stage through to the point at which farmers began to spend their own money on it and to adopt it on a large scale. In Figure 2.2, this journey is shown by the arrow from the development phase to the expansion phase. A further ten years could then be required before real impacts from the technology could be measured.[1] For example, IRRI's big agricultural engineering success, its axial flow rice thresher, which is now manufactured throughout Southeast Asia, had taken four years from the time research on it began in 1969 until the first commercial prototype was released. Its design is still evolving and improving over a quarter of a century later. Even a type of cassava dryer introduced to Colombia in 1981 from Asia, where it had been widely used for at least ten years, took three years from the time the pilot plant opened until the expansion phase.[2]

Despite this, in a staggering nine cases out of the eleven, the technologies I was following had been widely promoted in government programmes only three years after their development first started, and just nine months after the first example had been sold commercially. Half of these technologies were subsequently rejected by their potential users and only two are now demonstrably successful. What this meant was that everyone from the researchers themselves through to government mechanisation planners were working on the assumption that research institutes like IRRI could deliver new types of agricultural machinery in a fully developed, completed form in the same way that IRRI's plant breeders could deliver a 'finished' new rice variety.

There is a big difference between the two types of innovation, however. This is because people need to learn new skills to build and use new agricultural equipment, whereas farmers already know how to grow and save seed. In addition, although plant breeders can develop high-yielding varieties (HYVs) that work well without any real input from farmers, developing and introducing equipment technology cannot be done without a great deal of interaction and feedback from the manufacturers and users who stand to benefit from its adoption. This process obviously takes a lot of time. The reason everyone had been happy to overlook these differences and rush

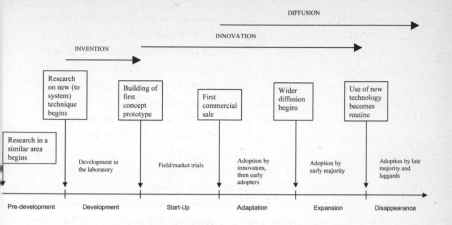

Figure 2.2   Stages and milestones in the invention, innovation and diffusion process[3]

equipment into large-scale use was clear: it had been in their interests to do so. One reason was that the foreign donors who had funded eight out of the eleven public sector innovation attempts I was investigating wanted to see some 'bang for their buck'. Such donors usually provide money for only about three years' work at a time and, if the researchers involved want to get further funding, they needed to show how successful they had been. What better way to show that your research output is relevant than by having a few farmers buy it and then get the technology included in a government promotion programme? The donors had colluded with this, too, because they did not want to wait the fifteen or twenty years required to assess the project properly. They had therefore purported to believe that what the researchers had achieved was 'a milestone on the adoption pathway' and a clear indicator that their money had been well spent.

Government planners had played the game by including the new technologies in their programmes because they knew their masters, the politicians, would approve. After all, supporting new technology, particularly an agricultural one, is a very visible way of showing that you are trying to help rural people and thus of improving your chances of re-election. Agricultural machinery manufacturers had collaborated, too, because they were always looking for new products to help them get ahead in a very competitive market in which few innovations come along. Indeed, in the Philippines, some of the larger manufacturers who regularly received government contracts had lobbied for new equipment to be included in government programmes because this meant more work for them, irrespective of whether they believed the technology was viable or not.

The extension engineers who commissioned the equipment knew that if they criticised the new technology they would get the reputation of being backward and obstructive. And, finally, the co-operatives, which were usually given the new technologies free or very cheaply by the government programmes, hadn't minded too much how they performed. As they had had to invest little effort or money to get the machinery, they had invested little effort or money in attempting to make it work. Indeed, if it failed, they quickly used the engine for something else. I have had several trips in the Philippines on motorised rickshaws powered by engines bearing labels showing them to have come from government-supplied farm machinery.

The flash dryer in the Philippines

The way the combined interests of all these stakeholders can lead to disaster is well illustrated by the story of the NAPHIRE flash dryer. This began in April 1986 when NAPHIRE (the National Postharvest Institute for Research and Extension, one of the many government agricultural agencies in the Philippines) started working with the Australian Centre for International Agricultural Research (ACIAR) on a high-profile rice-drying project. Unlike Burma, many farmers in the Philippines do grow two rice crops a year and the one they have to harvest during the rainy season can be literally dripping wet. The researchers therefore began the project by investigating the best way of drying very wet grain and concluded that the most efficient approach was to drive off the surface moisture with a fast, high-temperature process and then to follow this with a slower, more gentle drying cycle to get the moisture content of the grain itself down to a level at which it could be safely stored.[4] By 1989, NAPHIRE had built a prototype 'flash' dryer designed to do the first, fast stage. In other words, the *pre-development* and *development* phases marked on Figure 2.2 took three years and the project was entering the *start-up* phase.

The NAPHIRE team did not want to wait for the development of the second part of the technology package, the low-temperature dryer, before putting the first stage into use. This was because research had shown that a crop flash dried to 18 per cent moisture content[5] could be stored for up to two weeks before it spoilt, unlike very wet grain (26–30 per cent moisture content) which spoiled in a couple of days. Since wet season weather data showed there was a high likelihood of a few dry days occurring in any two-week period in the wet season, they reasoned that farmers ought to be able to finish the drying in the traditional way, by spreading the grain out on a pavement in the sun. They therefore concluded that the flash dryer could help farmers save their crops even without the companion low-temperature dryer.

The initial reaction to the prototype flash dryer was wildly optimistic, just as it had been with the stripper-gatherer in Burma, especially after a NAPHIRE publication, *Postharvest Digest*, claimed that the machine could dry dripping-wet grain in fifteen to twenty minutes. The article failed to make it clear that grain was only being half-dried. Another NAPHIRE publication reflects the organisation's early optimism: '[the flash dryer] offers vast potential advantage which benefit[s] farmers, commercial grain handlers and government grain operators. The reduced fuel energy required in heat generation remarkably cuts down the total cost incurred.'[6]

The first prototype was loaded by carrying sacks of wet rice up a ladder and emptying them through a hatch at the top, but the farmers involved in testing it thought an elevator should be fitted. Accordingly, the second prototype was built with a conveyor and sent for field testing at a co-operative in Agusan del Sur in Mindanao, about as far away from NAPHIRE as it is possible to get without leaving the Philippines. This co-op was chosen because, unusually, it rained in the area during both harvest seasons. This meant that the dryer was likely to be used more often than elsewhere and feedback would be faster.

When the results came back, however, the number of hours the co-op had used the dryer were disappointing because they meant that, even in a very wet location, the device would have a pay-back period of five years[7] and was therefore non-commercial. Nevertheless, in the belief that the machine would become more economical once the users had become more familiar with it, the team decided to press ahead, encouraged by the fact that other co-operatives in the area had shown an interest in acquiring their own units.[8] Its final test report concluded that NAPHIRE should introduce the dryer to other areas of the Philippines with similar weather conditions to Agusan del Sur without saying just how unusual this weather was. The team discounted alternative but perhaps more plausible explanations for the co-op's low usage rate. Among these was the possibility that the co-op's managers were using the dryer infrequently because it made their job less convenient as they had to oversee two separate drying operations – flash drying and sun drying – and two different groups of workers. (With sun drying, the same team would dry rice from dripping wet even if it took several days.) Another possibility was that, as the labour and fuel costs of using the flash dryer and then sun drying the rice were three times as high as traditional sun drying alone on a good day, the process was simply too expensive. (The researchers got round this problem by assuming that grain dried in the flash dryer would sell for a higher price, although in my study I found no evidence of a price differential). A third alternative explanation was that the dryer didn't work well. A survey of users I carried out showed that the conveyor jammed when loaded with dripping wet rice and that its installation actually made loading less convenient. Some users were even using a ladder and loading the dryer by hand.

A Vietnamese colleague once said that the Philippines had the longest grain dryers in the world because farmers, rice traders and millers sun-dried their grain on the roads, often closing one of the two carriageways for miles. While its flash dryer was under test, NAPHIRE actively tried to end this practice, the main competition to mechanical drying. It joined sixteen other government agencies in the Central Luzon Agricultural Resources Research and Development Consortium (CLARRDEC)[9] in 1992, and bans on grain drying on the roads began to be enforced two years later. Central Luzon is the main rice-growing area in the Philippines and is where the NAPHIRE research facilities are based.

A very ambitious government project was being planned just as CLARRDEC's campaign to ban rice drying on roads was getting started. Thai farmers are paid about half the amount that their Philippine counterparts are paid for rice and it was becoming clear to the Philippine government that when it was forced to lift rice import restrictions as a result of the Uruguay round of the General Agreement on Tariffs and Trade (GATT), which was being negotiated at the time, this price differential would disappear. The government therefore planned to use profits it had been making by importing Thai rice and selling it to consumers[10] to help Philippine farmers improve their productivity and enable them to compete when the market opened up. Accordingly, it launched the Grains Productivity Enhancement Program (GPEP) in 1993, which included in its budget well over $100 million to purchase and distribute twelve thousand mechanical dryers and twelve thousand drying pavements[11] to co-ops around the country. At least part of this spending was to replace drying capacity lost because of the bans on road drying.[12]

The government plan clearly stated that the mechanical dryers to be provided to the co-operatives should be 'mature', a term it defined to cover equipment that had been pilot tested and fine-tuned to be technically feasible, economically viable and socially acceptable in the areas into which it was to be introduced. NAPHIRE was appointed to co-ordinate GPEP and one of its first actions was to select four types of dryer to be offered to the co-operatives. Unsurprisingly, its new flash dryer was first on the list even though a realistic appraisal of the evidence from the test at Agusan del Sur showed that it had not been 'fine-tuned' even for one unrepresentative area. Dr Justin Tumambing, a lead researcher in the flash dryer project, later blamed the availability of the Thai rice money and political pressure for forcing him and his colleagues to promote the dryer prematurely in this way.[13] A competing flash dryer design was also included – the Ilonggo rotary flash dryer – but imported recirculating dryers, which were just beginning to become popular with rice millers, were disqualified by the setting of a price ceiling of $3,850.

Commercial production of the flash dryer began in 1991, ending its two year *start-up* period. The *adaptation* phase, in which most of the modifications from manufacturers and users are likely to occur, ended less than a year later when, in order to meet GPEP requirements, the start of large-scale production by several manufacturers meant that NAPHIRE had to finalise the design. This locked the design in stone because if NAPHIRE had continued to make major changes to the design later on, manufacturers and customers of the earlier designs would have complained about being given obsolete technology. Moreover, design changes might have caused high-ranking government officials to ask why NAPHIRE had not been aware earlier of the problems which necessitated the alterations. This could have called NAPHIRE's professional credibility into question, particularly as the institute had been instructed to select only 'mature' technologies.

By December 1994 twelve manufacturers had been approved to build the dryer after building samples to the standard design which NAPHIRE engineers then checked for compliance.[14] By 1995 about three thousand mechanical dryers, most of the NAPHIRE type, and six thousand drying pavements had been distributed. Over $120 million had been spent.[15]

In June 1997 I began a survey of owners of NAPHIRE and Ilonggo flash dryers to find out how all these thousands of dryers were being used. I went first to NAPHIRE to ask them to recommend some successful owners for me to visit. My plan was to follow up these visits by interviewing average users and then less successful ones identified from other sources. Unfortunately, though, my sampling method collapsed right at the start because the main NAPHIRE flash dryer engineer did not know any successful users. I therefore resorted to interviewing flash dryer owners I came across while carrying out the main stripper-gatherer survey. All nine of these are described in Table 2.3; the story they told was consistent and depressing. Neither the NAPHIRE nor Ilonggo flash dryers had worked well and the majority of owners, 60 per cent, had rejected the technologies completely. The most successful user in the sample, and probably in the country, was First Iloilo Area Marketing Co-operative, which had received special assistance from NAPHIRE in getting their flash dryer to work because the co-operative was a test site for the institute. However, even with this help, the co-operative had only been able to use the machine for a quarter of the time required for it to break even.[16]

Matalino Golinao, one of the two private individuals I interviewed who had paid the full price for their dryers, had made a real attempt to get his machine to work and pay for itself. However, after running it night and day for a season he said he realised that the most he could make in one day was about $20, which was not enough to pay for repairs and for his time. This was because the dryer could only dry a tonne of paddy an hour, a third of the rate claimed in the publicity material that had made people enthusiastic about the tech-

Table 2.3 Adoption status and seasonal
usage rate of flash dryers surveyed

Name	Type of adopter	Type of dryer	Status of adoption
Acuit	Co-operative	Ilonggo	Rejected
First Iloilo Area Marketing	Co-operative	NAPHIRE	In use
Balasan Estancia Carles	Co-operative	Ilonggo	In use
Pasbigtaba	Co-operative	Ilonggo	Rejected
Tamcom Illaud	Co-operative	NAPHIRE	Rejected
San Isidro	Barangay	NAPHIRE	Emergency only
Dulong Bayan	Barangay	NAPHIRE	Emergency only
Rogelio de la Cruz	Private	NAPHIRE	Rejected
Matalino Golinao	Private	NAPHIRE	Rejected

nology in the first place. Golinao might have made more money by
raising his prices but found farmers were reluctant to let him dry
their grain even at the low rate he was charging because they still had
the trouble and expense of finishing the drying off. Eighty per cent
of the flash dryer owners I interviewed complained about this.

The other private owner, Rogelio de la Cruz, gave up trying to use
his dryer when it caught fire and nearly burned his warehouse down.
When he asked the manufacturer to fix the fault he was told to have
sand ready to put out the next fire. He told me 'I could not sleep
feeling safe in my bed thinking my warehouse was going to burn
down.' His friends, Mr and Mrs Oh, had a similar experience. They
had bought a flash dryer at the same time as him but had stopped
using it when Mr Oh lost his finger in one of the dryer's belt drives.

Eventually, NAPHIRE and the designers of the Ilonggo dryer
realised that the cost of using their machines had to be cut to attract
potential customers, and both replaced the kerosene burners with
ones that burned rice-hull. This led to the second most common
complaint about flash dryers: that it was impossible to control the

rice-hull furnaces and the dryers ran so hot that they became giant popcorn, or rather poprice, producers.

In 1996, two years before the end of GPEP, the Secretary of Agriculture was sacked; one of his replacement's first acts was to cancel orders for seven hundred flash dryers.[17] However, government money for the purchase of flash dryers did not dry up completely, and it was still purchasing them in 1998.[18]

Nobody in NAPHIRE or the Department of Agriculture seems to know how many flash dryers the Philippines government had bought and supplied by the end of 1998. A very conservative estimate is three thousand – the number that Silvestre Andales, the then Executive Director of NAPHIRE, said had been distributed by 1995.[19] Nor is it easy to establish exactly how much money the government spent on them. Assuming an average purchase price of $3,500[20] per dryer applied, over $10 million must have been involved, not including expenditure on administration, promotion, liaising with the manufacturers and so on. Whatever the exact figure, it is at least an order of magnitude larger than the amount squandered by the Burmese government, and, as in Burma, it represents resources that could have been much better used. Certainly, the money did little if anything to help the small-area farmers whom GPEP was designed to support through their co-operatives.

Why were so many expensive dryers distributed for so long when a quick survey would have shown they were not working? I discussed this question at length with key dryer experts, including several members of staff of NAPHIRE, two manufacturers, a supplier of flash dryers and three engineers employed by the Department of Agriculture. The simple explanation was that the flash dryer was pushed into GPEP for political reasons to do with NAPHIRE's position in CLARRDEC and its wish, as a young organisation, to be seen by national and international funders to be having an impact. Then, once part of GPEP's six-year budget had been allocated to supplying flash dryers, it was in more peoples' interest for supplies to continue than to recognise the problems and put the further deliveries in jeopardy. Two of the larger flash dryer manufacturers I talked to relied on government orders for over 50 per cent of their turnover and were not going to endanger this by criticising the technology. The Australian researchers working on the project for ACIAR might have tried to delay the promotion of the dryer, but they seemed to have regarded it as NAPHIRE's baby and did not intervene.

NAPHIRE, of course, should have drawn attention to the dryer's problems very early on, but to have done so would have been deeply embarrassing because it had developed the technology. My team's own technology, the stripper-gatherer, was also included in GPEP so I think I have a reasonable insight into why the team which developed the NAPHIRE flash dryer put so much effort into defending it against criticism rather than sorting out its problems. With the stripper-gatherer, there was little or no money available for extensive pilot testing, but GPEP promised a lot for its promotion. Without the knowledge of the stripper's shortcomings that hindsight brought, I found it easy to say 'Yes, I think the technology is mature' and get it included in GPEP in the belief that having manufacturers build it and co-operatives use it was better than it being left out.

However, just as the NAPHIRE team had found with the flash dryer, once several manufacturers began to build the stripper on a relatively large scale, I found that it was difficult to change the design because to do so was an implicit admission that a product I had said was ready for mass production was flawed. Moreover, when criticisms started coming in, I became protective. I blamed manufacturers for using the wrong materials, for poor-quality construction and not training the operators sufficiently well, and I blamed owners for not using the machine properly. Looking back, though, I can see that before large-scale production began I had been proactively looking for improvements and accepting criticism, but that after it started I became more reactive and defensive.

In the 1970s, the Philippines government ran an agricultural development programme called Masagana 99 which, like GPEP, supplied rice dryers. A flatbed dryer was chosen for distribution to individual farmers through the scheme because an estimate of its profitability assumed, rather optimistically, that such dryers would be used for an average of ninety days a year and dry three hundred tonnes of rice in that time.[21] In most areas of the Philippines, however, the wet season harvest lasts no more than thirty days and, as a result, the thousand flatbed dryers installed were seriously underused and too expensive. So, as with GPEP, the intended recipients did not benefit; the only people to adopt the technology were commercial growers of high-value seed like maize.[22] The only lesson from Masagana 99 passed on to GPEP was that the simple flatbed dryer had not worked and should not be supplied again. No innovation management lessons were learned, such as the fact that as you do not have perfect knowledge at the planning stage, you need to build flexibility and responsiveness into the programme. Very little seems to have been learned from GPEP either. However, PhilRice, the Philippine Rice Research Institute, did learn that the farmers' co-operatives are not well managed enough to make innovative use of the new technology provided by government programmes. It has begun working with individual farmers instead.

All this leads me to believe that the blame for the millions of dollars wasted on the stripper-gatherer in Burma and the two types of dryer in the Philippines should not be attached to individuals or the individual organisations but to the system in which the mechanisation planners, engineers, extension workers and manufacturers operate. Moreover, I also believe that the main fault with the system is its in-built assumptions about the way in which technology is developed and transferred.

In her business management book *Wellsprings of Knowledge: Building and Sustaining the Sources of Innovation,* Dorothy Leonard surveys the development of thirty-two software programs in the USA and identifies two distinct approaches taken by the firms involved. In one approach, the R&D team assumes it has a good enough understanding of the target users' needs to be able to develop the new software without getting potential users to state what their needs are or to suggest an ideal product specification. The team simply goes ahead and develops the software and then tosses it 'over the wall' to users in the belief that: (1) there is a need for it; (2) the technology is complete and ready to use; and (3) the users are technically skilled enough to use it without help. Leonard calls this approach the *over-the-wall* model. She contrasts it with the *consultancy* model, in which the R&D team consults target users about their needs but does not involve them in the development process because it thinks that its own experience, together with its ability to ask users the right questions, will provide all the information it needs. It is confident that it will be able to develop all aspects of the technology itself, just as NAPHIRE was when it developed the flash dryer.

Leonard states that the consultancy model works well for upgrading existing technologies, but is a poor approach for developing novel technical systems – a category into which the flash dryer clearly falls. Radically new systems, she says, require the R&D team to 'co-develop' the technology in conjunction with potential users. Quite clearly the flash dryer was disseminated according to the 'over-the-wall' model, which, as we will see, is not surprising because government agricultural extension services throughout Southeast Asia are set up to transfer high-yielding varieties (HYVs) from research institutes to farmers. HYVs are like upgrades of existing computer programs and are suitable for over-the-wall transfer. We will discuss software development again in Chapter 5 and consider seed technology in Chapter 7.

The flatbed dryer in Vietnam

The development and introduction of the flatbed dryer to Vietnam provides clear evidence that co-development might be better than the over-the-wall model at improving agricultural equipment. Flatbed dryers are extremely simple. The grain to be dried is placed in a bin and heated air is blown through it until it is dry. Much lower drying temperatures are used than in the flash dryer,[23] so there is less risk of grain damage. The only complication is that the grain needs to be mixed to prevent the layer nearest the air inlet overdrying before the top layer is dry. A typical flatbed dryer is shown in Figure 2.1.

Flatbed dryers were first used in Asia in Japan but these machines were too expensive to be suitable for countries like the Philippines and Vietnam. Dante de Padua and his team at the University of the Philippines College of Agriculture (UPCA) built a copy of a Japanese design for a commercial maize farmer in 1966 and went on to develop a 2-tonne capacity flatbed dryer for paddy with money from an FAO project in 1969. IRRI jumped on the bandwagon in 1970 when it evaluated a Japanese flatbed dryer.[24] It built its own 1-tonne capacity model in 1972 and released drawings to manufacturers in the Philippines in the same year.[25] 'Our development of the flatbed dryer came at just the right time', Dante de Padua told me.

> Farmers who had begun growing IRRI's miracle rice were having a terrible time harvesting it in the middle of the wet season and began complaining to President Marcos. He ordered the Ministry of Agriculture to airlift all our flatbed dryers, even the experimental ones, to the north of the Philippines. After the airlift, Mr Tanco, the then Secretary of Agriculture, asked

me to brief him on the technology. A year later Mr Tanco made the flatbed dryer a linchpin of his programme to help farmers, Masagana 99.[26]

Tanco and President Marcos were not the only people to get excited about flatbed dryers. The Canadians began promoting de Padua's dryer in other Southeast Asian countries through their International Development Research Centre (IDRC). As a result, several countries including Malaysia, Indonesia and Thailand developed their own versions and tried to introduce them, but, as in the Philippines, very few were adopted by the small-area rice farmers who were supposed to be the programme's main beneficiaries. Only commercial seed growers or government grain-processing centres adopted the technology.

Oddly, Vietnam, the sole country in Southeast Asia in which IDRC did not attempt to promote flatbed dryers, is the only one where the technology has actually benefited a large number of small-area farmers. About a thousand flatbed dryers are currently in use in the Mekong Delta. They dry about 500,000 tonnes of paddy per year and prevent the loss of millions of dollars' worth of grain. All these dryers evolved from a single prototype built in 1983 by a university lecturer, Phan Hieu Hien, without any outside funding or government support. Hien told me in 1997:

> The salary of a university lecturer was very low back then. It still is. To survive we needed a 'side-line' – some other way of earning money. All I had were some drawings of a vertical-bin dryer that IRRI had sent me and some knowledge from my time as Dante de Padua's student at UPCA in the Philippines – all theory, no practice and no workers either. Looking back I would say that I was a foolish adventurer. I had nothing except my bicycle. I got an order from a seed company for a vertical-bin dryer. There was no allowance [in the price] for research, for trial and error. If the dryer did not work then I had to pay damages, whatever the cost. If I delivered late I was fined. I hired a carpenter and together we built the bin in three days and three nights. I gave a final-year student the project of building a fan. But the dryer worked. It solved their problem of drying corn for seed during the wet season. Now we see problems with it like non-uniformity [variations in the extent of the drying] of the dried grain and high kerosene consumption but back then it was already progress compared to nothing.
>
> After that I wrote a short note in *Popular Science* magazine about the dryer. Tran Van Hao from Soc Trang province read the article. He was an agronomy graduate from UAF and was running a government seed

farm. He was having big problems drying paddy in the wet season and asked me to build a dryer for him. Now that I had experience with the vertical-bin dryer I decided to build a UPCA flatbed dryer instead and he used it for one year in 1982. He said 'OK, the seed germination is good with the dryer but the capacity is too small. Now can you design a 10 tonne dryer? Nothing smaller will do.'

The problem was with the fan. So I went to the main Ho Chi Minh City library. I can honestly say that of all the American, French and Russian books only the German book by Bruno Eg was any good. In the book was the critical graph I needed to design the profile of a blower blade for a 10 tonne dryer. The trouble was that the graph was very small and that some of the characters describing the critical design step were illegible. My brother-in-law had a slide-rule which I borrowed and spent half a day doing the calculation. I didn't have a test duct to check the blower blade design but judging from the drying time and amount of water evaporated I judged it had a pretty good air flow.

Hien supplied Hao with the 10-tonne dryer and helped him commission it. News of the dryer spread by word of mouth. Three state-run food companies ordered dryers; one of them went bust, so Hao's father bought the blower from it and with Hoa's help built his own dryer in Phu Tam village, Soc Trang province, in 1985.

Phu Tam village became the cradle of the new technology. The need for mechanical dryers in the area was desperate as, two years previously, the farmers had had to throw nearly all their wet season crop away because they could not dry it. Most transport in this part of the Mekong Delta is by the canals, which, unlike roads, don't provide farmers with a surface on which to dry their grain. Indeed, to make matters worse, they flood during the wet season leaving no space on the nearby land either.

Farmers and village artisans quickly saw the potential of Hao's dryer and began copying it. Unfortunately, though, they made mistakes with the blowers. These reduced the airflow, which was consequently too hot and caused the grains to crack, reducing the proportion of whole grains when the rice was milled later on and lowering its sale value. Rice traders therefore imposed a 5 per cent price penalty on paddy they knew had been dried in a flatbed dryer, regardless of whether it had a good blower or not. Still, as the alternative was sometimes dumping their entire crop, most farmers continued to take their grain to be dried at the mushrooming number of flatbed dryers in the village.

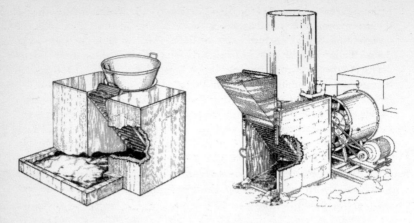

Figure 2.3 Diagrams of a local rice-hull cook-stove that was the source of inspiration for an inclined-grate rice-hull furnace exported from Vietnam to the Philippines and elsewhere

As more dryers were built and people became more experienced, performance improved. Local builders made improvements as well. For example, some makers adapted a local cook-stove that burned rice-hull on an inclined grate to replace the wood-burning furnace with a horizontal grate that Hien had designed (see Figure 2.3).

Hien did not know about any of this and, consequently, was not there to support it. Instead he was working with a friend and former student, Mr Kahn, the director of the government-owned Long An Mechanical Factory (LAMF). 'LAMF installed about 20 units in Long An province but at publicly owned rice mills where no individual owned the dryer and was responsible for it,' he says. 'These dryers were never modified as much or made to work as well as the dryers in Soc Trang province and their impact was much less. In Soc Trang the dryers were sold to private citizens who were much better motivated and got the dryers to work much better.'

Between 1989 and 1993 Hien worked at IRRI studying for a Ph.D. on rice-hull furnace design. On his return to Vietnam he heard of the 'nest' of flatbed dryers in Phu Tam village and went to investigate. He found 43 dryers working there and about 260 elsewhere in Soc Trang province, all of which had evolved from the one he had built for Tran Van Hao eight years earlier.

I found that over the years the skilled artisans in the village had modified the dryer into something that was clearly an improvement on my original design. So I picked up these improvements. For example they had reduced the layer depth from 45 cm to 25 cm. This meant they could dry very wet grain with good results. My design was based on the assumption that grain would be no wetter than 24 per cent moisture content but in fact it can be 30 per cent or even more. To dry grain this wet you have to have a shallow layer depth. The other modification I picked up was their inclined-grate rice-hull furnace.

Hien picked up more than this though. He also came away with a request to try and improve the uniformity with which the rice dried without having to reduce the layer depth any further. As a result Hien develop the side-duct bin that improved non-uniformity from 2.5–5 per cent to 1.8 per cent difference in moisture content. He and his dryer team sold forty of the improved dryers in 1995 and 1996, double the number Hien had sold between 1982 and 1989. He also improved the design on the inclined-grate furnace to reduce the amount of fly ash[27] in the drying air by almost 90 per cent.

Hien and I went to Phu Tam village together in July 1997. We found that the flatbed dryer had reached the *disappearance* phase – it had become mainstream. We met Mrs Sung, wife of one of the main dryer manufacturers, on the road. She told us: 'Dryers have become so commonplace that the local government decided to start to tax them this year. They are levying a 2 million dong ($200) fee per year. Many of the smaller operators will be forced out of business.' A dryer owner, Tu Sanh, explained to me that paddy drying was becoming big business for another reason.

> For many years it has been a buyers' market. Rice traders and rice mills left the problem of drying paddy to farmers because there was enough dry paddy for them to buy. But competition increased and now a rice mill with a dryer can buy more paddy than one without. It is a lot of trouble for a farmer to dry his own crop – if he can get a fair price he prefers to sell it wet and let the mill worry about drying. Competition is such that rice mills are paying $1,000 to hire a dryer for the whole season if they do not have their own.

There was clear evidence that the dryer was continuing to evolve. For example, some users had discovered that nylon mesh could be used to replace the steel perforated drying screen when it wore out. Admittedly, the nylon did not last as long but as it cost a twelfth of the price it was cost-effective. Moreover, building a new dryer with nylon mesh instead of metal screen reduced the price by 7.5 per cent.

Some operators had developed a way of increasing their drying capacity by as much as 50 per cent. Instead of bagging the grain inside the dryer bin after the grain had cooled for at least two hours, they would scrape it out of the side of the dryer onto the floor. This enabled them to begin loading again after just twenty minutes instead of the previous four hours. They bagged the grain on the floor at their convenience during the eight hours the second batch took to dry. Innovations like these, and the increasing competition, meant that the cost of drying had fallen from as much as 12 per cent of the value of the paddy when the dryers were first introduced to 5 per cent in 1993 to 4 per cent in 1997. Moreover, the progressive improvement in drying performance meant that rice traders started paying 5 per cent more for flatbed-dried paddy in 1994 rather than the previous 5 per cent less.

As the dryer improved, the market for it had spread out from Phu Tam and Soc Trang to the neighbouring provinces. 'There'll be 10,000 flatbed dryers in the Mekong Delta in the next ten years', Hien confidently predicted during our visit. 'Then rice mills will change over to recirculating dryers that take up less space and need fewer people.' His confidence was based on the fact that he was about to begin a new job as co-ordinator of a Danish International Development Authority project to install a thousand 'good' flatbed dryers throughout the Mekong Delta as ambassadors of the technology.

The flatbed dryer is clearly a success. By contrast the NAPHIRE flash dryer has been unsuccessful – hardly anyone has been prepared to spend their own money to buy it, and nearly all the adoption is through spending public money to give one free to a co-operative or farm. In my view, the way in which the two dryers were developed and promoted accounts for a great deal of this difference. The NAPHIRE flash dryer was developed and transferred using an over-the-wall approach to R&D. This happened because the GPEP planners assumed that researchers, rather than manufacturers and users, could develop new technologies and that the NAPHIRE R&D team knew enough about the needs and requirements of manufacturers and co-operatives to be able to build a technology that was 'mature'. No one considered whether innovations from manufacturers or users would improve the NAPHIRE design and if these might be necessary before the technology was fit enough for widespread use.

Like the flash dryer, the flatbed dryer was commercialised at a very early stage in its development and most of the knowledge it embodied initially came from researchers. Over time, however, the source-composition of the knowledge changed because the artisans in Phu Tam village added their knowledge to that from the researchers when they modified the dryer. The artisans' knowledge had been generated by 'learning by doing'. Users added to the knowledge base, too, by developing better ways of running the dryers. Their contribution came from 'learning by using'. Then, in 1993, Hien and his group learned from both manufacturers and users and made further improvements to the technology, hence increasing the researchers' contribution to the knowledge. In other words, the dryer was co-developed.

Another crucial difference between the two projects was their motivation. Dr Hien's primary motivation was to build a dryer he could sell to make money. If he failed to meet his customers' needs he was personally liable for their losses. The main motivation of the NAPHIRE R&D team might have been to meet farmers' needs at the beginning, but once the prospect of their 'baby' being included in GPEP arose, ensuring that it was became their main priority. They were lured into the numbers game: a game that I, the manager of the AMD factory, many donors, and most people who have worked in this area have joined or been forced to play at some point in their careers.

The game is played by making statements like 'between 1992 and 1997, two thousand NAPHIRE flash dryers were delivered to private individuals, co-operatives and local government units in forty provinces' or 'today our factory built fifteen stripper-gatherers and delivered them to tractor stations'. The delivery of two thousand dryers sounds much better than the twenty deliveries Hien would have been able to claim in 1989, before he found out about the developments in Phu Tam village. Nevertheless, his dryers spawned the construction of one thousand more and these are actually being used, whereas the two thousand NAPHIRE dryers ended as scrap. Those playing the numbers game trade on the fact that their audience will usually assume that delivering a dryer automatically leads to its adoption and a beneficial impact, and will fail to realise that they are just tossing the technology 'over the wall' to recipients and letting it sink or swim. In most cases the promoters' hopes are well founded because the people they wish to impress want to believe them.

In business jargon, Hien was much more 'customer-orientated' than NAPHIRE. He developed a flatbed dryer that worked. The customer tested it for a year and then specified a bigger one. This happy customer led to others. Local artisans and farmers in a village desperate for technology began to build and use it. As a result of learning by doing and learning by using they eventually improved the technology, although in the early days the changes they made led to increased grain damage and so reduced the fitness of the technology.

What happens when a technology is first adopted

I have attempted to illustrate in Figure 2.4 what happened to the knowledge associated with the flatbed dryer. A new technology consists either of knowledge that is new to the area into which it is introduced or of existing knowledge used in a novel way. In the figure I show schematically how the knowledge associated with the flatbed dryer changed between 1983, when Dr Hien built the first unit for Mr Hoa, and 1997. The phases of the innovation process shown in Figure 2.2 tell us that during this period the flatbed dryer moved from the end of the *start-up* phase through the *adaptation* phase to the *expansion* phase.

Any technology that has a physical manifestation, such as an agricultural machine or a computer, is made up of two types of knowledge. I show these in Figure 2.4. Just as an iceberg has a visible part above the water and an unseen part below, an agricultural machine has knowledge embedded in its hardware which is seen, and knowledge embodied in its software – by which I mean the knowledge needed to use it – which is not. An example of hardware knowledge was Dr Hien's use of Bruno Eg's graph in the design of the blower blade for the 10-tonne dryer. However, Hien and his workers also needed to know how to use their tools to build the dryer and then how to operate it. This was the software knowledge, a form that is not immediately visible but which can be more important than the visible part. For example, when you or I look at a dryer blower blade we cannot see the technique the manufacturer used to

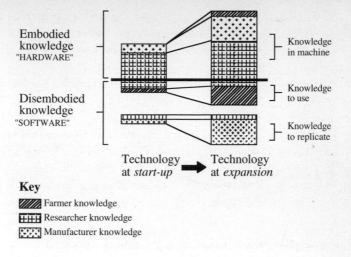

Figure 2.4 How the knowledge associated with the flatbed dryer grew when local manufacturers and farmers started making and using it

form the blade to exactly the right shape, time and again. But without this knowledge, the hardware knowledge of what is the correct shape for the blade would be useless. In the same way, unless we actually see a dryer being used we do not see the techniques that the users have learned to empty the dryer quickly so as to load the next batch in the shortest possible time. Nor do we see the operator bite a rice grain between his teeth to test whether it is dry. Without this software knowledge, though, the dryer will not work efficiently.

In Figure 2.5 I show a schematic representation of how the fitness – that is, the overall performance of the dryer – changed over time. The figure shows that the performance of the dryer was attractive at the beginning to the group of people who typically adopt new technologies – innovative adopters – of whom Mr Hoa was an example. The figure then shows fitness falling as local artisans began to copy the design and made mistakes with the blower. Then fitness improves as the artisans and users make improvements and learn more about the technology. Over time, too, customers become bet-

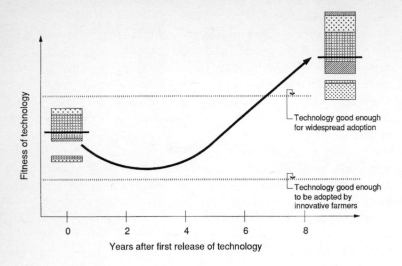

Figure 2.5 How the fitness of the flatbed dryer changed with local modification

ter at selecting beneficial modifications and avoiding detrimental ones and so the fitness begins to recover and improves to exceed that of Hien's prototype.

Hien was lucky because co-development happened without his planning for it or playing a part. He was also lucky because, although the mistakes with the blower led to a price penalty on flatbed-dried grain, the villagers persevered with the dryer since paying the penalty was better than losing the crop altogether. What would have happened if Hien had lived and worked in Phu Tam village rather than in Ho Chi Minh City, 200 km and five river-ferry crossings away? The answer is almost certainly that he would have helped local manufacturers gain the requisite knowledge about blower design, so fewer bad dryers would have been built and dryer fitness would not have suffered a dip. As a result, the adoption rate and diffusion beyond Phu Tam village and Soc Trang province would have been faster. Indeed, if the need for flatbed drying had not been so great in Phu Tam village, Hien's input could have made the difference between the technology reaching the expansion phase or failing. Perhaps if NAPHIRE had co-developed its flash dryer with potential manufacturers and users before promoting it widely, it could have been a success too.

Other innovation histories I have examined show that falls in fitness are the norm and are steeper the more the complex the design. Murphy's law applies: if something can go wrong it will, and the more complex a product is the more there is to go wrong. For example, there was a huge initial surge of excitement when IRRI tried to introduce its complex mechanical reaper in the early 1980s and an amazing total of twenty-seven manufacturers started building the machine within the first two years. However, in the third year the market for locally made reapers collapsed because poor-quality manufacture and inappropriate modifications had meant that the cutterbars broke frequently or became blunt very quickly. As a result, even though the Japanese-made reaper cost 70 per cent more, it completely replaced the Philippines-made machines.

If we can reduce or eliminate these falls in fitness, it ought to dramatically improve the adoption rate and impact of any new device. Accordingly, to get a better understanding of the phenomenon, I analysed modifications made by stripper-gatherer manufacturers in the first two years of production by checking their machines carefully against the original design IRRI had released to them. I rated the changes made according to the scale in Table 2.4 and then, to

Table 2.4 System for rating modifications to case study technologies

Effect of modification on machine attributes	Numerical rating
Breakthrough improvement in fitness	+5
Very beneficial	+4
Beneficial	+3
Fairly beneficial	+2
Slight improvement	+1
Neutral	0
Slightly detrimental	−1
Fairly detrimental	−2
Detrimental	−3
Very detrimental	−4
Catastrophic effect on fitness	−5

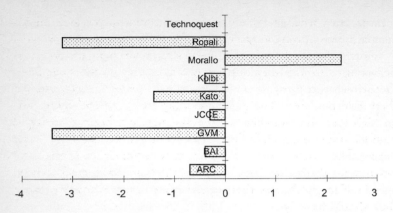

Figure 2.6 Net effect of manufacturers'
early modifications on fitness

make sure I was not being biased, asked a colleague to score them himself.[28]

The results revealed that manufacturers were making an average of twenty-four changes to the design, most of which were harmful. Figure 2.6 shows the net effect of summing the numerical ratings. Only one manufacturer had a positive effect on the design, while seven out of nine had a detrimental effect ranging from minor to extreme.

For example, ARC Engineering, the firm which has since sold more stripper-gatherers in the Philippines than anyone else, made one of the most seriously detrimental changes. The proprietor and chief engineer, Alejandro 'Boy' Campillian, agreed to a customer's request to adapt one machine so the customer could use a diesel engine he already had rather than buying a new petrol one. In making the change, Boy either forgot or did not bother to change the pulley size to allow for the fact that diesel engines run at roughly half the speed of petrol ones. When ARC Engineering tested the machine, Boy thought that the lower engine speed, which gave a lower stripper rotor speed and slower forward speed, was preferable because there was less vibration from the rotor and the machine was easier to control. He did not think that grain loss was any higher but did not measure to check. He therefore increased the pulley size on his standard petrol-powered machines so that they ran more slowly too.

Shortly afterwards, fourteen of the slower stripper-gatherers were delivered to regional demonstration centres run by the Philippines Department of Agriculture. A farmer who saw one demonstrated there told me later: 'The grain loss from the stripper-gatherer was so high that after watching the demonstration I decided to buy a Kubota reaper instead.'[29] Many other farmers came to the same decision, because one of the fundamental characteristics of the stripper rotor is that losses increase sharply as rotor speed and forward speed fall and in this case both speeds were only two-thirds of what they should have been.

I gave this modification by ARC a rating of –4. However, ARC and Boy Campillian also scored +4 for a very beneficial innovation. 'I almost had the money in my pocket', Boy told me while explaining the reasons for his innovation, 'but then the farmer asked me to show him the machine work in one of his lower fields. It was still waterlogged and the stripper-gatherer got stuck. It took four of his men to pull it out. I had lost the sale.'

Boy wanted to stop the same thing happening again. After much head-scratching he built a prototype wheel very different from the one I had specified on the machine that had got stuck. It consisted of two rubber tyres to spread the weight of the machine out over a big area, and two paddles to dig into the mud and drive it forward.

Boy told me about his wheel design and offered to let me test it. 'The wheel does the same thing as other equipment designed to operate in mud', Professor David Gee-Clough, an expert in machine mobility in muddy fields, explained when I described the wheel to him at a conference in Australia.

> There is a part of the machine that carries the weight and another part that moves the wheel forward. Conventional wheels do both – they carry the weight and move the machine forward. The problem is that in very soft ground conditions mud is squashed against the wheel and sticks there. Layer sticks to layer and very quickly the tread becomes covered and does not grip any more. The machine stops moving forward and then becomes bogged down because the spinning wheels just dig the vehicle deeper into the mud. ARC's wheel works in mud because the paddles are not carrying the weight of the machine and so mud doesn't stick to them.

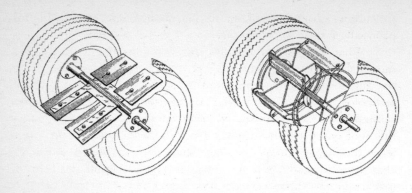

Figure 2.7   A manufacturer's first prototype wheel with just two sets of paddles that give little traction and no lift in soft field conditions, and the IRRI-modified version that works better

With Boy's agreement a colleague, Philip Cedillo, and I added more paddles to give the wheel better grip. We also used wider tyres to give a lower ground pressure. ARC's wheel and our modification to it are shown in Figure 2.7. We then sent these drawings to other manufacturers so they could copy the wheel and fit it to their machines.

Conclusions

The story of the flash dryer and the flatbed dryer is rather like the fable of the hare and the tortoise. As we saw, the flash dryer was promoted too quickly and too widely and gained such a bad reputation that it is doubtful if it will ever become widely adopted. At least $10 million was wasted. By contrast the flatbed dryer's humble beginnings and slower start gave manufacturers and users the time to adapt it so that its performance improved. Consequently, its sales increased by word of mouth and, although a large-scale programme to promote it only began fifteen years after the construction of the first prototype, it won the race to become 'mainstream'.

Anyone with a welder and an angle grinder can modify the relatively simple agricultural equipment we have considered in this chapter. Once made, though, these changes tend to persist and this makes a palaeontology of innovation possible. We can seek to explain why farmer X or manufacturer Y fused this lump of metal to that. What the fossil record has shown in this chapter is that the most successful researcher-developed technologies were those that the key stakeholders – the people who built, bought or used the technology – modified most. This seems counter-intuitive at first sight. Surely researchers should know their jobs well enough to ask the right questions and develop a prototype that doesn't inconvenience the manufacturers and users so much that they have to make changes to it? And surely the more finished a technology is when it is released into the world, the more successful it should be? But, as Dorothy Leonard points out, the many engineers, scientists, policy-makers and extension workers who think this way are implicitly assuming a 'consultancy' development model that US experience shows is good for improving an existing product but is not suitable for developing new technologies. Instead, the development of something like a flash dryer needs a 'co-development' model in which the key stakeholders and researchers construct the technology together during the early adoption phase, which we call the adaptation phase. Accordingly, we will attempt to develop such a model in the next chapter.

3

Seeing inside the black box

Modelling early adoption
(with Darwin's help)

It is not just public-sector agricultural research establishments in Asia that have handled innovation badly as a result of a faulty mental map of how the process happens. In his book *Sources of Innovation,* Eric von Hippel accuses US industry of doing exactly the same thing:

> It has long been assumed that product innovations are typically developed by product manufacturers. Because this assumption deals with the basic matter of who the innovator is, it has inevitably had a major impact on innovation-related research, on firms' management of research and development, and on government innovation policy. However, it now appears that this basic assumption is often wrong.[1]

This mistaken assumption has wasted millions of dollars. In the next chapter we'll look at how the US government paid aerospace firms such as Boeing $330 million to research and develop huge wind turbines to generate electricity. Twenty years later, however, there was no commercial product to show for the money spent.

Searching for a good mental map

If our map of the innovation process is wrong, can we develop a better one? More particularly, can we use the 'fossil record' of changes in agricultural equipment I mentioned in Chapter 1 to help us do so? For example, take Figure 2.4 in the last chapter (p. 37), the diagram of the development of the flatbed dryer in terms of the knowledge embodied in it. A good map ought to be able to explain the processes by which the manufacturers and farmers in Phu Tam village made changes to the way they built and used the flatbed dryer. In other words, it ought to describe how knowledge is built in to a technology during the adaptation phase.

Conventional economists treat technological change of the type represented by the modifications made to the flatbed dryer in Phu Tam village as a 'black box' – something they cannot see inside and cannot therefore understand or use as the basis of predictions. Fortunately, a handful of more adventurous economists have challenged this unsatisfactory attitude and suggested that the apparent similarity between technology change and the way living species evolve might help us see inside the box and explain the technology change process.[2] Certainly, the idea of using our understanding of Darwinian evolutionary theory to help understand technical change makes intuitive sense and would appeal to Dr Hien, who already talks about the development of the flatbed dryer in terms of a twenty-year evolutionary process.[3]

Natural selection is the heart of Darwin's theory of biological evolution. It is the process by which, because of constant competition for the necessities of life, only the fittest individual plants or animals, those best-suited to their environment, survive. Differences between individuals in a population arise because of random genetic mutations and sexual reproduction; if any of these differences proves advantageous, it will enable those possessing it to produce more offspring. Some of the offspring will inherit the beneficial trait and produce more offspring too, and so, over time, the genetic composition of the population will change. As Richard Dawkins wrote: 'Never were so many facts explained by so few assumptions. Not only does the Darwinian theory command superabundant power to explain. Its economy in doing so has a sinewy elegance, a poetic beauty that outclasses even the most haunting of the world's original myths.'[4]

The analogy between technical evolution and biological evolution is therefore no ordinary one. If we could find a process in technology change akin to natural selection we might be able to develop a very powerful mental map indeed.

Natural selection consists of three mechanisms. These are:

- *Novelty generation*   As a result of random genetic mutations and sexual recombination of differing genetic material, differences between individual members of a species crop up from time to time.
- *Selection*   This is the mechanism which retains random changes that turn out to be beneficial to the species because they enable those possessing the trait to achieve better survival and breeding rates. It also rejects harmful changes.
- *Diffusion and promulgation*   These are the mechanisms by which the beneficial differences are spread to other areas.

If we follow the steps by which changes in the flatbed dryer came about in Vietnam, we can quickly identify a process akin to natural selection which draws on what actually happened in Phu Tam village. Suppose a farmer finds that the rice mill pays her a low price for the grain dried in her dryer because some of it is not properly dried. If, when drying the next batch, she experiments by loading to a depth of 20 cm rather than the 40 cm specified in the operator's guide, she has *generated a novelty*. She notices that, as a result, fewer wet patches[5] develop during drying. *Selection* will occur if she decides whether the additional price paid by the rice mill is worth the cost of running the dryer at only half capacity. *Diffusion* of the modification will occur if she tells her neighbour, who also has a dryer, what she has learned. Equally, she might tell a researcher or manufacturer, who, as a result, would learn that the grain that farmers actually dry in Mekong Delta is much wetter and has more impurities than the paddy on which the dryer was originally developed in the Philippines. As a result the researcher or manufacturer might alter the operating instructions supplied with the machine, which would also lead to diffusion of the novelty and a gradual improvement in the performance of the dryer.

The first change in the way the dryer is used might lead to someone making another modification, for example adding an extra blower to increase air supply so the dryer can be loaded more deeply, which could then follow a similar sequence, becoming widely adopted and further improving the fitness of the machine. As a result, the machine's hardware (its physical characteristics) and its software (the way and the skill with which it is used) would both evolve.

Learning selection – analogue to natural selection

Rather than natural selection, let us call this whole interactive and experiential learning process *learning selection*. Figure 3.1 is a diagrammatic representation of learning selection in which participant *i* is our experimenting farmer. She learned from *experience* that the dryer did not work well when loaded as specified, *made sense* of the implications of this, *drew her own conclusions* about what might be the cause and then took *action*. This led to another experience – the outcome of the change she had made – which she also had to interpret and then use as the basis for a new set of conclusions. This cycle is essentially the same as D.A. Kolb's experiential learning cycle developed in 1984 and W. Wallace's 'wheel of science' developed in 1971, although they used different terms for each of the stages.

However, as we have seen, the farmer is not going through her learning cycle in isolation. The action taken by the miller in paying her a low price for her unevenly dried paddy helped her make sense

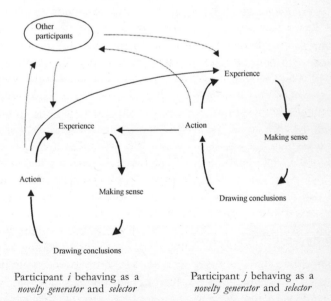

Participant *i* behaving as a
novelty generator and *selector*

Participant *j* behaving as a
novelty generator and *selector*

Figure 3.1 Learning selection – an analogue in innovation to natural selection in biological evolution

of the implications of the problem. The miller took this action as a result of a previous learning cycle in which he discovered that unevenly dried paddy does not mill or store well. This interaction is represented in Figure 3.1 where the miller is participant j. The farmer and the miller will be discussing the problem with their network of friends and colleagues, whose advice may also influence and reinforce their own learning cycles. In practice, of course, our farmer and miller will be among many participants interacting and learning in this way. The fact that many people are involved and trying different things creates the conditions for the 'recombination' of differing observations and experiences and can lead to the generation of novelties that have 'hybrid vigour'. In the process the technology evolves and with it the participants' opinions and knowledge of it, and the way they organise themselves to use and promote the technology. These processes are all involved in learning selection.

The analogy I am suggesting between natural selection and learning selection is not perfect. Rather, it is an 'analogy as a heuristic'; an analogy that suggests ways of thinking about innovation processes from the much better understood evolutionary process. One obvious difference between natural and learning selection is that natural selection is 'mindless' while learning selection is not – genetic mutations occur at random but farmers make changes to their dryers for a reason. This difference means that to make learning selection into a useful tool for understanding and predicting the outcomes of the early stages of innovation processes, we need to understand the motivations of people involved in learning processes. We need to know what motivates people to want to interact with new technology in the first place, and then what is likely to influence the outcomes of the learning selection iterations they go through, some of which will help the technology evolve and others that will hinder it.

Opening up the black box

Two important thinkers from different fields can help us understand what motivates people. In 1951, Kurt Lewin, who was born in Prussia in 1890 and is recognised as the founder of modern social psychology, came up with what is, in hindsight, the stunningly obvious idea that the actions people take as a result of the things they learn depend on the characteristics of the individuals themselves and on the characteristics of the environment in which they are working. Putting it simply, Lewin said that the outcome of learning was a function of the interaction of the people involved with their environments. Everett M. Rogers, who wrote one of the most widely quoted texts on the adoption of new technology, *Diffusion of Innovations*, helped identify the types of people most likely to want to interact with new technology. Rogers claimed in his book that the characteristics of those adopting new technologies fell into five categories ranging from innovators, the first group to adopt a new technology, through early adopters, early majority and late majority to laggards, the last.[6] He described innovators as venturesome, enjoying the technical challenges posed by new technologies and actively seeking them out. Laggards, by contrast, are the last people to adopt because they do not like taking risks and are conservative in their outlook. Rogers also said the characteristics of the environment that affected motivation and learning included the benefits of using the technology, the cultural and physical environments and the number and quality of interactions that individual participants had with other people.

So far, so good. We have identified a process we have called learning selection and understand how it works well enough to be able to explain what happened inside at least one of the conventional economists' black boxes of technological change. We know, as Figure 3.2 shows, that many cycles of the learning selection process lie inside the black box of the flatbed dryer. The diagram also shows that these cycles improved the fitness of the dryer. The figure shows the essence of the flatbed dryer innovation history in the previous chapter. It shows that when the dryer – depicted as a gear wheel – was first introduced, the knowledge associated with it came from the researchers, IRRI and Dr Hien. At this point the technology was not 'finished' and was good enough to appeal only to relatively few in-novative individuals who saw it had some potential. Over time, though, the manufacturers and users adapted the technology to local conditions, and adapted local practices to the dryer, through 'learn-ing by using' and 'learning by doing'. The 'meshing in' of the flatbed dryer to local, cultural and economic practices is depicted in Figure 3.2 as the change from a single gear wheel to interlocking wheels, while the innovations that occurred after first introduction are rep-resented by an increase in their overall area. The figure shows that most of this innovation, or 'knowledge construction', came from the

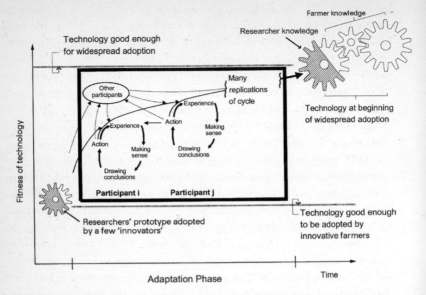

Figure 3.2 What is inside the black box – the *learning selection* model of the early evolution of new technology

manufacturers and users. It came from modifications and innovations to the machine itself (the hardware), the ways it was built, the ways it was used and how the technology fitted into the existing farming, social and cultural systems (the software).

As I said earlier, my research showed that the most successful technologies – the fittest – were the ones that had been most adapted. In other words, they were the ones where the knowledge increase and 'meshing in' after first introduction was the greatest. The story of the axial-flow thresher told later in this chapter gives a good example. Consequently, although Figure 3.2 is based on the flatbed dryer, it represents the way in which many technologies were adapted and adopted just after they were released onto the market. The diagram represents what frequently happens when a technology is first introduced to the commercial world.

The learning selection model therefore implies that if we suspect that a technology we have developed is not 'finished' in the sense that it is not fit enough to be widely adopted immediately (and only a fraction of new technologies are), then we need to encourage learning selection to complete its development. My experience with the stripper-gatherer and the survey work I've done on other technologies convince me that the best way to do this is to do exactly as Dr Hien did with the flatbed dryer and produce a prototype that shows real potential to solve a problem and introduce it to an area where the problem is acute, so that people are prepared to go to some trouble to help develop the technology and it can survive its fitness dip as they build their own versions.

This early part of the adoption stage needs to be managed to prevent mistakes being made which would kill the technology by stopping the learning selection process in its tracks. For example, the technology could be nurtured by a 'product champion' – someone who works with manufacturers and users to spot any detrimental changes as soon as they appear and who 'plugs their knowledge gaps' by explaining to them why the variations are reducing the fitness of the technology. The product champion would also look out for beneficial modifications and attempt to promote these.

In their international bestseller *In Search of Excellence: Lessons from America's Best-Run Companies,* Thomas Peters and Robert Waterman identify product champions as a key factor in successful innovation. They write:

> Recently Texas Instruments conducted a fascinating survey, reviewing its last fifty or so successful and unsuccessful new-product introductions, and found that one factor marked *every* failure: 'Without exception, we found we hadn't had a volunteer champion. There was someone we had cajoled into taking on the task.' The executive who told us this added: 'When we take a look at a product and decide whether to push it or not these days, we've got a new set of criteria. Number one is the presence of a zealous, volunteer champion. After that comes market potential and project economics in a distant second and third.'[7]

In my own survey I found that eight of the thirteen innovation attempts had a clearly identifiable product champion. My team and I played that role for the stripper-gatherer; all six other product champions from the public sector were individuals or small groups from the original R&D teams.[8] It was quite natural for me to become a product champion because I had a large personal stake in seeing my machine survive and thrive.

But should the R&D team, even if they are motivated and have the required knowledge, leave the research laboratory to work in the field with manufacturers and farmers? Is this really the best use of resources? Research – at Texas Instruments again – seems to show that it is. Ten years before Peters' and Waterman's survey, Christopher Layton, Christopher Harlow and Charles de Horton carried out a similar study of the factors affecting the success of ten key innovations in Europe and the USA. They wrote:

> Texas Instruments systematically hives off cells of development engineers who have developed a product to become a small production/profit centre of their own.... Our studies showed that an important factor in successful innovation is the transfer of information from development to production; and here we found no substitute for the movement of people, including highly qualified ones.[9]

In my view, the R&D team needs to be involved in the commercialisation of its technology in order to fill the knowledge gaps that prevented it 'finishing' its development in the first place. Working with the *key stakeholders* – the manufacturers, users and those who might suffer from the innovation such as manual labourers – gives the research team a chance to increase its knowledge and improve the technology by doing some learning selection itself.

This seems so obvious that many readers might well feel that nurturing is just another term for on-farm testing or adaptive research that any good research project would carry out before releasing a finished technology. This is not the case, however, because the nurturing required for a complex technology like a flash dryer cannot be done, or would be prohibitively expensive to do, before the technology is released. 'Finishing' a technology requires innovations, particularly organisational ones, that can only made by farmers when they adopt the technology for real – in other words, when they have invested their hard-earned cash and are committed to make it work. For example, the mechanical reaper was sabotaged in the Philippines for years by labourers who saw the machine as a threat to their livelihoods. Reinventing a method used by British labourers in the early 1900s, they stuck iron rods among the rice stems to break the reaper's cutterbar. Today, though, the sabotage has stopped and the reaper is being widely used in some localities because the owners have agreed to rent their machines to the harvest labourers rather than competing directly with them. This arrangement enables the labourers to harvest more, and earn more. Through 'constructive conflict' a settlement has been reached that shares the benefit of the new technology, something that would not have happened if a research institute had merely lent a farmer a machine to try out for a season or two. 'Why should I upset my neighbours and the people I rely on to transplant and weed my crop for a machine I don't own?' the farmers would have thought. The environment in which the machine was to have been used would not have changed.

This example illustrates the truth of Lewin's observation that learning outcomes are a function of the interaction between learners and their environments. It suggests that we should choose the people – the *key stakeholders* – and the environments in which we first attempt to commercialise a new technology. We need to work with people who have the characteristics of Rogers' innovators[10] because this will ensure they are motivated, prepared to take risks and will enjoy the challenge of making the technology work. They are also likely to be technically proficient.

I found that newspaper articles describing the stripper-gatherer were a very effective way of finding innovators with these characteristics. So did Dr Hien and his team when they made their first sales of the SRR dryer. The approach works because it requires potential adopters to invest time and effort to seek out further information, a step which eliminates all but the most motivated of them. A random sample of nineteen individual farmers who had bought the stripper-gatherer revealed that over half had either graduated from tertiary education or had an engineering or technical qualification. They were also relatively rich, with farms seven times larger than average. Some of the reasons a purchaser gave me for adopting the stripper are set out in Box 3.1. They show that he was keen to try the machine even though he expected problems with it.

Eng. Santiago's words reveal the extent to which an individual farmer who has paid his own money to buy a new technology is prepared to go to make it work. Besides having the characteristics of Rogers' innovative adopter, Eng. Santiago is also what Eric von Hippel calls a lead user, by which he means someone who faces problems that will become general months or years later. As his account shows, Eng. Santiago was well aware that it was becoming increasingly difficult to find labourers to harvest his rice fields. He

Box 3.1 Excerpt of an interview with an innovative stripper-gatherer harvester adopter, Eng. Santiago

Most of the farmers' children in the country today, and even other children, like to get an education. After which they shun farming. Hence the scarcity of harvest labour, and even farmers. Everybody leaves [the countryside]. After high school, they enter college or vocational schools. Instead of farming they get jobs in the towns and cities.... So manual labour in the field becomes scarce.

If harvesting and transplanting technologies are not improved, most people will some day stop farming. So I bought the stripper-gatherer. There aren't enough manual harvesters here during the peak [harvest] season. Our crops would become over-mature and then only two or three people would show up to harvest. It is really difficult for us.

Before only the [Kubota] reaper was used [in this area], apparently made in Japan. I learned from Department of Agriculture technicians that IRRI in Los Baños had a more advanced reaper. I asked my brother who's in Manila to ask [IRRI] for the design. The Department of Agriculture people told me it was simple and easy to build. My brother was not given the design but was referred to Ropali. So I visited Ropali and they recommended the machine to me. I asked them who had bought the machine already and they referred me to Mr [Eng.] Reyes.

Mr Reyes discouraged me from buying the stripper because Ropali's production [quality] still needed much improvement. Manual labour is scarce here during the peak harvest season. When I saw the unit, I liked the operating principle, but not its inferior craftsmanship. When I visited Ropali again they wanted to demonstrate–deliver to me, meaning they'd demonstrate it and consider it sold.

I weighed things up. If it breaks often can I fix it? ... I saw during the demonstration that the principle was feasible – the way it gathered grains. But could I maintain it? I wondered. I thought I could maintain it so I bought a unit. The first time I used the machine I didn't follow their [Ropali technicians'] advice to put the grains [stripped material] on a canvas [before threshing]. I put [the stripped material] straight from the box into sacks. Two operators alternated; and also two helpers.

A disadvantage is that if the machine breaks down after only one hour you pay the operators a full day. Most of the parts are pipes. Most of the pipes crack in or near the joints. My main problem was the frame.... I weld [the pipes] and they crack again. So I welded flat bars [on the frame]. Near the joints I welded GI [metal] sheet-stiffeners. After this, welding wasn't a problem anymore.

The handle also twisted since it is only pipe. So I put two stiffeners, which improved it. The new problem is that it [the handle height] can't be adjusted anymore.

The skid shafting also twists. So I put a $1^1/_4$ [inch] flat bar and a stopper to control the twisting. The rotor also bent so I welded a stiffener inside and outside. Even at fast rotor speeds it [the rotor] does not bend any more.

As the stripper is a new innovation in harvesting, those of us who bought the first units should be entitled to free renovation. We have had to introduce a number of innovations. Given this, other improvements should be made to our machines. Making improvements ourselves costs money. Our machines will become more expensive. The manufacturer should be responsible for making these improvements. At least they could pay us to make the improvements. This will make us pioneer buyers feel that we are being properly acknowledged and supported.

was also in a position to benefit from a solution because his farm was nearly four times larger than average.[11] Significantly, although Von Hippel's book was written primarily for readers in first-world industries, he says that lead users should be part of the product development process.[12]

The difference between an innovative adopter like Eng. Santiago and unmotivated adopters became clear when I interviewed nine co-ops which had been given stripper-gatherers by the Philippines government and found that they were much more likely to give up on the technology as soon as a breakdown or problem emerged. Antonio Atienza, a line engineer working for a flash dryer manufacturer, told me later that he had reached a similar conclusion. 'People who are given the machine as a dole-out [for free] don't value it,' he said.

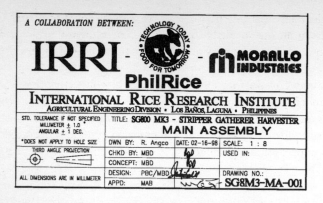

Figure 3.3 Title box used on IRRI's drawings of the Mark III stripper-gatherer showing the joint ownership of the design

The same applies to the manufacturers who are going to make the new equipment – if they are given government orders too easily they won't attempt to improve the technology. Just as there are innovative adopters, there are innovative manufacturers, and the stripper built by Morallo Metal Industries was so good that we decided to base our Mark III design on it. The firm's owner, Eng. Lawrence Morallo, even allowed IRRI to release his design to other manufacturers 'because the stripper-gatherer can still be improved and we can benefit from other manufacturers' innovations'. Indeed, Morallo had already benefited from the manufacturers' innovations included in the first IRRI drawings of the stripper-gatherer he had received. He explained to me that if the manufacturers, IRRI and PhilRice, could collectively solve the problems with the stripper-gatherer then the market would be big enough for him and his competitors. The shared ownership of the Mark III is shown in the title box used on the drawings shown in Figure 3.3.

What made Morallo Industries special? First, as it was a relatively small family-run business where the main engineer was also the joint owner and manager, there were no bureaucratic impediments to novelty generation. Second, the company did not depend on government orders and was on the lookout for new products it could sell to farmers at an unsubsidised rate. Third, the company prided itself on quality and, finally, Lawrence Morallo himself was an excellent engineer.

The lesson I took from all this was that, although the early users and manufacturers of a new technology select themselves, innovation managers can influence the selection, and hence the result of the learning selection process, by not making the technology too easy or cheap to adopt. Erecting a barrier or two favours the self-selection of the right sort of people. Innovation managers should also introduce the technology somewhere where there is a real need for it in order to ensure it benefits from an environment that provides lots of motivation to the key stakeholders.

Clearly an R&D team, or anyone else for that matter, should not champion a new technology indefinitely. Nurturing and product championship can stop when three conditions are met:

1. The technology is fit enough to be adopted by the early adopters (the group who adopt after the innovators).[13]
2. The key stakeholders are motivated to continue to promote, sell and improve the technology. The profit motive and the forces of competition will normally ensure this is the case once the technology has become fit enough to capture a market.
3. The key stakeholders have had their knowledge gaps plugged sufficiently well to be able to carry out learning selection themselves in a way that increases the fitness of the technology.

We can therefore define the end of the adaptation phase as either the point where these three conditions are met, or the point at which it becomes clear that they won't be met and the R&D team should stop flogging a dead horse. In other words, the adaptation phase ends when an adoption process that began with the first commercial release either becomes self-sustaining or fails.

Putting it another way still, the adaptation phase ends when learning selection turns into market selection. Joel Mokyr, Professor of Economics and History at Northwestern University in the USA, has already said market selection is analogous to natural selection.[14] Market selection occurs when the market is big and knowledgeable enough to provide an effective selection mechanism and manufacturers are numerous and knowledgeable enough to generate

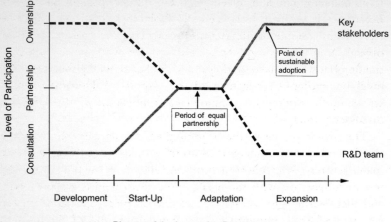

Figure 3.4 How levels of stakeholder participation change during innovation

beneficial novelties themselves, or spot an improvement when they see one elsewhere. In other words, market selection is learning selection that does not require nurturing – it is learning selection controlled and carried out by the key stakeholders after the R&D team has withdrawn. Figure 3.4, which is based on my research findings and experience, shows how the participation of the two stakeholder groups – the public sector R&D team and the key stakeholders – changes during the innovation cycle.

When a public sector R&D team is developing its ideas initially, manufacturers and users – the key stakeholders – find the project somewhat speculative and abstract. They are therefore not prepared to invest much more than their time to talk to the team about its ideas. In other words, they will act as its consultants. These two levels of involvement are illustrated above in the development phase. However, once the R&D team has produced a prototype that shows it has market potential by meeting a need, attitudes change, particularly because it is easier for the key stakeholders to visualise what the R&D team is trying to do. 'Because prototypes are physical or visual objects, they can communicate with people who have no special training but whose untutored eye may predict general public response much better than the judgement of the "experts",'[15] Dorothy Leonard writes in the survey of technological innovation in the USA we discussed earlier.

The prototype marks the beginning of the start-up phase during which the key stakeholders build up their stake by, in the case of the manufacturers, investing some time and money in building a market-test prototype, or, with the users, agreeing to field-test a prototype and then learning to use it. The adaptation phase begins when the key stakeholders' commitment is roughly equal to that of the research team. This is usually when the first innovator–adopters start buying the machine and the first manufacturers begin commercial production.

At this stage, the learning selection model tells us that the participants are acting as novelty-generators and selectors, and that their interactions are leading to the diffusion of the technology. As the adaptation phase continues, the key stakeholders learn more about the technology and, with the help of the R&D team, improve its fitness. As this happens, the beneficiaries begin to take over ownership of the process. They gain full control when the R&D team can reduce its involvement to that of consultants. Sustainable adoption is then achieved and market selection starts to work.

This learning selection map of the innovation process was developed in relation to technologies invented and introduced by the public sector, which, because of its customary short funding cycles, were handed over to manufacturers and users well before they were mature. This being so, does it have any relevance to a private-sector company which pioneers a new technology? After all, a private company cannot afford many failures and still stay in business. Nor can it afford the bad publicity that release of an immature and unproven technology would undoubtedly bring.

Only one harvesting technology, the Kubota reaper, and one drying technology, the Suncue dryer, had been introduced to the Philippines by private companies and were included in my survey. In both cases, the firms were based outside the Philippines and had far greater financial resources than any Philippines machinery manufacturer.

Moreover, both technologies were tried and tested before being introduced to the Philippines because they had already been developed and launched elsewhere. As a result, the first buyers of the privately developed machines had far fewer problems with them than did the first adopters of the new technologies introduced by the public sector. For example, when the publicly developed mechanical harvester – the CAAMS/IRRI reaper to which I have already referred (p. 39) – was introduced to the Philippines in 1982, it initially enjoyed a phenomenal success and by the end of 1983 twenty-seven manufacturers had built 430 machines. However, Kubota, a Japanese company, introduced a very similar machine in 1983 and this, although 70 per cent more expensive, was outselling the CAAMS/IRRI design by the end of 1984 because, as I mentioned, the locally made machines had developed a very bad name for quality and reliability. Indeed, the quality of the Japanese machine was so superior that production of the CAAMS/IRRI type soon ceased completely.

So, if people have fewer problems with privately developed machines, should the public sector be involved in agricultural R&D at all? Some donors seem to have come to the conclusion that it shouldn't be, and have cut their funding so severely that now none of the sixteen CGIAR centres has a separate agricultural engineering division. Even IRRI's Agricultural Engineering Division, where I used to work, has been downgraded to a unit and the number of engineers employed has fallen from twenty-six in its heyday to seven.

According to the learning selection model, though, these funding cuts were a mistake for two reasons. One is that stakeholder motivation is very important; the other is that it is best to have multiple sources of novelty generation. Let us look at motivation first. Companies obviously want to see a good return on their investment in R&D. Consequently, they will keep R&D costs and risks to a minimum in peripheral markets like the Philippines or Vietnam by transferring technologies that have been proven in other countries rather than adapting or developing new ones. The case studies bear this out: no local adaptations were made to either the Kubota reaper or the Suncue dryer when they were introduced to the Philippines. In the case of the Suncue, the Philippine importer, Henry Go, risked comparatively little because he knew the technology was already working in Taiwan. Consequently, neither he nor the manufacturer carried out any pre-launch tests in the Philippines market. The same

Table 3.1 The private sector is less inventive than the public sector

Level of inventive activity		Public sector	Private sector
High	**New embodiment**	SRR dryer SG harvester Flash dryer	
	Local adaptation	Flatbed dryer CAAMS/IRRI mechanical reaper	
Low	**Direct transfer**		Kubota mechanical reaper Suncue recirculating dryer

was true for the Kubota reaper, which was developed and proved for the Thai market.

By contrast, Le Van Bahn's design for the SRR dryer was unique and had never been tested anywhere in the world. Consequently, the University of Agriculture and Forestry, for whom he worked, and the German government, which funded the project, were taking much more risk than Suncue had in the Philippines when they invested money and resources in the project.

Table 3.1 grades the level of inventive activity of the technology introductions I surveyed. The private-sector introductions rate low because they were technology transfers. Of course, the public sector transferred technologies from one country to another too, but when this happened the agency involved did not just ship finished machines to be sold, as had happened with the Kubota and Suncue products. Instead the public agencies either sent drawings or shipped a prototype of a technology that, in most cases, had not been commercially proven, and the recipient agency then invested resources in pilot testing and local adaptation. This intermediary level of invention is described in Table 3.1 as 'local adaptation'.

If a private company does decide to undertake research and development on a new product, one would expect it to concentrate on technologies suited to large, prosperous markets in which it can hope to make and continue to make a large profit. Poor farmers do not constitute such a market. Moreover, the maintenance of a healthy profit requires that no one comes out with a similar product which undercuts them and, as many developing countries lack enforceable patent laws, this means that companies tend to confine their development efforts to products with a 'natural patent' that hinders copying. In practice this means developing machines that are too complicated to be copied easily. Both the Kubota reaper and the Suncue recirculating dryer fall into this category – they are complex machines that require manufacturing processes, materials and skills not readily available in the Philippines and elsewhere. Naturally, their complexity makes both machines so expensive that they can only be afforded by rich farmers and rice millers. It also makes them difficult to maintain and repair. I visited a factory in Vietnam that was trying to develop its own version of a Japanese combine harvester because its complexity made it hard for their competitors to copy, even though the manager I talked to admitted a simpler design would be better for farmers because it would be easier to find spare parts and fix.

Table 3.2 shows the limited portion of the developing-country market that private companies are likely to supply with new technology. Without access to new technology poorer farmers are not going to be able to adapt to changing economic conditions and are likely to go out of business, with serious implications for their country's culture and its urban and rural environments.

Now let us look at how public-sector involvement can catalyse and foster multiple sources of innovation and learning selection in ways that purely private-sector involvement does not. This is because, as public research institutes want private companies to use the new technology, they make it as easy as possible for them to do so. A private company, by contrast, wants to become, and remain, the only manufacturer in order to get the maximum return on its investment. If it is successful, it inevitably remains the only novelty generator, with the result that the technology evolves less quickly. Indeed, it may not evolve at all in markets where geographic distance restricts feedback or which the manufacturer considers peripheral. No changes whatsoever were made to adapt the Kubota reaper to Phil-

Table 3.2 Shaded area shows the different types of technologies categorised by level of inventive activity required in their development and the potential value of sales. Private sector companies are most likely to meet the need for technologies that can be directly transferred from another country, are complex so they cannot be easily copied, and where profit potential is high

Level of invention	Design complexity	Profit potential	
		High	Low
New embodiment	High Medium Low		
Local adaptation	High Medium Low		
Direct transfer	High Medium Low		

████████████ Subset of main interest to foreign companies

ippines conditions in the fifteen years from its first release in 1983. The machine has remained expensive and sales have remained fairly constant at only about a hundred a year.

Our model also helps us see that the provision of prototypes is only part of what the public sector and government can do to tackle the low rate of learning selection that is at the heart of the problem. Creating the right environment for learning selection is also critical, and can make the difference between whether private manufacturers are 'selfish' or 'generous', and whether they take part in learning selection or not. Lawrence Morallo gave some clues to what the right environment for co-operation might be when he explained to me why he had allowed IRRI to distribute freely the drawings of his improved SG800 harvester: 'the technology can still be improved, I can also learn from other manufacturers and the market is big enough for all of us once we get the machine working to farmers' satisfaction.'

He knew that the technology would evolve faster through co-operation and sharing. Morallo gave his ideas to his competitors for free because IRRI had set up conditions in which it was beneficial for him to do so. IRRI had done this by working with a group of manufacturers, including Morallo, where an unwritten rule was that IRRI gave its intellectual property for free on the understanding that the manufacturers would reciprocate, and not try to patent any aspect of the technology.

There are many other ways in which government and the public sector can create a nurturing environment for learning selection. For example, the government could provide manufacturers with grants and access to information to help them develop new technology, or it could help develop local credit sources so farmers can borrow money more easily and cheaply.

One of the implications of the learning selection model is that peoples' needs are best met when there are many novelty-generators close to the problem and each other. This implies that the government and public sector should be working to support local workshops. The case of the mechanical reaper in Vietnam supports this. The CAAMS–IRRI reaper was also sent to Vietnam; after an initial spurt of enthusiasm, as in the Philippines, it was rejected by the market because of its poor quality. In Vietnam, though, there were no Kubota reapers to put local manufacturers out of business. Several manufacturers continued producing and learned how to build better machines. As a result Vietnamese farmers can now buy locally made reapers of similar quality to the Kubota reaper but at 40 per cent of the price, a factor which means that users find the Vietnamese machine highly profitable while the Kubota reaper is not. Moreover, the development of this reaper has given Vietnamese manufacturers experience with cutterbar technology. They are consequently in a much better position than their Philippines counterparts to follow the Thais in developing their own combine harvester industry (see Box 3.2).

Conclusions

We have learned so far that people are more likely to benefit from agricultural equipment if they can understand it and modify it themselves, or suggest modifications to manufacturers with whom they

Box 3.2 Invention of an axial-flow thresher by IRRI in the 1970s helped create a multi-million-dollar combine harvester industry in Thailand in the 1990s

Land reform in the Philippines in the 1970s broke up many of the feudal *haciendas* [estates] and gave the land to the tenants. Before the break-up, so that their rent could be extracted 'at source', the tenants had been forced by their landlords to bring their rice crops to be threshed by large McCormick threshers imported from the USA. In response to the needs of the new class of small landowners, IRRI developed a low-cost, lightweight axial-flow thresher in 1972 that was cheap enough to be owned by the farmers themselves and light enough to be moved to their crops rather than the other way around. The design was phenomenally successful – in just ten years, seventy-five manufacturers set up in production and built over 19,000 units in the Philippines alone.

Some economists argue that the need for small threshers was such in the 1970s that the Philippines private sector would have developed them[16] without public-sector R&D. The patent records suggest this is true, but all the designs patented at the time used the same tangential-flow principle as the McCormick thresher. IRRI's axial-flow thresher was much simpler and eliminated the bulky and expensive straw walkers required by all the tangential-flow designs. It is therefore reasonable to believe that, left to the private sector, a technically inferior design would have been introduced which would not only have been more expensive but would have failed to extract more of the farmer's crop. Economists with whom I have discussed this say that it wouldn't have mattered too much because sooner or later market forces would have led to technically superior designs. However, recent developments in economic thinking have recognised that, once well established in the market, inferior technologies can keep better ones at bay,[17] just as they are said to have done with the QWERTY keyboard and the VHS video system.

IRRI sent blueprints of the axial-flow thresher to Thailand and manufacturers built the first machines there in 1976. They found that the design had to be extensively modified to meet Thai conditions, which they were able to do successfully; by 1985, twenty-five manufacturers had built over 25,000 machines.[18] This helped create a dynamic, experienced agricultural machinery industry which was able to develop a combine harvester in the early 1990s, when, as a consequence of rapid economic growth, farmers could no longer find people to hand harvest their crops. The axial-flow thresher was an integral part of the combine's design and contributed in no small way to the market acceptance of the machine. By January 1998 over two thousand combine harvesters had been built, worth over $60 million, and exports had begun.[19] In short, a design developed with public-sector money in response to changes in one country was pivotal to the development of a multi-million-dollar industry in another.

can communicate closely. In other words, agricultural engineering technologies evolve more quickly the more people there are in a position to generate novelties. Private ownership of a technology through legal or natural patents consequently slows down technological evolution because it reduces the number of novelty-generators. It therefore reduces the potential benefits that a new technology can bring. Furthermore, as private companies are motivated primarily to earn money rather than to meet people's needs, they are likely to introduce overcomplex technologies which are not in everyone's best interests. Once introduced, these suboptimal technologies can prevent better solutions being reached. Learning selection and the evolution of optimal solutions is best served by an environment in which the key stakeholders – manufacturers and farmers – are motivated to interact with each other and share knowledge. Government and the public sector have important roles to play in creating this environment.

If these conclusions hold for non-agricultural types of technology, then they have far-reaching consequences about how we attempt to manage innovation and the way we look at public and private sector roles in R&D. In the next four chapters we examine the extent to which the learning selection model applies to very different types of technology in developed as well as developing countries.

4

Blowing in the wind

How 'bottom-up' beat 'top-down' for the
billion-dollar wind turbine industry

When the climate of the west coast of Ireland became wetter five thousand years ago, the ground got so waterlogged and acidic that most trees died. Although some were then blown over in gales and others were burned in huge forest fires, a substantial quantity of their wood still lies preserved under a blanket of peat. This wood, whether the remains of pine or of oak trees, is wonderful to carve. The oak is matt black while the pine – bog deal – has a lovely reddish-brown colour when dried. Its particular attraction for me is that the weathering and erosion each piece underwent before it was covered by the swamp means that fantastic shapes develop when you cut the damaged material away.

The best place to find bog wood is obviously where peat is being removed so, while writing this chapter, I drove to a bog in north County Mayo which is being cut to supply a peat-fired power station at Bellacorick a short distance away. The peat is harvested by shaving a thin layer from the surface of the bog and leaving it in the open to dry. It is then burned like coal to raise steam to drive turbines. Ireland produces 16 per cent of its electricity this way.[1]

It is hard to imagine Mayo getting wetter but the peat being burned at Bellacorick might be making it so. The combustion of fossil fuels – of which peat is one – has been the major source of the extra CO_2 and the other 'greenhouse gases' in the atmosphere which are causing the whole planet to warm up. One effect of this could be to make Ireland drier in summer and wetter in winter.[2] The Arctic, the

Figure 4.1 Danish wind turbines generating almost 10 per cent of the electricity produced by the Bellacorick peat power station

'thermostat of the world', is already the fastest warming area on Earth. The average temperature there has risen by 1.5°C since 1965[3] and an area the size of France has melted in the last twenty years. If the thaw continues, sea levels could rise by 54 cm in the next fifty years,[4] threatening many of the world's largest cities with flooding.

The power station's huge cooling tower can be seen from forty miles away. Next to it are two chimneys that pump out more that 200,000 tonnes of CO_2 per year.[5] As we drove closer, however, we began to see another kind of tower – those of twenty-one wind turbines which have been erected in a piece of dug-out bog near the power station, their white blades turning steadily in the stiff breeze from the sea. These machines provide enough power for 4,500 households – equivalent to 8.5 per cent[6] of the output of the Bellacorick power station – without producing any carbon dioxide at all. Of course wind turbines do require some fossil fuel energy to build them but they 'repay' this within three months to a year, depending on the average wind speed at the site they are erected. Indeed, in its life, a wind turbine can produce thirty-three times more energy than it took to build,[7] making wind power one of the most environmentally friendly means of generating electricity.

We found the bog deal we were looking for at the foot of one of the turbine towers where a bulldozer had pushed the remains of the ancient trees into a large pile. As I looked at the trunks it was hard to believe that they were five thousand years old. Some pieces still had their bark or were charred by the forest fires. The evidence that climate change happens was there in front of me, while overhead the blades of a technology that could help prevent a similar catastrophic change in the environment today swished in the wind.

It is over 130 years since an Irish scientist, John Tyndall, became the first person to show that the water vapour and carbon dioxide in the atmosphere maintained the world's temperature by absorbing infrared radiation. It is three decades since a UN report first referred to the potentially 'catastrophic warming effect' that an increase in atmospheric CO_2 might have on the world's climate.[8] And it was in 1988 that the Intergovernmental Panel on Climate Change was set up to co-ordinate the world's response to this problem, with the result that some 170 countries undertook to limit or reduce their greenhouse gas emissions. Their need to do so has been a driving force behind the rapid development of wind turbines during the 1990s.

By the end of 2000 there was 13,500 MW[9] of wind power generating capacity installed world-wide producing about 23 TWh of electricity.[10] This is about as much as Ireland, with a population of 3.5 million, uses in fifteen months[11] and 1,350 times more than the Bellacorick wind farm produces. These turbines are reducing the amount of CO_2 emitted into the world's atmosphere by 19.4 million tonnes each year.[12] BTM Consult ApS, a Danish consultancy specialising in wind energy, expects that this capacity, and the amount of CO_2 emissions saved, will double between 1999 and 2002.[13] Indeed, wind energy capacity has been expanding, on average, by 27 per cent per year since 1992, making it the fastest growing form of energy production in the world. According to *Windkraft Journal*, between 30,000 and 45,000 people are employed in the industry in Europe, up from just 5,000 in 1990, and the magazine predicts that 500,000 people could be employed by 2010 if present growth rates continue.[14] At present, installation rates are faster than those of nuclear power in the 1960s and 1970s and today's capacity is equivalent to that of nuclear power stations in 1968. Unlike nuclear power, though, it doesn't take a lot of energy to decommission wind turbines, and there are no potentially catastrophic environmental consequences from doing so. In 1996, an independent survey in Denmark found that when external costs and benefits are incorporated (including the CO_2 emissions saved) electricity generated by the wind is cheaper than gas- or coal-fired power stations.[15] By 1999 electricity from large windfarms was competitive with 'clean' coal power stations. It cost about $0.05 per kilowatt-hour.[16]

The reason I chose the runaway success of the wind turbine industry as a case study for this book is that its innovation history is strikingly similar to those of the flash dryer and flatbed dryers we discussed in the second chapter. For example, millions of dollars were wasted on public-sector-funded wind turbine R&D in the USA, Sweden, Germany and the UK over the years, just as it was squandered on the flash dryer in the Philippines. Wind turbine engineers were also driven too much by their theoretical models and too little by practical realities and the needs of users, just as the dryer developers had been.[17]

Another similarity is that the successful wind turbine design and the organisational changes and innovations required to adopt it came from the adopters and from the small manufacturers who built the first machines rather than from the research labs, just as they did in Vietnam with Dr Hien's flatbed dryer. This attracted me because it meant that the learning selection model developed for the very visible technological evolution that occurs with relatively simple farm machinery in developing countries might also apply to the evolution of a highly complex and sophisticated technology that has spawned a multi-million-dollar industry. So, let us test the extent to which the learning selection model can explain why the bottom-up approach led to the development of successful wind turbines in Denmark and why the top-down approach failed in the USA. We'll look at the history of the industry in terms of novelty generation, selection, diffusion and stakeholder motivations.

Early history

The wind provides one of the oldest sources of mechanical power known to man. The first written evidence of the existence of windmills comes from Hero of Alexandria in the second century BC.[18]

They were used in England in the eleventh century and spread throughout Europe. In the Netherlands in particular they became cultural icons – it is hard to think of the country without thinking about them too.

The development of steam engines that could provide power at any time and in any location, not just on a windy day in a windy place, led to the relative decline of windmills,[19] but while coal and steam power remained relatively expensive, windmills were still used and the technology continued to improve incrementally as it had done for the previous two thousand years. For example, the Dutch-type windmill was improved by replacing its broad canvas sails with adjustable narrow vanes. The improved mills were called *klapsejlsmølles* (clap-sail windmills). Then in the nineteenth century, the multi-bladed steel windmill, used for pumping water in so many cowboy films, began to appear. These are known colloquially as 'wind roses'. These improvements meant that wind power was still widely used at the beginning of the twentieth century, and Denmark had 30,000 'wind roses' and *klapsejlsmølles* working as late as 1931.[20]

The Danish experience

Development phase

With one exception, the inventors whose work made possible the widespread use of electricity for light and power ignored the wind as a source of energy for generators because of its unreliable nature. Michael Faraday invented the first dynamo in 1831[21] but electricity was not widely used for lighting until 1872 when filament lights were installed in St Petersburg docks. (The first electric streetlights in London were only switched on in 1878 and in New York in 1880.) Although an electric railway was demonstrated by Siemens in Berlin in 1879, the first practical AC electric motor was not invented until 1888 – Nicholas Telsa was responsible and George Westinghouse put it into production. The first public power station in New York was opened by Edison in 1882. It had six steam-powered generators, each of which could light 1,750 50-watt lamps. The first hydroelectric generating station was opened at Appleton, Wisconsin, the same year.

The single exception was the 'Danish Edison', a secondary-school teacher, Poul la Cour, who successfully generated electricity using a windmill in 1891 and used it to light his school and some neighbouring houses by electrolysing water into hydrogen and oxygen and then burning the hydrogen in converted gas lights. The system operated for many years, although not without a few explosions. La Cour was also remarkable because he was the first person to carry out systematic experiments in a wind tunnel to improve windmill design. He recommended two to four blades for generating electricity, far fewer than on the 'wind rose'. Several hundred La Cour-inspired wind turbines were in use in Denmark in 1925 generating between 5 and 25 kW. La Cour also trained 'wind electricians' and some of his former students helped continue the technology development path he began. This was particularly the case during the two world wars, when coal imports were difficult. Denmark does not have its own coalfields.

Although the resumption of cheap coal imports effectively killed off the use of wind turbines for generating electricity after the Second World War, worries about the wisdom of reverting to near-total reliance on imported energy led a Danish electricity company to invest in wind power research. Johannes Juul, an ex-student of La Cour, led the project and spent the years between 1947 and 1957 developing his design. Juul was a practical engineer and learned much from the field performance of earlier wind turbines. The design he eventually fixed upon was very simple. It had three blades mounted up-wind of the generator. These were fixed rigidly to the rotor, which turned at a slow speed but was coupled through a gearbox, which increased the rate of rotation, to the generator. The machine was built to prevent its blades spinning too fast if the drive mechanism between the blades and the generator somehow became uncoupled. This was done by 'stall regulation' – the blades were designed with an aerofoil (wing) shape which caused the air passing over them to become increasingly turbulent as the rotor speed increased above normal, thus dissipating the energy that could otherwise break the turbine up in strong winds. Another important feature of Juul's design was that it was not limited to supplying the needs of off-grid sites; it generated AC power that could be fed directly into the national power grid.[22]

Juul's machine, known as the Gedser wind turbine, after the village where it was built, generated 200 kW and set the design characteristics for the 'Danish wind turbine' that had 55 per cent of the world market in 1999. It ran continuously from 1958 to 1967, when a chain broke and was not replaced because an economic calculation had shown that electricity produced by the machine was twice as expensive as that generated by a power station run on oil.[23] The real reason for ending the experiment, however, was that the electricity companies had become more interested in nuclear power than the wind as an alternative to fossil fuels. The 1960s were the low point for wind power in Denmark. Cheap oil and the promise of nuclear energy 'too cheap to meter' killed nearly all wind research activity. The tide began to turn in 1973, however, when the first OPEC export restrictions tripled oil prices and led some countries to introduce rationing. Alternatives to fossil fuel became attractive again.

Adaptation phase

The emerging Green movement played a key role in wind energy's rebirth. Its members, often characterised disparagingly as hippies, challenged the conventional view that nuclear power would replace oil when it ran out and that wind power was not an option because it was too unreliable and had been tried before and failed. Among them was a carpenter from west Jutland, Christian Riisager, who set out to build his own wind turbine based on Juul's machine. 'He was a wild man, full of ideas who was prepared to try and try and try', says Flemming Tranæs, chairman of the Association of Danish Wind Turbine Owners (Danske Vindkraftwaerker, or DV). After several accidents and setbacks Riisager built a 22 kW machine with wooden blades mounted upwind of the generator, as on the Gedser turbine, and held in place by wire guy ropes. He also followed Juul in building the machine out of standard, cheap parts, such as car components. Eize de Vries, a wind power consultant and contributing editor to *Windstats Newsletter*, describes Riisager's method as a blacksmith's approach. 'The use of scrap or readily available materials often results in [technically] sub-optimum solutions, unfit for series production', he says. 'This intuitive approach also depended a lot on common sense, craftsmanship and luck.'[24]

After a lot of negotiation, Riisager persuaded an electricity company to connect him up to the grid, an achievement which played a big part in shaping the technical developments that followed. He and his wife Boe set up a company to build their machines and by 1978 there were thirty Riisager turbines installed throughout Denmark. Unfortunately their products proved unreliable and damage claims by twelve owners drove the couple out of business.[25]

While Riisager and others were building relatively small wind turbines, the Tvind schools, an organisation of folk highschools set up to promulgate socialist values, embarked on a much more ambitious enterprise. The schools wanted to build a 2 MW machine, nearly a hundred times bigger than Riisager's, and adopted a communal self-help approach to the job, complete with equal gender work quotas. Outside experts who sympathised with the group's ideology offered their help for free. For example, Helge Pedersen, who had been designing turbine blades since before the Second World War, built the 54-metre diameter three-bladed rotor in glass-fibre reinforced resin rather than wood. The major departure from Juul's design was that the blades were downwind of the tower. It was built between 1976 and 1978; although it has never generated more than 1 MW, at the time it was the largest wind turbine in the world. It is still running today and cost only $1 million to build.

The success of the Tvind turbine, built with no public money, stands in sharp contrast to the simultaneous government-sponsored efforts to develop a large wind turbine. The Danish Technical University received the best part of 50 million kroner ($7 million) – 75 per cent of the public money spent on wind power between 1976 to 1982 – to carry out research and development on wind power. The university designed two 630 kW machines, known as the Nibe turbines, which were commissioned in 1980 but soon taken out of use, again because economists calculated that the cost of the electricity they were generating was too high. Opponents of wind energy used their failure to argue against further government funding for wind power development. However, the university's work did benefit the industry by leading to a better understanding of the load patterns on wind turbines in different wind conditions.

If economists had been anywhere near the Tvind turbine it would probably have been shut down for not being cost-effective too; however, it was built by a community that had values other than narrow economic measures of worth. The community wanted their turbine, felt pride in their creation and kept it running. In other words there was a nurturing environment for the Tvind turbine but not for the Nibe and Gedser machines. This underscores a fact scientists and engineers often overlook: that history judges a technology not on any absolute scientific criteria but on whether people used it and benefited from it. Adapting the parable of the seed and the sower, a technology, however good it is technically, will only be adopted and prosper if it falls on fertile ground.

An important component of the nurturing environment for wind turbines that currently exists in Denmark dates back to 1978, when wind turbine owners, who had been holding regular 'wind meetings' since 1975 to exchange ideas and experiences and to motivate each other,[26] formed themselves into the Association of Danish Wind Turbine Owners. It set itself two goals: to negotiate satisfactory connection and payment rates with the electricity companies to which its members sold their electricity; and, through a magazine it set up called *Naturlig Energi* (Natural Energy), to distribute information on wind turbine performance, problems and solutions.

DV's first members were people who bought wind turbines largely for idealistic reasons rather than to make money. They were prepared to put a lot of time into repairing and modifying their machines but were naturally upset if the machines were destroyed in strong winds, as happened to a number of machines made by one manufacturer – Kuriant – when the brakes failed. DV and *Naturlig Energi* helped the owners realise that this was a common problem and lobbied the manufacturer to incorporate stall regulation as a second fail-safe air brake, as Juul had done on his Gedser machine. These negotiations failed, according to Flemming Tranæs, because Kuriant thought the modification would be too expensive. 'In any case, the owner of the firm didn't really give much credence to a recommendation from a bunch of owners', he says. 'He thought that the market for wind turbines was small and he wanted to make money as quickly as possible. At the time his sales were increasing in spite of the problem.'[27]

After due warning, *Naturlig Energi* published a news story about the design fault and six months later Kuriant was bankrupt. A similar episode occurred when AJ Windpower's machines were found to fall apart because the manufacturer had increased the diameter of the rotor by 20 per cent. Again the manufacturer refused to make the recommended change and went bankrupt after a warning was published. *Naturlig Energi* had proved itself to be a 'fantastic tool' for owners to identify problems and exert leverage on manufacturers to make changes.[28]

DV and *Naturlig Energi* were able to identify common problems by getting members to send in monthly reports on the performance of their wind turbines. These were used to assemble statistics on the amount of electricity generated, the numbers of non-operational machines, and the reasons for component failures. A table of the results was printed in the magazine every month, giving potential buyers and manufacturers a very clear picture of where problems were occurring. In terms of the learning selection model, *Naturlig Energi* was a very efficient selection and promulgation mechanism. DV and the wind meetings provided motivation, and the members of DV themselves generated novelties, assisted in their experiential learning by the information provided by *Naturlig Energi* and contacts with others.

Trænæs stresses that the manufacturers, represented by the Wind Turbine Manufacturers Association (FDV), quickly realised that DV was having a beneficial effect on the industry by showing how its products could be improved, and DV and FDV now have an excellent relationship. 'One of the problems we identified [with a particular manufacturer's product] was with the yawing mechanism which keeps the wind turbine facing the wind', he says.

> A wind flag on the top of the turbine housing set the direction that the turbine should face. We found that in certain winds the flag flapped. We told the manufacturer about the problem and we suggested placing the flag in a different position. The manufacturer sent us a set of flags with different-length flagpoles. We crawled up on the top of the turbine and installed them until we finally found a height that was acceptable. We told the manufacturer, who was very happy. This is just one example of how we've worked together. Collaborations like this are still happening.

Two people in particular enabled significant improvements to be made to the design. Erik Grove Nielsen, an engineering student at the Danish Technical University, built a scaled-down copy of the mould that Pedersen had used for the glass-fibre Tvind blade. Karl-Erik Jorgensen, a skilled mechanic, then took this mould and used it to build wind turbines with glass-fibre blades incorporating the Juul–Pedersen stall control that stopped a rotor from destroying itself if the speed control provided by the asynchronous generator ever failed. Jorgensen also developed an active yaw system that used an electric motor to turn the turbine to face the wind, thus overcoming the problem of slow response times to changes in wind direction.[29] He then sold a licence for the use of his improvements to Vestas, now the largest wind turbine manufacturer in the world. The Danish design of a three-bladed, upwind, active yaw, stall-controlled machine on a horizontal axis with glass-fibre blades had evolved.

In hindsight it might appear obvious that the 'Danish design' was superior to its peers, but this was not at all obvious at the time and people invested time and effort experimenting with other designs. Vestas, for example, built a vertical-axis machine but decided that the Juul–Riisager–Pedersen–Jorgensen concept had pulled so far ahead that it would be too expensive to develop a competitive vertical-axis machine. Per Dannemand Andersen, who did his Ph.D. research on wind turbines and now works at the Danish government's wind energy laboratory at Risø, tells how the Risø laboratory had six different types of wind turbine under test when he started work there in 1986, only one of which proved successful. In hindsight these five failed innovations seem a waste, but at the time 'all major and minor inventors operated in complete uncertainty about whether their projects would succeed, and thus were all part and parcel of technical creativity'.[30] If people learn from failed innovations and tell others this creates guideposts of where not to go. We can only become certain about the correct path when we are sure the others are dead ends. The free flow of information through *Naturlig Energi*, DV conferences and wind meetings helped a successful design path to evolve through learning selection. It is only with hindsight that the path appears obvious.

Another organisation that helped create a nurturing environment for wind energy in Denmark was the Renewable Energy Committee of the Danish Parliament. This was set up in 1975 in response to public environmental concern to support entrepreneurial activity in the renewable energy field. Interestingly Riisager applied unsuccessfully to the committee for a grant to develop his wind turbine, so perhaps the selection role it played was not as good as it might have been. However, it did much to make wind power respectable, and established networks within ministries and political parties which helped shape government policy towards wind energy in a favourable way, as we shall see later.[31] *Naturlig Energi*, which was sent free to politicians and policy-makers from the time it was first published, also contributed to the growth of a favourable public policy environment for wind power.[32]

From the perspective we gained in previous chapters, DV and the Renewable Energy Committee can be seen as software innovations born out of the Green movement's championing of wind power from the early 1970s onwards. Once in place, these organisational innovations evolved through learning selection themselves. The effect of the innovations was to change favourably the environment for wind turbines.

Most wind turbines installed in Denmark from 1974 to 1979 were small – between 22 and 30 kW – and were erected by individuals on their own property. Owners did not even have to apply for planning permission because few people thought they detracted from their 'visual amenity'. However, the more reliable second generation of 55 kW machines that came onto the market in 1979–1980 cost more than one family could easily afford, and turbines have been increasing in size and cost ever since. By the end of the 1990s most installations in Denmark were 600 kW machines costing roughly $600,000.[33] Local ownership of wind turbines, and with it local tolerance of them, could have ended had another organisational innovation not come along – the wind guild, a group of people from the same area who jointly buy and operate a wind turbine, a product of the Danish co-operative tradition.

Once established, wind guilds were shaped by the culture of the time and then helped shape that culture, just as DV had done. They helped keep wind power a technology of the people and so helped maintain political support. This was critically important, as a comparison between Denmark and the UK shows. In 1999 Denmark generated 10 per cent of its electricity from the wind, and plans to double its capacity by 2002,[34] while the UK generated less than 2 per cent and its installation rates have been falling because local people have developed increasingly effective ways of opposing planning requests.

The problem in the UK is one of ownership. Anonymous investors and electricity companies, rather than groups of ordinary people from the immediate area, as in Denmark, have been proposing large wind farms instead of small clusters of turbines. Most of the early applications for planning permission in Britain were granted, but

Figure 4.2 Wind turbines have become an accepted part of the Danish landscape, unlike in countries such as the UK, where lack of local ownership has led to the 'not in my back yard' opposition to wind power

gradually opinion against them hardened when it became clear that local people did not benefit from the 'bog brushes in the sky' which some thought disfigured the countryside. Twelve large windfarms went before planning inquiries between 1991 and 1993 and nine won approval. Between 1994 and 1999, however, eighteen windfarm inquiries were held and all but two were rejected[35] thanks to the 'not in my back yard' or NIMBY phenomenon.

In Denmark, by contrast, private people own 80 per cent of the wind-generating capacity, and 10 per cent of the population own shares in wind turbines, a situation which came about through the interaction between grassroots activists like the Lauritsen family, who live in Ny Solbjerg near Århus, and central government. In other words, Denmark's healthy mixture of top-down and bottom-up created an environment in which the country can hope to double its installed capacity of wind turbines in only three years.

It happened like this. When OPEC tripled oil prices for the second time in 1979, the Lauritsens wondered what they should do. 'As we used oil to heat our house we looked for ways in which we could save money', Per Lauritsen, an architect, says.[36] The wind, blowing almost unchecked over the low-lying Jutland peninsula, was the obvious answer given the legacy of La Cour and Juul. The Lauritsens suggested to their neighbours, the Vangkildes and the Sorensens, with whom they already shared a snowplough, that they buy a wind turbine together to meet their energy needs and sell any surplus to the national grid. A lot of money was involved: 350,000 kroner – about $81,000 or $27,000 per family – for a 55 kW turbine. Although the two other families needed loans secured on their properties to raise this, they said they would go ahead.

But several things needed sorting out. One was the legal basis for their joint ownership of the wind turbine, and the three families eventually set themselves up as the first wind turbine guild. This was technically a partnership rather than a co-operative because Danish law does not allow the members of a co-operative to set the interest they pay on loans against their personal income tax. It was, however, a co-operative in all other respects and established an important principle, the criterion of residency, which stated that all members had to live within 3 km of the wind turbine. This was to ensure that anyone benefiting from its electricity had also to suffer any inconvenience that its siting might bring.

Another problem the three families had to tackle was getting a connection to the national grid. During the 1970s the ninety-eight electricity companies operating in Denmark had connected owners like Riisager on a case-by-case basis. Not all these firms were keen on wind power and those that weren't didn't make connection easy. New turbine owners had to negotiate the charge for their connection to the grid and the sale and buyback price for their power individually, which led to tremendous variations. For example, some companies imposed an electric motor levy on wind turbines even though motors consume electricity and wind turbines produce it. DV took this case to the Renewable Energy Committee and won, as it did with several others, but the electricity companies did not necessarily comply with the Committee's rulings. This created uncertainty among people considering buying turbines and sales were sluggish even after a 30 per cent government grant towards their cost was introduced in 1979 to support the emerging industry.

'The resistance of the electricity companies [to wind energy] arose because they were opposed to anything that could prevent them using nuclear energy', Flemming Tranæs says. 'They wanted central management of electricity production. Turbine owners can tell incredible stories about the way power companies did whatever they could to prevent erection of wind turbines. We founded DV on 4 May 1978, the anniversary of the day Denmark was liberated from Nazi occupation, as a statement about this obstruction.'

The Ny Solbjerg families had particularly bad luck with their utility company, which refused to connect their recently formed wind guild. Per Lauritsen fought back by raising the issue of the connection of wind turbines in the Danish parliament. DV and *Naturlig Energi* were lobbying the government at the same time with the message that the utilities were running their own energy policy despite the public's continued support for wind power. Both campaigns were helped by the 1981 National Energy Plan, which proposed the installation of ten thousand wind turbines within ten years. This convinced DEF, the umbrella organisation for the electricity companies, that the case-by-case connection arrangements could not continue and it began negotiations with DV on a national agreement covering connection charges and purchase and buy-back rates. Agreement proved impossible, however, until Poul Nielsson, who had recently been appointed as Denmark's first Minister of Energy, 'hinted' that if the utilities did not reach agreement then a law would be passed which set the terms for them.[37] As a result, the utilities agreed in 1983 to pay one-third of the costs of all grid connections, with the turbine owners paying one-third and the state subsidising the rest. The power firms also undertook to pay 85 per cent of the retail electricity price to large producers and 70 per cent to owners who were producing for their own consumption and selling a surplus to the grid.[38] This agreement was binding for ten years.

In spite of the pressure they had put on DEF, many politicians shared its desire to confine wind turbines to large windfarms that could be centrally controlled. Accordingly, around the time the connection agreement was hammered out, the government borrowed an idea from California and introduced an additional 15 per cent investment subsidy for large windfarms. This created a 'wind-rush' and sales of turbines in Denmark jumped from 8 MW in 1984 to 25 MW in 1985[39] (see Figure 4.5). However, the rapid installation of large windfarms, particularly in West Jutland, alarmed many people, just as it did in Britain a decade later. A political consensus developed that providing private investors with large subsidies with which to get richer was not a legitimate use of public funds, especially if the investors were not local and did not have to live beside their machines. Consequently, and very importantly, a law passed in late December 1985 added a criterion of consumption to the criterion of proximity that the Ny Solberg families had helped establish. It restricted individual ownership of wind turbines by limiting people to selling no more than 35 per cent of their annual electricity consumption. In addition, the government withdrew the 15 per cent subsidy.

This was a major blow to the turbine manufacturers, who saw orders representing one-third of their annual domestic production cancelled.[40] Peter Karnøe, an associate professor at Copenhagen Business School who studies the wind turbine industry closely, believes the government was being cruel to be kind and saved Denmark from a serious outbreak of nimbyism which would have done much more serious damage. The only thing the government did to soften the blow was to agree with the electric companies that the latter would install 100 MW of wind power capacity between 1986 and 1990, thus making them turbine owners for the first time and raising the possibility that they might develop a more positive attitude to wind energy. However, as these installations did not start immediately, the turbine makers still faced a very difficult time.

Denmark had another important selection mechanism for wind turbine technologies in addition to DV and *Naturlig Energi*. This was the Risø Test Station for Wind Turbines, which was set up under the leadership of Helge Pedersen in 1978 with a government grant of $1 million per year for three years. Pedersen brought with him over thirty years of practical wind energy experience, and the staff he recruited were also predominantly practical rather than theoretical.

The test station was set up at a nuclear power research centre, where, housed in a small wooden shed, it was the laughing-stock of the nuclear scientists. Its relatively restricted funding and three-year time horizon meant that it kept clear of long-term research projects and made itself useful to industry as a way of ensuring further funding. As a result, the station only produced one paper for an academic journal in its first five years but, according to 'Woody' Stoddard, an American windpower pioneer, half of the twenty-five most useful wind energy reports from the 1980s.[41] A measure of the success of this strategy is that today the nuclear scientists are in a small ugly building and the wind test station occupies pride of place.

Pedersen's team was helped by world events. In 1979 the second oil crisis reminded the Danes of the dangers of their dependency on fossil fuel, and the Three Mile Island nuclear accident in the USA showed the dangers of nuclear energy. The government responded to these by passing a law giving a 30 per cent subsidy to people installing wind turbines that Risø had approved, thus forcing the station to develop and publish its evaluation criteria. The team consulted widely and eventually adopted some of DV's standards, to which it added some structural criteria from the building industry.

In hindsight, some of the specifications were very conservative, the result of uncertainty that still existed at the time over the forces to which wind turbines would be exposed. This meant that the resulting machines were solid and heavy, but this suited the culture of the mechanical and agricultural engineering firms building them.[42] In learning selection terms, the Risø criteria altered the environment to favour the rugged, relatively simple Juul–Riisager–Jorgensen design, a design which was not only well understood by the engineers and mechanics building the machines, but by many of the turbine users as well. As we will see later, keeping the design simple, rugged and hence relatively forgiving favoured learning selection and thus helped the rapid evolution and improvement in fitness of the technology that occurred in the first half of the 1980s.

It might be thought that requiring manufacturers to conform to conservative building regulations would have discouraged novelty generation and hence hampered the evolution of the industry, but fortunately it worked the other way because it encouraged manufacturers to interact so closely with the researchers at Risø that the two groups learned from each other. In a chapter in his Ph.D. thesis, Per Dannemand Andersen, a test engineer at Risø, gives the development and licensing of one component of a wind turbine – a damper flange to reduce wind turbine noise levels to keep the machine within specified limits – as an example of how the interaction worked. He describes how over a period of ten months at least four different designs were proposed, discussed and rejected. In the process, he says, he learned more about the need to balance technical perfection with cost, while the manufacturer learned something about load calculations and had a better design at the end. Andersen realised that his science-based approach was limited and that practical experience had great value. He concluded that if Risø had been staffed by theory-driven scientists then the Danish wind industry today might be as weak as the British or Swedish industries.[43]

Expansion phase

Peter Karnøe says that if the period from 1973 to 1978 was the infancy of the modern Danish wind industry then the period 1979 to 1985 was when it learned to crawl.[44] The 30 per cent subsidy for wind turbine installation introduced in 1979 and the establishment of the Risø test centre a year earlier encouraged new manufacturers to enter the market. There were ten manufacturers by 1980. Three of today's market leaders moved in about this time – all agricultural engineering firms[45] seeing to diversify in response to a dangerous slackening of their European market.[46] Their main asset was a core group of practical engineers and technicians with a lot of experience in developing machinery with a working life of fifteen to twenty years despite the fact that it got a minimum of maintenance and was exposed to tough, unpredictable conditions. These firms had a development culture of learning from field experience, or 'learning by using' as Nathan Rosenberg, author of the highly acclaimed book *Inside the Black Box*, calls it. Paul Gipe, one of the foremost consultants on wind energy, says that the 'learning by using' process was made easier because the manufacturers were geographically close to the wind turbines they had built and could service them directly from their factories. In 1996, for example, Vestas was servicing half the turbines it had ever built.[47]

Flemming Tranæs also points to the special relationship that developed between manufacturers and the first adopters of their machines at this time as being important to learning selection.

When I helped set up a co-operative in 1981 to buy a wind turbine we voted that one of our members, a chief ship's engineer, should visit all the wind turbine factories and give us a report. A new manufacturer, Bonus, impressed us. We really felt that they had come to stay. The company philosophy was to build just ten 55 kW machines and then wait one year to see how they worked. We knew we were buying a new technology and breakdowns might occur but we also knew we could expect excellent support. We bought Bonus turbines 3 and 4.

The three Ny Solbjerg families also chose to buy a 55 kW wind turbine but from Vestas. Other manufacturers also started producing these so-called 'second generation machines' which were based on a 15-metre-diameter rotor rather than the first generation of 22–30 kW machines' ten-metre rotor. Thanks to the Risø specifications and the agricultural machinery culture, the initial designs were conservative and heavy but, as their manufacturers and users learned more about them in operation, the large safety margins were reduced, often by fitting larger rotors. The 55 kW turbine, for example, was upgraded to 75 kW by increasing its rotor diameter by two metres to 17 metres.

This became the pattern for the development of wind turbines in Denmark: manufacturers incrementally improved one generation before jumping up to a new power band. Per Dannemand Andersen has helped his Risø co-worker Lars Hansen to collect data that shows clearly that there have been six generations of wind turbine in terms of their nominal power, as Figure 4.3 shows. Figure 4.4 shows how, over time, manufacturers made improvements to rotor and generator design to allow them to get more power from a given swept area. With these and other incremental improvements, manufacturers were able to reduce the cost of wind-generated electricity in 1996 to one-quarter of the 1980 cost, as Figure 4.4 also shows. Interestingly Nathan Rosenberg described the same incremental improvement process in the aircraft industry. He found that as manufacturers and users learned more about a type of aircraft, they were able to use their knowledge to improve its performance – for example, by stretching the fuselage to fit more passengers inside.[48]

While Eize de Vries of *Windstats Newsletter* agrees that the overall picture is of incremental improvements and quantum leaps, he points out that the quantum jumps did not always follow after the careful optimisation of a power band. For example, in 1993 a German

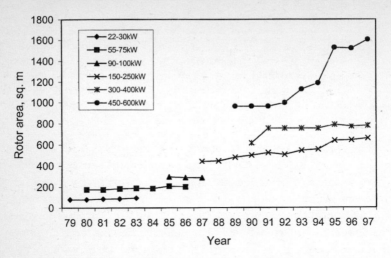

Figure 4.3 There have been six generations of Danish wind turbines in terms of power output. In the first five generations, the power the turbine develops, shown here by the size of the swept area of the rotor, has increased incrementally through learning by using, before the quantum jump to the next generation.[49] In the sixth generation, learning-by-modelling began to replace learning-by-using, giving designers the confidence to increase the rotor-swept area in the same power band

company took the Danes by surprise when it brought out a 600 kW machine at a time when the Danes were selling mainly 250–300 kW machines and trying to optimise the 500 kW power band. In another case, EU research subsidies for multi-megawatt machines prompted Vestas to make a quantum jump and build a 1.5 MW turbine with a nacelle weighing 75 tonnes, 25 per cent lighter than turbines of the same capacity built by competitors, whose designs were based on the then current 250–300 kW turbine technology.[50]

While the Danish wind turbine manufacturing industry was set up to meet domestic demand, exports provided the main development impetus in the expansion phase. Most of these overseas sales came about because the Renewable Energy Committee commissioned a consultant, Aage Højbak, to assess the export potential of the US market during the sluggish period for domestic sales before the 1983 agreement with the utilities on pricing. After Højbak reported that California was a good prospect because a 50 per cent subsidy to-

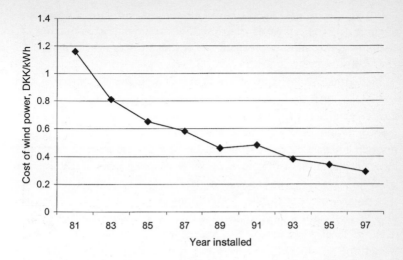

Figure 4.4 As Danish wind turbines have evolved, the annual energy production per square metre of the area swept by the rotor has increased linearly due to improved design. The cost of producing electricity has fallen logarithmically as a result of this increasing turbine efficiency, better reliability, and reduced manufacturing and installation costs (based on 20 years' depreciation, 5 per cent interest rates and siting in roughness class)[51]

wards a turbine's purchase price was being given there,[52] many Danish manufacturers flew out to investigate and found that they had a fitter product with a much better track record than their US rivals. They took the market by storm and between 1982 and 1986 their share rose from nothing to 65 per cent. In 1985 alone, Danish manufacturers sold two thousand wind turbines in California, ten times as many as they did in Denmark the same year. Employment in their factories increased from 300 to 2,500.

When the Californian tax incentives ended in 1986, however, the production boom went bust. This was not just because wind energy was no longer so attractive an investment but also because, although the Danish turbines had proved more reliable than their lighter US competitors, they were by no means 'perfected', and half the machines[53] installed in the first phase of the wind rush had suffered major breakdowns. This had led to long periods in which they were not generating and therefore not repaying the capital invested in them. In the early 1980s, many California wind farms were non-operational 40 per cent of the time. This made investors much more cautious about wind power and the installation rate halved in 1987 and again in 1988.

Nevertheless, the export boom helped the Danish industry mature quickly. Their insurance companies started requiring better certification criteria and, partly as a response to this, the firms set up more formal product development teams which did much to improve reliability. Reliability was also improved by US wind mechanics making local modifications to Danish machines. 'The success of the Danish wind turbines in California is as much due to American perseverance as Danish engineering and craft tradition', says Paul Gipe.[54] Gipe may be right, but a design that is simple and rugged enough to lend itself to local adaptation – in other words, learning selection – has something to do with it too. As a result, all projects installed in California after 1987 were operational 95 per cent of the time. Most of the improvements in productivity shown in Figure 4.4 came from improved reliability.[55]

The collapse of the Californian market led to a deep depression in the Danish wind industry. Every firm had serious financial difficulties and several went bankrupt. The industry did not collapse completely though, and Peter Karnøe believes that the rationalisation was beneficial as the surviving firms hired the best people from the bankrupt companies. R&D continued and the third new generation of wind turbine was born with a nominal capacity ranging from 150 to 250 kW.

The market recovered in 1988 when the Danish electric companies started to install the 100 MW capacity they had agreed with the government to erect before 1990. Exports also began to pick up as European countries such as Greece, Germany, Sweden, the Netherlands and the UK began to place orders as a result of new government policies favouring wind power. The Chernobyl accident in 1986 also helped wind power by re-emphasising the dangers of nuclear power as an alternative energy source. By 1990 the industry employed 1,600 people. Though this was less than at its peak five years earlier, it was nevertheless optimistic about its future, particularly because the government's Energy Plan 2000 had set a goal of 1,500 MW of installed wind power capacity before 2005. In 1989 and 1990 the first prototypes of the fourth and fifth generation machines were built with nominal generating capacities of 300–400 kW and 450–600 kW respectively.

This optimism was dashed in 1991 with the fall of the Green-led coalition government that had been so supportive of wind power in the Energy Plan 2000. The new government was less enthusiastic about wind power[56] and uncertainty grew about what would happen to connection prices and buy-back rates after 1994 when the 1983 agreement came up for renegotiation. As Figure 4.5 shows, the rate of capacity installation fell by a third in 1992 and remained at the 50 MW level for three years. DEF made it quite clear that it wanted to pay market rates for the electricity it bought and to charge the full cost of connecting new turbines and any grid strengthening required. Only strong exports saved the industry from another round of bank-ruptcies. These overseas sales have continued, with the result that by 1999 55 per cent of the world's 10,000 MW wind generating capacity came from Danish turbines.[57] In 1997 Denmark exported over three times more capacity than it sold locally.

DV and FDV, the manufacturers' organisation, withdrew from negotiations on a new agreement when they realised DEF would not agree to a package that would leave a viable home market.[58] Fortu-nately for the wind industry, the Greens won the election in 1993 and formed a new government. Svend Auken, the new Minister of Energy and the Environment, came down enthusiastically in favour of wind and expanded Energy Plan 2000 into E–21 (Energy for the Twenty-first Century). Fed up with DEF's intransigence, the govern-ment passed the 'Bill for Wind Turbines', which made the electricity companies legally responsible not only for delivering electricity any-where in the country but also for collecting it. The electricity com-panies had therefore to shoulder the costs of strengthening the grid to take wind energy while wind turbine owners were responsible only for the immediate connection costs. Single turbines were about to be excluded from these provisions because both DEF and the government planners still wanted to direct development towards large windfarms; however, after heavy lobbying, Flemming Tranæs, who had become chairman of DV by this time, managed to get them included at the eleventh hour.

The Act set a flat purchase price for wind electricity of 85 per cent of the utilities' production and distribution costs (85 per cent of $0.058/kWh in 1997[59]). In addition the government paid turbine

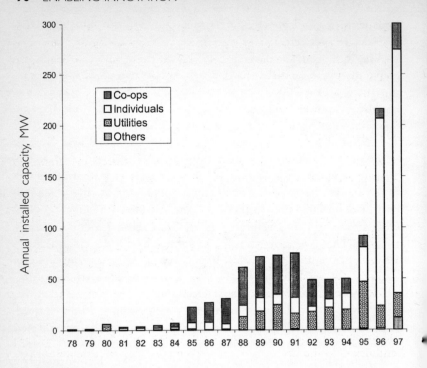

Figure 4.5 Annual installations, measured in rated capacity, of wind turbines in Denmark has grown nearly a hundredfold in twenty years, but not without a major setback in 1992

owners $0.015/kWh for the CO_2 they saved and added $0.026/kWh in direct subsidy, giving them an average selling price in 1997 of $0.10/kWh.[60] DEF was resentful and its chairman said that the Act had 'created a certain bitterness in electricity companies that electricity consumers as a whole are still being punished economically for the wind turbines of the individualists'.[61] Worse was to come for DEF, as in early 1994 the government relaxed the criteria of proximity and consumption. This, together with the Act, lower interest rates and cheaper wind turbines made investment in wind generation both possible and profitable for individuals rather than neighbourhood wind guilds. Figure 4.5 shows the beginnings of a huge increase in individuals – mainly farmers – installing wind turbines.

According to DEF, 4,784 wind turbines, with a capacity of 1,129 MW, were connected to the grid at the end of 1997, which generated about 6 per cent of Denmark's electricity.[62] By 1999 this had risen to 10 per cent. The Danish parliament has now agreed that this should rise to 20 per cent by the end of 2002, and is planning to make further changes to the financial support system to ensure that this happens.[63]

Disappearance phase

Eize de Vries believes the wind industry has matured and entered a new phase in the last few years. He explained to me:

> The wind turbine industry started by building 'advanced blacksmith' designs that users could modify. Now manufacturers are building 2 to 2.5 MW machines with rotor diameters of up to 80 m. No one attempts to modify these. The people buying these machines are investors interested in money whereas before they were people interested in technical things. More sophisticated machines with pitch control and variable speeds are now gaining ground on the simpler Danish-type design.

If de Vries is right then wind turbine technology is entering the disappearance phase. It has moved from the domain of the technical enthusiast to the domain of the accountant, and from being viewed as a fringe or 'crank' activity to being normal and mainstream.

This move to mainstream has gone hand in hand with an accumulation and codification of knowledge, which has allowed better predictive models to be developed. 'Learning by using' is giving way to 'learning by modelling' where learning from experience from the field gives way to learning from virtual tests carried out on a computer. In so doing the learning selection model of the early stages of innovation becomes less relevant, and conventional economic demand and supply models begin to fit better. Interestingly, de Vries believes that while the Danish industry has benefited tremendously from learning selection in the past, it is now suffering from relying on an approach that is too iterative and hence too slow to respond to technological developments in other countries. He cites as an example the fact that Danish manufacturers, with the exception of Vestas, have been very late in shifting from their classic fixed-speed rotor with passive stall protection to designs where rotor speed and the angle of the blades (blade pitch) vary in response to changes in wind speed. This new design, favoured by the German competition, allows a wind turbine to capture more energy from the wind. Nevertheless the Danes themselves have recognised the large net advantages of using a learning selection approach in developing new technology. The Danish Wave Energy Programme, established by the Danish parliament in 1996, 'will adopt the "bottom-up" approach that was so successful in the early development of Denmark's wind energy industry by appealing to a broader base and seeking new ideas from inventors ... with a step-by-step technical evaluation program to test the new ideas'.[64] Perhaps in ten or twenty years Denmark will have a billion-dollar wave industry as well.

The American experience

Like Denmark, the USA had a strong wind power tradition. Walter Prescott Webb, one of America's most prominent historians, wrote that three innovations made the settlement of the Great Plains possible: the Colt 45, barbed wire, and the water-pumping windmill,[65] over one million of which are still in use worldwide. Then, when electricity became widely adopted, windchargers provided the core of 'home light plants' sold to the 90 per cent of US farms that were not connected to central-station power during the 1930s.

After a lean period for wind in the 1950s and 1960s, the first OPEC oil embargo in 1973 encouraged people with similar motivations to the pioneers in Denmark to want to generate their own electricity in a renewable way. Many did so by buying old and junked windchargers and getting them working again. As in Denmark, these people were not 'way out', but the front runners of a growing Green movement which had begun asking serious questions about the sustainability of a capitalist system based on economic growth. This group found political representation in the National Energy Act of 1978, part of which, the Public Utility Regulatory Policies Act (PURPA), guaranteed a market for electricity generated by independent producers. It required the electricity companies to pay a fair price and sell backup power to producers at non-discriminatory rates.[66] In short, PURPA put into law something that people like Tranæs and Lauritsen had to fight long and hard to achieve in Denmark.

The National Energy Act also included a tax credit amounting to a 10 per cent subsidy on the capital cost of installing wind turbines and other types of generator. This was boosted to 15 per cent in 1980 after the second oil crisis. California offered an additional 25 per cent tax credit subsidy to encourage the use of renewables, bringing the total subsidy available in that state to nearly 50 per cent. This sparked the Californian 'wind rush' and millions of dollars were poured into solar power and wind farms. While this helped the Danish wind industry to mature quickly, only one company, US Windpower, remained in business after the tax credits were phased out in 1985 and 1986 and even that went bust in the 1990s, leaving Denmark in 1999 with 55 per cent of a $1-billion world market.

So why was the US industry so much less successful than the Danish? The simple answer is that the US manufacturers failed because their products were less reliable – in other words, less fit – than those of their Danish competitors. The Danes started with Juul's 'low-tech' machine that was adapted by 'hobbyists' and agricultural engineers who knew little of aeronautics but who applied intuition, tinkering and trial and error instead. In other words, they took a first approximation – something that worked and that they could sell – and, little by little, learning by doing and learning by using, they improved the product, just as Dr Hien and the manufacturers and users of the flatbed dryer did in Vietnam.

In the USA, by contrast, technology development was mainly top-down and designs were subjected to very little selection pressure in the real world, exactly as happened to the flash dryer in the Philippines. True, there were bottom-up attempts to develop wind turbines in the USA too, but these did not occur in as nurturing an environment as in Denmark and were therefore much less successful than they might have been despite getting $120 million in funding.

The scientists and economists who drove the top-down approach in the USA made two mistakes. One was that they underestimated the technical difficulties in designing wind turbines. Infused with the success that Big Science had enjoyed with achievements like the moon landings, they believed that technical challenges could be overcome with enough R&D and money. Their other error was that they calculated that wind turbines would have to be huge to be cost-effective. As a result, they failed spectacularly and squandered $330 million over twelve years.

US-designed wind turbines are generally much lighter than their Danish counterparts. They have two blades rather than three and these are mounted downwind of the tower rather than upwind. They are set on a teetering (movable) hub rather than bolted on solidly,

Danish-style. These differences can be attributed to the high science, as opposed to practical, backgrounds of the two people from whom the design emerged. One of these was Palmer Putman, who worked building water turbines for the Morgan Smith Company during the Second World War. Anxious to diversify, Morgan Smith became interested in supplying electricity companies with wind turbines too and believed that they would demand large machines. Accordingly, Putman, who had no experience with wind power at all, assembled a highly qualified team of engineers and scientists and set out to build the largest wind turbine in the world.

His team took as its point of departure the 'home light units' on US farms that used wind turbines rated at only a few kilowatts. Putman did not believe in a gradualist approach and built a 1.25 MW machine with a huge 53-metre-diameter rotor – over twice that of Juul's turbine, and ten times the diameter of commercially available wind turbines of that time. This failed spectacularly soon after commissioning when a 25-metre blade broke away because the structural loadings were higher than the team had calculated.[67] The machine was dismantled in 1946 when, like the Gedser turbine, accountants worked out it was not economic. Still, the team had established that, technically, a two-bladed downwind rotor would give the lightest weight machine, thus planting the US flag on the concept. It had also built the world's first wind turbine of over a megawatt capacity that was grid connected and designed for the electricity company market.

The other source of the US approach to wind power was Ulrich Hütter, a German working for the Ventimotor Company as chief designer. Hütter had an aeronautical background and designed gliders before joining Ventimotor, where he completed his Ph.D. on optimal wind turbine design in 1942. In glider design light weight and aerodynamic efficiency are of paramount importance and so it is perhaps not surprising that he came to the conclusion that the same would hold true for wind turbines if they were ever to generate electricity cost-effectively. He proceeded to develop a design similar in concept to Putman's – two-bladed and downwind – but designed with better data based on more experimentation. Hütter's design was ahead of its time in several ways: it used glass-fibre blades and a teetering hub; it was very light and had active pitch control. According to Paul Gipe, the technical elegance of the machine 'has captivated the dreams of many German and American engineers since the 1960s'.[68]

When increasing environmental concern rekindled interest in wind energy in the USA at the beginning of the 1970s, NASA, eager to find something to do after putting a man on the moon, organised the first wind power workshop since the 1950s in conjunction with the National Science Foundation. This was held with impeccable timing in June 1973, just as the OPEC oil shortages were beginning to bite.[69] Putman and Hütter attended and may well have been instrumental in steering the participants to the conclusion that wind power had a big future if large turbines were built for the power company market. In any event, shortly afterwards, NSF asked NASA to prepare a five-year development plan for wind energy, which NASA began by conducting an extremely thorough literature search and translating useful texts into English. The agency also rehabilitated and tested the Gedser turbine with the help of the Danish Technical University, and commissioned two aerospace companies to carry out conceptual design studies using computer design optimisation. These found that Hütter's design was technically the best approach and NASA bought the design from him for $55,000.

The conceptual studies also considered the optimum size, and both concluded that bigger was better – for example, they calculated that a 1,500 kW machine would be three times more cost-effective than a 500 kW one. There is some evidence that this finding was the one NASA wanted. Karnøe, in his Ph.D. research, found that although the first report actually said that 30-metre-diameter rotors – not much larger than those on the Gedser turbine – would be the most economic,[70] the authors were told to go away and do their calculations again. Karnøe believes that NASA was driven by the American 'breakthrough' innovation culture,[71] which seeks to hit the innovative equivalent of a home run rather than moving incrementally from base to base. The agency therefore had to build the biggest wind turbine in the world, just like Putman had before it.

Even so, NASA did not immediately jump in the deep end. It took Hütter's design and changed it, in Woody Stoddard's phrase, from 'a sports car into a truck' by making it stronger and heavier. In so doing some of the aerodynamic efficiency of the blades was lost. NASA also decided to replace the teetering hub, which dissipated some of the uneven loadings caused by the wind shadow of the upwind tower,[72] with a fixed hub similar to the Danish design. The modified Hütter design, MOD–0, with a 100 kW capacity, was ready for testing in 1975. No real test runs were made, however, because of the alarming amount the blades bent because of the wind shadow and the unteetered hub. Nevertheless, NASA learned some lessons and subcontracted Westinghouse and Lockheed to build four modified versions, MOD–0A, with larger rotors and generators rated at 200 kW. These still presented blade fatigue problems but ran much longer than the first prototype. According to Karnøe, some people involved in the programme believe that if NASA had continued to improve the MOD–0A the US would have had a design to compete with the Danes in the Californian wind rush of the early 1980s.

But NASA didn't continue this work because developing a small turbine was not its objective. Before the test results had even been properly analysed, it began to scale the MOD–0 up by a factor of 10 and construct a 1.5 MW machine, the MOD–1. Rather like NAPHIRE with the flash dryer, NASA defined the design specifications and placed a tender. General Electric, which had not been involved with MOD–0, was given the contract, thus ensuring that very little learning was carried over from the earlier work. MOD–1 was erected in 1978 at a cost of $6 million. It was dismantled in 1980 after operating for just a few hours.

MOD–1 failed but the US wind energy programme barely noticed, rather as the Ministry of Agriculture in Burma failed to discover that farmers did not want the machines its workshop was producing. In August 1977, two years before the MOD–1 machine was up and running, NASA awarded Boeing the contract to build MOD–2. This was the home run NASA wanted to hit. It was supposed to be the pre-market prototype of the machine that, when mass produced, would produce electricity at a price competitive with that from coal. The machine was quite different to MOD–1 – it had an upwind rotor to eliminate the blade fatigue due to wind shadow, a teetering hub, and, while having twice MOD–1's capacity at 3 MW, was supposed to weigh no more. Three machines were installed between 1980 and 1981, but four years later they had only operated for 4,100 hours between them. Boeing and NASA had one last try and built the much-improved MOD–5B. Nevertheless, high maintenance of its transmission system meant that it was not cost-effective and there was no commercial uptake of the technology. None of the products of this programme is operating today and none of the companies involved is building wind turbines.

In total NASA spent $330 million trying to develop macho mega-watt machines. Just as in Burma and the Philippines, top-down government development programmes seem to squander large amounts of public money because of lack of feedback and learning.

The bottom-up approach fared little better. A few members of the grassroots movement to re-establish wind power, a 'motley bunch of hippies' as Paul Gipe disparagingly describes them, formed what is now the most powerful and well-funded wind energy association in the world, the American Wind Energy Association (AWEA), in the basement of a Detroit church.[73] The AWEA then lobbied the federal government to fund the development of small wind turbines and in 1977 the Rocky Flats test station was set up, a year before the Risø wind test station in Denmark.

Rocky Flats was unlike Risø in several important respects. In particular, as its funding was much more secure, it did not have to set out to make itself as useful as possible to industry. One of its main functions was to assess R&D proposals and to grant-aid the best of them. It awarded $14 million in grants to companies between 1978 and 1982 but, unlike the grants provided by Renewable Energy Committee in Denmark during the same period, this money went mainly to the large aerospace companies like McDonnell–Douglas and Grumman which were able to submit proposals couched in aircraft engineering terms. This was because the Rocky Flats staff agreed with NASA and Hütter that low-weight turbines with high-efficiency blades were required to produce electricity competitively and they therefore used the same criteria that NASA employed for its large turbine programme when making their small turbine grant assessments. Their awards therefore went to firms attempting to build very light, downwind machines with two blades, even though the market was not interested in technical efficiency or design elegance *per se*, but whether the machine would work long enough and reliably enough for investors to make money. Not surprisingly, then, of the thirteen companies that shared the fourteen $1-million grants awarded by Rocky Flats, only one, Enertech, sold many machines in the California wind rush. All the other US companies involved in the rush were not linked to Rocky Flats at all apart from Energy Sciences International (ESI), which had been set up by one of its engineers. The institution was therefore almost entirely irrelevant to the real world.

Rocky Flats was also required to test turbines and to disseminate the results but, in comparison with Risø, it failed here too because its reports were too academic for most of those hoping to use them and they only came out two years after testing began. The US did not have the equivalent of DV or *Naturlig Energi* to provide monthly performance data from machines that were actually being used around the country.

After the California wind rush, four of the five US companies that had made significant sales in it, Enertech, ESI, Carter and Fayette, collapsed because, unlike their Danish competitors, they did not have orders from their home utility companies to support them and they were unable to compete in export markets because of their reliability problems. Only US Windpower staggered on for another ten years.

Using learning selection to explain why the Americans failed

The learning selection model says that a technology is more likely to be of benefit and the benefits will be achieved faster in circumstances in which there are many novelty-generators and an effective selection and promulgation mechanism. The evolution of the Danish wind turbine industry in comparison with that in the US bears this out. Quite simply, the Danes provided the circumstances in which learning selection could take place, while the Americans didn't.

In fact, the evolution of the Danish wind industry was very similar to the evolution of the flatbed dryer in the Mekong Delta. Both technologies had been used successfully elsewhere (or previously in the country concerned) and in both cases an individual – Juul in Denmark and Hien in Vietnam – adapted one of them for current conditions and showed that the adaptation worked. Both men then succeeded in interesting other people in the technology and, because it was understandable and filled a need, in both cases people started to copy and to modify it. In other words, each technology's simplicity and lack of enforced patent protection encouraged novelty generation by manufacturers and owners. In both cases, too, mistakes were made in the copying – Riisager did not design his blades to stall at high speeds and the Phu Tam village manufacturers were not able to copy the blower on Hien's machine properly. These mistakes caused a fall in fitness that was eventually corrected by users, manufacturers and researchers interacting and learning from each other.

Figure 4.3 shows how manufacturers began on the learning curve with small 22–30 kW wind turbines that were relatively cheap. After optimising this design by learning selection they had learned enough to build the next generation, which had twice the capacity. This process has repeated itself five times so that most of the machines installed by the end of the 1990s had a capacity of about 600 kW. Figure 4.4 shows how the cost of generating electricity with wind turbines fell by three-quarters. The flatbed dryer in the Mekong Delta improved incrementally, shown by the increase in price of mechanically dried paddy compared to sun-dried paddy, but did not make the same quantum jumps in capacity as have Danish wind turbines. In this respect the wind industry shows an added dimension of learning selection and fitness change.

In the case of the flatbed dryer, the early release of the technology by Hien was unavoidable because he did not have the funding to develop it any further himself before releasing it. He had to use his first customers as guinea pigs. Bonus had to do much the same and it is interesting that Tranæs and his co-operative were knowing guinea pigs when they bought two turbines from the first batch of ten Bonus built. The way Tranæs describes working with Bonus to improve the yaw system shows the benefits of the approach to the manufacturer. The owners benefited because they were able to have their ideas and innovations included in the design and get a better product. Karnøe believes that when high levels of uncertainty exist about a new technology this iterative development approach is superior to a top-down one in which the customers play little part. Evidence from the top-down attempts to develop wind turbines in the USA supports this conclusion.

People in R&D sometimes forget that it is not enough for a product's performance to be highly technically efficient for it to be a success – there must also be a market for it. They also seem to think that if they can get an innovation to work well then it is 'finished,' and they can throw it 'over the wall' and it will be adopted. The learning selection model holds that adoption of new technologies doesn't work like this because the market evolves with the new technology; thus it is impossible to develop a 'finished' technology straight off. The best you can do is develop your 'best bet' and then work with the key stakeholders as co-developers during the adaptation phase. Successful early adoption involves the key stakeholders in learning about the technology, changing it as well as changing their opinions and their methods of working until they get the technology working well for them and begin to feel that the technology is theirs. Gaining ownership of the technology in this way can have particularly important beneficial effects on the environment and market for the technology. This process is shown in Figure 3.2 as the 'meshing in' of a new technology to its key stakeholders and environment. The Danish wind turbine story shows just how important this process is to the success of an innovation, and how indeterminate it is. The interaction of people interested in wind power led to the organisational innovation of the Association of Danish Wind Turbine Owners, which in turn helped learning selection by providing people with evaluation information about wind turbines. DV also helped change the environment to the benefit of wind energy by negotiating to keep connection costs down and buy-back rates up.

Another institutional innovation that helped create a nurturing environment for wind turbines was the wind guild ownership model. The model allowed ordinary people to own wind turbines jointly without the hassle endured by the Ny Solbjerg families and so helped a large broad-based market for wind turbines to develop. This in turn helped create a much higher level of grassroots political support for windpower than exists in other countries. The wind guild model and DV itself were the fruit of the Danish co-operative cultural tradition but their emergence was not inevitable. They required creative vision and the intensive effort of people like Per Lauritsen and Flemming Tranæs.

This grassroots support in turn created and sustained a nurturing environment for wind turbines that was as important to the success of the industry as the technical performance of its product. It is the reason why Denmark can plan to double installed wind generating capacity by 2003, while in the UK planning approval for wind farms is blocked by local people who feel they have nothing to gain from them.

On the other hand, the stories of the government-funded attempts in the USA and Denmark to develop and introduce large wind turbines bear striking similarities to the story of the flash dryer in the Philippines. Like the flash dryer, the introduction of wind turbines in both countries was conceived and planned by people working in the central research establishment, not by people who wanted to build and use the technology. Both the US and Danish centrally planned programmes failed, as did similar programmes in Germany, Sweden and the UK.[74] What is particularly telling is that the only early attempt to develop a megawatt machine that has been recorded as a success is the bottom-up effort of the Tvind schools in Denmark. The Tvind machine is still producing electricity not because it is technically 'better' than the efforts of the research community but because it was created by the people who were going to use the power it generated and to maintain it. This highlights the importance of environment and technology co-evolving together, something which is more likely to happen if the primary stakeholders are partners in the development process from an early stage and are able to carry out learning selection.

There is only one case in which publicly funded wind R&D has worked well. This was the EU project to develop a 1–1.5 MW turbine between 1992 and 1995. Funding was given to six or seven manufacturers to help them develop machines of this size despite criticism that the grants were subsidies and not market-driven. However, there is now a strong market for turbines as big or bigger than this for use offshore and, as a result of the project, Europe now leads the world in their design and manufacture. The lesson is that subsidies can work if applied well and with vision.

In general, though, government-driven R&D programmes have run into problems because they were put together by scientists who underestimated the difficulties of what they were proposing to undertake because they had overestimated the value of their scientific knowledge in relation to the necessary inputs from other groups. These projects were then run to timetables set by their financial budgets and not to capitalise on feedback from the field. This is clearly shown by the way the successive MOD phases did not wait for the results of the previous one to be known. Experience was undervalued to such an extent that Boeing, which had no previous experience with wind turbines, was given the MOD–2 contract rather than the two companies involved in MOD–1.

In terms of the learning selection model, the NASA programme had limited sources of innovation, little or no interaction between the researchers and the key stakeholders, and a very poor selection mechanism. The main selection criteria were the lowest installed cost and designs that could be seen as technical 'breakthroughs'. This favoured the selection of the Putman–Hütter lightweight, high-tech design path. Little or no consideration was given to what the market wanted, which was a range of machines that worked reliably and could give a competitive return on the capital invested in them.

The bottom-up development of wind turbines in the USA also suffered from a poor selection mechanism because Rocky Flats was not nearly as effective as Risø in generating useful knowledge and guidelines and circulating them quickly. As we saw, it took two years to get its test reports out whereas *Naturlig Energi* published performance data from machines purchased the previous month.

People are obviously affected in the way they act as novelty-generators, selectors and promulgators by their backgrounds and work culture. In the case of wind power, however, the US 'breakthrough' innovation culture was particularly damaging. 'The government program actively discouraged us from adopting the Danish design because it had been done before', Woody Stoddard, a windpower pioneer in the 1970s, told Peter Karnøe. 'In any case we thought the Danish approach was pedestrian and in our typical American way were sure that our engineering tools would lead inevitably to a breakthrough. We trusted our tools too much but we simply did not believe the problems were as hard as they were.'[75] In other words, the NASA people who planned the federal wind programme – scientists who had put a man on the moon just a few years before – were unwilling to take someone else's design even if it did work well. A breakthrough culture works against learning selection and evolution because it looks for a giant leap forward rather than incremental improvements over time based on what has been learned before.

The tools and models that Stoddard and his colleagues were so sure would produce a technological breakthrough came from the aeronautical industry. While it was initially reasonable to think that people with this background ought to be excellent novelty-generators, it turned out that formulae developed for helicopter blades or aeroplane wings were 'hopelessly inadequate'[76] for designing relatively slow-moving wind turbine blades. Another difference that was overlooked was that aeroplanes have 5.5 man-hours of maintenance for every hour of operation[77] while wind turbines need to operate for thousands of hours with hardly any maintenance at all. Denmark might have made this mistake, too, had it had an aerospace industry. As it was, though, its wind turbines were built by agricultural machinery manufacturers well used to building machines to last a long time with little maintenance in a highly variable environment. Moreover, these 'agricultural' turbines fostered more novelty-generation because they were simpler and more forgiving and so could be understood, repaired and adapted more easily by owners and technicians.

Another problem in the USA, Karnøe believes, was the culture of trying to keep discoveries from competitors, thus inhibiting inter-action and learning selection. US patents are granted to the first person through the door of the patent office, even if other people have had the idea first and are using it already. The position is quite different in Europe, where, once an idea has been made public, it can no longer be patented. Karnøe describes how in the early days of the development of wind turbines in Denmark, ideas were shared liberally among manufacturers and others, especially at the wind meetings. The Danish manufacturers also formed a trade association for themselves, something the US manufacturers have so far failed to do. The Danish culture of co-operation is also shown by the fact that many Danish firms have ended up making almost the same machine without battles over patents breaking out. In short, because all were relatively small and they could see that together they might be able to develop a product for a market big enough for all of them, the Danish manufacturers seem to have adopted the same attitude as Lawrence Morallo and the other manufacturers of stripper-harvesters. As of 1998, when Denmark had over half the world market, only 1.5 per cent of wind energy patent applications were being made by Danish firms.[78]

This might be changing now, though. In January 1998 Sore Hansen of the Danish Patent Office warned the country's wind industry of its vulnerability to aggressive business tactics from overseas and in particular from the USA. He said: 'Companies must realise that patents can be granted for solutions which have quietly functioned in practice in a Danish wind turbine for years. It might be unfair but those are the rules.'[79]

Another factor affecting the environment for a technology and the ability of learning selection to operate is the degree of subsidy on the purchase price of the machine. As the flash dryer in the Philippines and the SG harvester in Burma were both given away, there was little or no incentive to improve the machine. Then, later on, the thousands of machines rotting in back yards soured the prospects for the future development of these technologies. The Californian wind rush did much the same. The 50 per cent subsidy on the purchase price led to thousands of machines being purchased within a few months. As a result, manufacturers found their products easy to sell and there was little motivation for them to improve their designs.

As we saw, many of the machines installed in the first years of the wind rush broke down and were decommissioned. Others were erected hastily with no regard for the natural environment. Both these factors led to a hardening of attitude towards wind power in California. The subsidy was stopped and boom went to bust. In other words, inappropriate incentives to adopt a new technology worked against learning selection and damaged the technology's long-term prospects. Conditions were made so soft that technologically inadequate devices were able to reproduce whereas evolution, by its very nature, requires 'cruel' selection mechanisms in order to be 'kind' to the survival and promulgation prospects of the species (or technology).

Conclusions

The stories of wind power in the US and Denmark shows that public-funded research can produce white elephants many times larger than those in developing countries. In both developed and developing countries, however, the reasons for the waste were the same: learning selection was constrained by factors such as:

1. a bias towards breakthroughs and against incremental innovations that met customers' needs;
2. researchers who were overconfident that their knowledge and tools would be enough to get something to work;
3. researchers who undervalued practical knowledge and innovation from other sources;
4. development programmes driven by budgetary time frames rather than how the technology actually works;
5. machines that, because they were technically sophisticated, were unforgiving and difficult to adapt;
6. patents and trade secrets that restricted interaction between different participants.

Open and closed

Linux versus Windows

If the ideas about learning selection we have developed so far are even partially correct, we would expect to find that technologies develop more rapidly when there are a lot of novelty-generators who are able to communicate quickly and easily with each other and who are highly motivated to pass improvements on. And if that is so, then computer software development ought to demonstrate it well because of the large numbers of 'hackers' (people who modify computer programs) who constantly send their modifications ('patches' in their jargon) over the Internet to each other so that they can be tested immediately by the recipients. Moreover, every hacker seems to be motivated by the drive found in other technological pioneers. They are fascinated by technical puzzles and gain great fulfilment from solving them and having their achievements recognised by their peers.

So what would be the most convincing proof we can imagine that learning selection is a really effective way of developing a technology? Would we be impressed if we found that the largest software company in the world, the monolithic and centrally controlled Microsoft with annual sales of almost $15 billion and profits larger than those of the world's next five hundred software firms combined, was losing its dominance in a key market to a program developed by an unpaid, disorganised bunch of hackers? Yet that is what seems to be happening. Microsoft's core product, the Windows operating system, is installed on 90 per cent of the world's personal computers and there is no sign of that changing. However, NT, the version of Windows that Microsoft developed to run servers – the computers that run networks, including the Internet itself – is now facing stiff competition from Linux, 'a world class operating system' that has coalesced 'as if by magic out of part-time hacking by several thousand developers all over the planet connected only by the tenuous strands of the Internet'.[1]

The position at the end of 1998 was that Windows NT had been installed in 36 per cent of the servers commissioned during the year, while Linux was the operating system in 17 per cent of them, up from 7 per cent the previous year.[2] Microsoft was pretending in public to be unconcerned at its rival's growth. In private, however, the firm was very worried and, according to the *Wall Street Journal*, had set up an attack team whose job was to keep tabs on Linux and provide the corporation with information which could be used to discredit it.[3] This was because Linux had two big things going for it: it is free and most of the programs that run on it are free, and it is evolving much faster than Windows because, as leaked internal Microsoft documents have outlined, it has harnessed more computer talent world-wide than any single company could muster.[4] Learning selection might therefore prove itself the best way of developing software before very long.

Linux: open-source innovation

Development phase

Linux differs markedly from the technologies we have looked at so far – agricultural machinery and wind turbines – because it is all software, while they have large hardware components. Its development began in 1991 when Linus Torvalds, a Finn, was a 21-year-old, second-year computer science student at Helsinki University.[5] Torvalds wanted to understand how the Intel 386 chip in his personal computer worked and, in order to do so, he set out to write a program to control it.

Torvalds knew quite a lot about programming already. He had spent many hours as a teenager programming a Sinclair QL, an eccentric British computer launched in 1984 that had many faults but one real virtue: it allowed advanced hacking. The previous year he had also taken a course on Unix, the operating system that ran most of the Internet, as it was used on a new computer that had just been installed at the university. At the time Unix was every hacker's favourite operating system because the code in which it is written – the source code – is open. This means that it can be read and, most importantly, modified.

An operating system is simply a set of instructions that can be used to control a computer without having to worry about how its hardware – its central processor and memory chips, for example – operates. In Unix, the core of the operating system, the kernel, controls the hardware and also supervises and schedules data input, processing and output. Because most of the hardware information is in the kernel, the other parts of the operating system can work independently of the hardware. This makes Unix relatively easy to run on a wide range of computer types.

One of Torvalds' Unix course books was Andrew Tanenbaum's *Operating Systems: Designs and Implementation,* which provided a guide to a kind of baby Unix called Minix. Tanenbaum, a professor of computer systems at the Free University in Amsterdam, wrote Minix purely as a teaching tool. Although it was very simple and very limited in what it could do, it struck a chord and within two months of its release in 1987 a newsgroup with over 40,000 subscribers throughout the world was discussing it.[6] One of the reasons for its appeal was that it could run on ordinary PCs, whereas Unix proper required computers costing tens of thousands of dollars. Torvalds bought a 386 PC himself so he could run Minix at home and avoid queuing for a terminal on the university's computer, which could support only sixteen users at a time.

Even though the operating system Torvalds wrote for his 386 drew heavily on his knowledge of Unix and Minix, it took him two months' effort to stop it constantly crashing. During this time, a project that had started out as a learning exercise grew into something more and he began to see that he had something that other hackers might like, too – a free operating system. Unix and Minix had both to be purchased and their source codes were subject to stringent copyright restrictions.

In October 1991 Torvalds released the 0.02 version of his operating system (the 0.01 version was never published and became 0.02 when Torvalds added a patch to it himself) by e-mailing a message about it to the Minix newsgroup. The program did not have a name at this stage and was christened Linux by a website manager later on. Part of Torvalds' message read:

> Do you pine for the nice days of Minix–1.1, when men were men and wrote their own device drivers? Are you without a nice project and just dying to cut your teeth on an OS [operating system] you can try to modify for your needs? Are you finding it frustrating when everything works on Minix? No more all-nighters to get a nifty program working? Then this post might be just for you.
>
> As I mentioned a month (?) ago, I'm working on a free version of a Minix-lookalike for AT-386 computers. It has finally reached the stage where it's even usable (though may not be depending on what you want), and I am willing to put out the sources for wider distribution. Full kernel source is provided, as no Minix code has been used.
>
> ALERT! WARNING! NOTE! … you need Minix to set it up if you want to run it, so it is not yet a standalone system for those of you without Minix. I'm working on it.
>
> This is a program for hackers by a hacker. I've enjoyed doing it, and somebody might enjoy looking at it and even modifying it for their own needs. It is still small enough to understand, use and modify, and I'm looking forward to any comments you might have. I'm also interested in hearing from anybody who has written any of the utilities/library functions for Minix. If your efforts are freely distributable (under copyright or even public domain), I'd like to hear from you, so I can add them to the system.[7]

This makes it clear that Torvalds had no inkling that Linux was about to become a major success. He saw it simply as a program that might be of interest to hackers interested, like himself, in learning about operating systems.

The Free Software Movement was the reason Torvalds was wrong. This had been started in 1983 by Richard Stallman, who had worked as a programmer in the Artificial Intelligence Laboratory at the Massachusetts Institute of Technology in the days when programmers were free to interact with each other even if they worked for different companies and the programs they developed could be copied and modified by anyone. Then 'pollution', as Stallman called it, began to become a problem as software increasingly became the property of owners who prevented modifications by keeping the source code secret. When, in 1982, the Lab's premier operating system was licensed to a computer company and turned into a proprietary tool for making money, Stallman resigned in disgust and started a charity, the Free Software Foundation (FSF), to maintain and nurture the free software ethos. One of FSF's achievements was to promote the idea of copyleft, a form of copyright which allows anyone to copy and modify a program if they then allow others to copy and hack their modification, but which makes it illegal for someone to take copyleft software and make it proprietary.[8]

Another Stallwood project was to produce an operating system, GNU, which users would be free to copy, improve and share with others. He decided to model the new system on Unix because of its proven and portable structure, and to make it compatible with Unix too so that Unix users, of which there were many, would be able to change over easily. Unix also had the advantage of being an open-source program and the Unix world was friendly to code-sharing.[9] Unlike Torvalds, however, Stallwood did not start by writing GNU's kernel but with the other components of an operating system such as compilers, editors, text formatters and mail software. Only after dozens of these programs had been completed, many by volunteers, did he decide to base the kernel – Hurd – on a microkernel developed at Carnegie Mellon University. Unfortunately, the university's lawyers kept him waiting for two years while they worked out the terms for the software licence, thus leaving the way open for Linux to adopt GNU's non-kernel components and become the first non-proprietary open-source operating system suitable for use on PCs.

Torvalds had no idea that this would happen. At one point in his launch message he says 'I can (well, almost) hear you asking yourselves "Why?" Hurd will be out in a year (or two, or next month, who knows?), and I've already got Minix.' In other words, why should anyone bother to spend their time learning to use it when a better system was about to come along? In another e-mail he wrote: 'Linux will never be the professional operating system that Hurd will be.'[10] He underestimated his system's potential, too. 'Simply, I'd say porting [making a program work on hardware other than that for which it was written on] is impossible'[11] he once wrote. How wrong he was.

Minix's creator, Tanenbaum, was not overly impressed with Linux either. 'Minix is a microkernel-based system. The file system and memory management are separate processes, running outside the kernel. Linux is a monolithic-style system. This is a giant step back into the 1970s.... To me, writing a monolithic system in 1991 is a

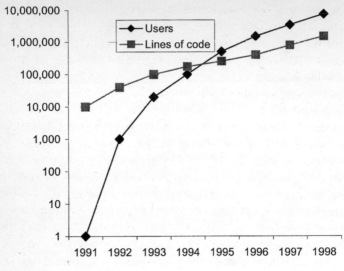

Source: Data from www.tamos.net/ieee/history.html.

Figure 5.1 The phenomenal growth of Linux shown in terms of users and lines of code

truly poor idea,' he said in a post to the Minix newsgroup. Torvalds replied:

> True, Linux is monolithic, and I agree that microkernels are nicer. With a less argumentative subject, I'd probably have agreed with most of what you said. From a theoretical (and aesthetic) standpoint Linux loses. If the GNU kernel had been ready last spring, I'd not have bothered to even start my project: the fact is that it wasn't and still isn't. Linux wins heavily on points by being available now.
>
> If [being microkernel-based] was the only criterion for the 'goodness' of a kernel, you'd be right. What you don't mention is that Minix doesn't do the micro-kernel thing very well, and has problems with real multi-tasking.[12]

In other words, Torvalds had produced something that, like the Danish wind turbine design, was not technically very elegant, but it was ready and it worked. Also, because other people could work on it, it soon became very reliable. Although Version 0.02 was not very stable, within three months Torvalds had made major corrections and released version 0.12, which was. He later wrote: '0.12 was the kernel that "made it": that's when Linux started to spread a lot faster.'

The GNU project not only provided the Linux operating system with a lot of ready-made components; GNU also helped create a favourable environment for it, just as Unix had created a favourable environment for GNU. In this environment, tens, then hundreds, and then thousands of novelty-generators and selectors – hackers with copyleft as their constitution and guiding principle – were happy to become involved in testing Linux and writing code improvements for it. And by doing so, they made it the success it is today.

Figure 5.1 shows the phenomenal growth of Linux in terms of numbers of users and lines of code. Linux began with just one user – Torvalds himself – and 10,000 lines of code. Although Torvalds stressed in his early e-mails that Linux did not have any Minix code in its kernel, Minix provided the structure – the scaffolding if you like – on which Linux was built. If 10,000 lines of code is roughly what one person can write, with help, in about six months, the 1.5 million lines of code that Linux had in 1998 is equivalent to at least 75 person-years of programming.

Start-up and adaptation phases

In Linux's development phase – the six months which Torvalds took to write the first program – he did not attempt to come up with a 'breakthrough' – that is, something new and without precedent. Instead he built on something that was already there. Then, in the start-up phase, which began with his first e-mail to the Minix newsgroup about the system, he set out to be useful. He asked Minix users what they liked and disliked about Minix and what features they would like to see included in the new operating system.[13] This met a real need. 'I was getting hundreds of e-mails a day asking to add this feature and that feature [to Minix],' Tanenbaum says. 'Many people were getting frustrated with me constantly saying no.'[14]

Torvalds' main role in the development of Linux after the release of version 0.02 was not to write code for features people wanted but to select and propagate improvements to the system from the ideas that streamed in. Ten people downloaded version 0.02 and five of these sent him bug fixes, code improvements and new features.

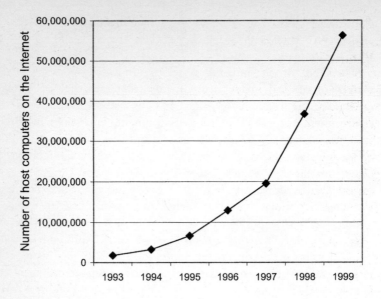

Figure 5.2 The growth of the Internet has exploded since 1993 and has driven the unprecedented growth of Linux by helping learning selection and promulgation

Torvalds added the best of these to the existing program, along with others he had written himself, and released the composite as version 0.12, thus beginning the adaptation phase only three months after the start-up phase had begun.

The rate of learning selection accelerated as the number of Linux users increased; to cope with the volume of hacks coming in, Torvalds began choosing and relying on 'a few trusted lieutenants from whom he [would] take larger patches and trust those patches. The lieutenants more or less own[ed] relatively large pieces of the kernel.'[15] When Linux 1.0 was released in March 1994 a Credits file listed the names, addresses and contributions of more than a hundred people – novelty-generators in our terms – who had contributed to its 170,000 lines of code.

The Internet enabled Torvalds to issue new versions of the kernel as often as once a day, driving learning selection along at a pace that would have been impossible if he had had to put diskettes in the post or send out his reworked code in some other way. The explosion of the Internet since 1993, shown in Figure 5.2, was therefore a key factor in Linux's rapid development.

Eric Raymond, a champion of the open-source software movement, believes that the main reason Linux succeeded was the way Torvalds handled the feedback he got from users via the Internet. His strategy of releasing improvements early, trusting others and delegating responsibility was particularly important. Other writers agree. 'He amazed me,' says Phil Hughes, publisher of the *Linux Journal*. 'He's very low on the ego end. [Participation] snowballed because of his attitude and because he was willing to accept what others wanted.'[16] Torvalds himself says,

> In order for Linux to succeed, there has to be someone to make the judgement of what's correct. In some sense I am the boss over Linux developers, and they don't want me to be the snake that bites them. What I want is for people to trust me, and obviously part of that is the image that I am not corrupted.

For Torvalds, remaining pure means having no commercial interest in Linux's success or failure. He must have no involvement beyond making selection decisions that improve the program's performance.

When deciding what was to be included in the major releases, Torvalds seems to have been very successful in walking the thin line between losing control of the development process completely and being too selective and frustrating his co-developers so much that they gave up. How was this possible, since one person cannot vet all 1.5 million lines of code in the latest Linux release, let alone all the material suggested for inclusion? The answer is that a two-stage process has developed which brings the cream to the top so that Torvalds can skim it off. In the first stage of the process, Linux enthusiasts pass new hacks among themselves; in the second, Torvalds chooses code for incorporation not on the basis of his personal assessment of what might be best for the system, but in line with the feedback he receives from people who have already tried the new material out. The more members of the Linux community who adopt a hack, the more likely it is to be in the next release. In terms of our evolutionary model, then, Torvalds chooses novelties on the basis of their fitness measured by the promulgation rate.

Without this two-tier process Linux could not evolve an order of magnitude faster than commercial closed-source software and still remain coherent. 'One thing that has surprised all of us is how quickly the applications have been developed', says Wayne Sennett, general manager of Motorola Computer Group. 'This thing has a mind of its own,' he adds, a phrase which gives a strong indication that a real evolutionary process is behind it.

Vinod Valloppillil, a Microsoft engineer, analysed the open-source software movement in a confidential memorandum that was leaked and posted on the web at Halloween, 1998. He suggested that Linux has avoided splitting up into different competing versions in the way Unix and its main open-source competitor BSD–Unix had done because, rather counter-intuitively, its development has been more open and has allowed splits ('forking') to occur. He explained that FreeBSD was intended as a free, unrestricted version of Unix. However, the programming team that developed it did not allow outsiders to change the code. As a result, those frustrated with the direction FreeBSD was taking went off and developed their own variations such as OpenBSD, NetBSD and BSDI.

In evolutionary terms, the decision to restrict the size of the group that could contribute code effectively restricted the size of the environmental niche that BSD could evolve to occupy. Moreover, once forking occurred, its development path stayed forked because, as the BSD variants had been created as a reaction against FreeBSD, none of those responsible for them was interested in having the original FreeBSD programmers evaluate their changes. This was the equivalent of a geographic separation in the natural world. Because interbreeding didn't happen, different species of Unix evolved.

Linux escaped this fate because Torvalds and his lieutenants are happy to consider changes from anyone. As a result, anyone could adapt the system to their own needs, and, if others found their novelty useful, it would be promulgated and, if it proved popular, eventually released in an official version. So, although forking happened, the open nature of Linux development made recombination common and added 'hybrid vigour' to the project.

Early in 1999, an institutional innovation to prevent forking in Linux was launched by the company for which Torvalds now works, the Transmeta Corporation. This is the Linux Standard Base (LSB), which is intended to 'develop and promote a set of standards that will increase the compatibility among Linux distributions and enable software applications to run on any compliant Linux system.'[17] The current membership of LSB includes four vendors of Linux-based software and IBM. This has raised fears that LSB might stifle the open-source software community's 'best development model wins' model by allowing commercial considerations to take precedence over what is best for the user.

Linux is not the only program developed by the free software movement. Sendmail, which routes about 70 per cent of all e-mails, is another. It was originally written by Eric Allman in 1981 and is now developed and maintained over the Internet by several thousand volunteers. Another example is Apache, which was developed by a loose group of twenty programmers. IBM has made Apache the cornerstone of WebSphere, its Internet commerce package, but the Apache programmers were paid nothing. Instead, in line with the free software ethos, they made IBM promise to keep the Apache code open, along with any modifications the firm might make. The only other thing the group got from IBM was a patch that made Apache run faster on Windows NT.

A third example is Fetchmail, which was launched by Eric Raymond to test Torvalds' development model. Before Linux came along, Raymond had believed that, above a certain level of complexity, a centralised, top-down approach to computer programming was required. He describes that level of work as cathedral-like, with in-dividuals or small bands of programmers carefully crafting software to an overall plan in splendid isolation.[18] Linux, however, showed that under the right conditions even the most central and complex of programs, an operating system, could evolve from the efforts of an anarchic mishmash of volunteers. He describes this bottom-up development model as a bazaar – a babbling multitude of people with differing agendas and opinions which somehow creates a coherent and stable system. Raymond's bazaar model is very similar to learning selection and to Dorothy Leonard's co-development.

After Linux had proved him wrong, Raymond set out to identify and understand the factors that had made the bazaar approach work. He reached some tentative conclusions and tested them with Fetchmail, thus developing his ideas further and gaining valuable insights. His first conclusion was that a participatory, bazaar-like development needed a good base from which to start. 'Your nascent developer community needs to have something runnable and test-able to play with', he said. Just as the first draft of Linux had come from Torvalds and Fetchmail from him, this had to be developed in the cathedral mode by an individual or small team working in isolation. This starting point had to make a 'plausible promise'. In other words the program could be crude, full of bugs, incomplete and poorly documented but it had to 'convince potential co-developers that it could be evolved into something really neat in the foreseeable future'.[19] In our terms, it had to be good enough to persuade the key stakeholders – the potential users – to jump in, adopt it, gain ownership of it and move from being just consultants to equal partners. In other words, Raymond is describing the change in stakeholder participation levels fundamental to our learning selection model. These are shown in Figure 3.4. During this period of the adaptation phase, the R&D team from the cathedral and the key stakeholders from the bazaar become equal partners in the development.

Raymond also identifies the need to have someone good to select the modifications. 'It is absolutely critical that the co-ordinator be able to recognise good design ideas from others', he writes. He also identifies the need for a product champion who can motivate people and keep the show on the road. He specifies that 'a bazaar project co-ordinator must have good people and communication skills. In order to build a development community you need to attract people, interest them in what you're doing and keep them happy with the work they're doing.'

His recipe for keeping the show on the road is KISS, or Keep It Small and Simple. Co-ordinators need to avoid being seduced by their egos and making the project 'cute and complicated'. He quotes Gerald Weinberg's[20] observation that when program developers are not territorial about their code and encourage others to look for bugs and potential improvements, progress speeds up dramatically. This certainly squares with my experience in agricultural engineering. An enormous amount of time and effort can be wasted when an R&D team devotes itself to defending its baby against criticism rather than sorting its problems out.

Raymond presented his conclusions in a paper called 'The Cathedral and the Bazaar' at the Linux Kongress in Würzburg in Germany in May 1997. Since then the paper has taken on a life of own with effects Raymond could never have imagined. One of these was to encourage Netscape, a major software company, to try to capture the power of the bazaar – or learning selection as we call it – for itself.

In January 1998, the company announced that it was publishing the source code for its flagship client software, Netscape Communicator,[21] because it wanted to 'benefit from the best of both worlds, using its own development team to innovate new features and functionality, while selecting the best enhancements from the open-source development to create Netscape-branded versions of software.' Netscape added that, 'while several factors lead to success, including a compelling need for the software and a good base of code from which to start, the most important is a person or group trusted by the development community to lead and guide the development effort'. This role is identical with that of selector and promulgator in the learning selection model. The company created mozilla.org to fill it.

Expansion and disappearance phases

Development in information technology occurs much faster than in any other technical sphere, thanks to 'Moore's law', the rule-of-thumb which states that the number of transistors on integrated circuits – and hence the performance of computers – doubles every 12–18 months. Figure 5.1 shows how software development has matched and even surpassed that development rate.

Early in 2000, Linux was very much in its expansion phase, although its adaptation phase was far from over because the improvements being made to it were fitting it for wider markets. For example, as Linux improved many managers of corporate IT systems began to run their networks on it because of its stability – it crashes infrequently. Boeing, the aircraft company, adopted it for another reason. According to Bob Young, the president of Red Hat Software Inc., which sells Linux programs, whenever Boeing has a complex application it wants to get access to the source code to make modifications. '[With closed source software,] if there are some inconsistencies in how the application interfaces with the operating system, they have no way of fixing it because they have bought a car with the hood welded shut',[22] he says.

Netscape's decision to publish one of its software codes so that it could be co-developed was important for Linux because it encouraged another software firm, Corel, to announce in May 1998 that it was writing a version of WordPerfect 8 to run on Linux. Its CEO, Michael Cowpland, said:

We really encourage the idea of the free and open operating system, but we also encourage the idea of Linux being a very good commercial platform for software developers such as ourselves to port to [write programs in] and end up with a very economical and attractive accommodation. The analogy would be having the interstate highway system where the roads are free, but you have shopping centres on them, as opposed to toll roads, which is the Microsoft model, where you have to pay for the road and the application.[23]

Cowpland's mention of the Microsoft model is telling because the move by Netscape and Corel to open-source software can be seen as a their way of attacking the near-monopoly the Windows operating system enjoys in the personal computer market. Windows runs 90 per cent of PCs[24] compared with Linux's 1 per cent. This gives Microsoft a large number of testers in the form of its customers and it is said that the launch of Windows 95 was the biggest-ever release of an imperfect, unfinished version of a computer program so that users could improve it. In the industry, these prematurely released programs are known as beta versions, but Windows 95 was not announced as such. Forty million copies were sold to people in the first year who expected it would work properly, and they complained loudly when it did not. Microsoft remedied many of the problems with Windows 98, which it sold as an upgrade to Windows 95 for an extra $100. An indication of the unreliability of machines running Windows is that study after study has shown that Apple Macintoshes are four to ten times cheaper for computer departments to service and run.[25]

By working with open-source software enthusiasts, Corel and Netscape are hoping to compensate for their more limited resources and smaller customer base. The strategy might be working. For example, within hours of Netscape liberating their Communicator code, a team of Australian programmers had produced a cryptographic add-on that enabled the program to handle secure Internet transactions. Other improvements poured in from all over the world, and in less than a month a new version of the program was posted on the project's website, ready for free downloading.[26]

But even if open-source software enthusiasts can muster more talent and develop better products than Microsoft, there is no guarantee of their commercial success. Inferior technologies have often become dominant either because they were first on the market or because they were promoted more aggressively. For example, JVC's VHS video system ousted Sony's technically superior Betamax; while, in the computer world, the Apple operating system lost out to Microsoft's Windows even though it worked better and was available earlier.

Windows NT: closed-source innovation

As Linux moves further into the mainstream, it will have to compete increasingly with Microsoft's Windows NT (now also known as Windows 2000) operating system. Let us therefore use the learning selection model to look at the way Microsoft develops its software so that we can compare and contrast the strengths and weaknesses of the cathedral and bazaar development models.

The history of Windows NT and the nature of the program cannot be separated from Microsoft's corporate strategy. The company was set up by two computer programmers, Bill Gates and Paul Allen, in 1975. Neither shared the 'software-should-be-free-to-all' spirit of the time even though, as Microsoft's own history says, 'building software as a business was an odd notion in 1975'. In 1976, Bill Gates even wrote an open letter to pioneer owners of personal computers protesting at the 'it-should-be-free' attitude: 'As the majority of hobbyists must be aware, most of you steal your software. Hardware must be paid for, but software is something to share. Who cares if the people who worked on it get paid? Is this fair?'[27]

Gates's and Allen's initial project was to write a computer language, BASIC, for the first personal computer, the Altair. Then, as other computers were introduced, they produced compilers – programs that translated BASIC into machine language so that its commands could be executed – for them too, so that by the end of 1979 Microsoft had one for virtually every personal computer on the market and BASIC was becoming the industry standard.

The company's big break came a year later when it won a contract from IBM, the biggest computer firm at the time, to develop languages and an operating system for the personal computer IBM was planning to introduce. This was launched on 12 August 1981 running Microsoft Disk Operating System version 1.0, which was quickly abbreviated to MS–DOS 1.0. The IBM PC quickly became the industry standard as IBM allowed other companies to copy its architecture, thus enabling Microsoft to license MS–DOS to other manufacturers as well. The competition between IBM-compatible PC manufacturers made their machines much cheaper than Apple computers. As a result, Apple, which had refused to allow its architecture to be copied, eventually lost its position as market leader in spite of then having a much better, easier-to-use operating system.

Anyone who ever used MS–DOS will recall its counter-intuitive characteristics and the large number of commands one had to remember and type in to make one's PC work. In 1984, however, Apple introduced a Graphic User Interface, or GUI as it is usually called, that allowed users to click on icons with a mouse rather than remember commands to type. It was intuitive and studies found that people were more productive using an Apple Macintosh computer than a PC running MS–DOS. In order to match its rival, Microsoft developed a GUI of its own, which it added to MS–DOS and released as Windows 1.0 in November 1985. Apple complained about copyright infringement and struck a deal with Microsoft covering the first version. However, when Windows 2.0 was released it sued for infringement of copyright and lost.

Microsoft's marketing strategy has always been to maximise its market share by trying to make its products the market standard. Because Apple lost sales to cheaper IBM PC clones, more and more programs were written for Windows rather than Apple, even though many thought the Mac's operating system was superior. This created a positive feedback because people increasingly decided to buy PCs as there was a lot more software available for them. As a result, Microsoft gained a near-monopoly in the PC operating system market and its co-founder, Bill Gates, became the world's richest man by the end of the 1990s.

Microsoft now benefits from the QWERTY keyboard phenomenon – that even if a better operating system comes along, people have invested so much time and effort in learning Windows programs that they will be reluctant to change. However, to maintain this advantage, Microsoft has to make each new version of Windows compatible with the previous one, thus maintaining a lineage all the way back to early 1980s versions of MS–DOS. As a result, the company has never been able to 'spring clean' the program and clear out all the relics of its past which make it buggy and unstable. 'Internally Windows 95 is a complete mess,' says Torvalds. 'Even people

who have worked for Microsoft and who have had years of experience just don't know how it works internally. Worse, nobody dares
change it. Nobody dares to fix bugs because it is such a mess that
fixing one bug might break a hundred programs that depend on that
bug.'[28]

In the mid-1980s Microsoft realised that MS–DOS might not be
the ideal basis for an operating system, particularly one for computers
other than PCs. In partnership with IBM it developed a more powerful DOS replacement, which it released as OS/2. At the same time
the firm began developing its own Unix-like operating system. Initially this was called OS/2 NT because it used some OS/2 code. NT
stood for new technology. In 1991 it decided to give OS/2 NT a
Windows personality by marrying it to the Windows GUI. The
resulting program was released in July 1993 under the name Windows
NT. It was labelled version 3.1 not only to stress its compatibility
with the MS–DOS-based Windows 3.1 that was current at that time,
but also to make people think it was more developed, and hence
more reliable, than a version 1.0 tag would have implied.[29]

Because Windows NT was aimed at the network-server market,
it needed to be more stable than Windows 3.1, which was becoming
notorious for producing error messages like 'Your program has
committed a fatal error' and forcing users to reboot – that is, to shut
down their computers and then open them up again. While NT
managed this, it was still less stable than Linux, and NT newsgroups
began to complain about a 'blue screen of death' when the program
locked up.

In August 1996 Microsoft released NT version 4.0, which contained a staggering 16 million lines of code, over ten times more
than the 1999 version of Linux and thus with more potential for
going wrong. Microsoft followed this in 1998 with version 5.0, which
has 25 million lines of code. A year later, the firm surprised the
computing world by announcing that version 5.0 would be renamed
Windows 2000 and replace the MS–DOS-based Windows series.
'Windows NT will be the basis for all Microsoft PC operating systems
from consumer products to the highest performance servers', Jim
Allchin, a senior vice-president at Microsoft announced. 'Windows
NT is going mainstream.'[30]

Unfortunately, its stability problems remain and a 1999 survey
found that organisations of all shapes and sizes planned to wait from

six to eighteen months before adopting Windows 2000. This was mainly because they thought the operating system they received would be unstable and they wanted to leave more time for the worst bugs to be eliminated.[31]

Nicholas Petreley, editor-in-chief at *NC World* magazine and contributing editor for *InfoWorld* magazine, believes that Windows NT is unstable because of the sometimes conflicting evolutionary pressures exerted on it by Microsoft's overriding drive to mantain its monopoly. 'Some of [these] have absolutely nothing to do with serving the customer', he comments. It was these pressures that Torvalds was thinking about when he spoke of his need to remain uncorrupted by commercial interests so that people would trust him in his role as main selector and Linux product champion.

As each PC can work by itself, independently of any other computer, it has to have its own, relatively expensive, operating system installed on it. This is what has made Microsoft rich. Windows NT was designed for use on a computer network, which can consist of a number of PCs connected together so that they can communicate with each other. However, the cheapest way to build a network is to have terminals connected to a powerful central computer – the server. The terminals are sometimes called 'thin clients' because they are not designed to operate alone and hence can have less hardware. While this might be the best solution for the customer, it threatens Microsoft's core monopoly – its sales to PC users – because each networked computer would not need its own version of Windows. Moreover, as even people working at home on the Internet are connected to a network, network-based computing is likely to mean that Windows will cease to be as ubiquitous as at present.

Microsoft would obviously prefer that, if networks are built, they consist of linked PCs, each running its own copy of Windows. Its design specification for Windows NT therefore envisaged that each client computer would run its own full operating system and do much of its own data processing. But, by designing Windows NT in this way, the firm created problems for itself, because, as we have just seen, this is not the best way to run a network. Its competition – Unix and now Linux – were designed from the start to expect more to be done on the server and less on the clients.

Microsoft has introduced patches to overcome this inherent design problem and allow Windows NT to compete with a resurgent Unix by serving thin clients. In doing so, however, it has introduced bugs to the program, Petreley thinks. As Torvalds says, 'They're [Microsoft] just adding things on top of each other and hoping the end result is stable instead of trying to really build up a very stable base that everyone can depend on.'

Other bug problems may have come from Microsoft's attempt to win the standard speed tests set by computer magazines. Petreley says this is the reason NT has a 'dangerous kernel model that invites driver crashes'.[32] He thinks NT also crashes because of the way Microsoft has overwritten competitors' dynamic link library (DLL) files with its own. A DLL file consists of one or more small programs that lets a larger program communicate with a specific device such as a printer or scanner. By overwriting DLL files, Windows can sabotage its competitors' programs. Microsoft resists removing this source of instability because the company wants to keep the competitive advantage that an 'unfair' practice, in the view of others, has given it.

The findings of the anti-trust case brought against Microsoft by the US Justice Department at the end of the 1990s show that Microsoft's 'unfair' practices go far beyond corrupting their competitors' DLL files. The presiding judge, Judge Jackson, wrote this damning indictment of Microsoft's anti-evolutionary effect:

> Most harmful of all is the message that Microsoft's actions have conveyed to every enterprise with potential to innovate in the computer industry. Through its conduct to Netscape, IBM, Compaq, Intel and others, Microsoft has demonstrated that it will use its prodigious market power and immense profits to harm any firm that insists on pursuing initiatives that could intensify competition against one of Microsoft's core products. Microsoft's past success in hurting such companies and stifling innovation deters investment in technologies and businesses that exhibit the potential to threaten Microsoft. *The ultimate result is that some business innovations that would truly benefit consumers never occur for the sole reason that they do not coincide with Microsoft's self-interest.*[33]

Microsoft counters criticism of Windows NT by pointing out that it would not be the market leader if its instability was as bad as its detractors say. Moreover, NT is faster than Linux if used on powerful servers with four or more processors. Linux has not yet made much of a dent in this market: it is more often installed on low- to mid-range servers – the machines used to manage departmental, rather than whole-company, networks.

The main reason businesses buy Windows NT is the level of after-sales service and support available and the program's compatibility with desktop Windows. There is a third consideration, too. 'Organisations whose lawyers want to make sure that they can sue someone if their applications crash are not likely to consider Linux vendors sufficiently deep-pocket', says *Software Magazine*.[34] In addition, Walter Nelson, vice-president of software engineering and product management at Fair, Isaac and Co. Inc., explains that many companies, his included, don't plan to adopt Linux because it would require them to employ better qualified IT personnel. Using Linux 'means that you are using a wide range of multi-vendor components to try and construct your system', he says.[35]

But things are changing. As Linux has become the program many computer science students use at university, expertise in it and other open-source software is becoming more widespread. Second, pockets are deepening. Red Hat, which sells Linux systems, was floated on the stock market in August 1999 and the value of its shares tripled in the first day.[36] On 15 December 1999 the company had a market capitalisation of an incredible \$15 billion.[37]

As Microsoft sold 20 million licences for Windows NT between 1994 and 1999, the system's sales performance clearly cannot be compared with that of the flash dryer or the US government's wind turbines. Even so, its technology generation and transfer model is very similar to the over-the-wall one used by governments because it assumes that there is a central source of innovation – the Microsoft campus in Seattle, its cathedral. Microsoft does better than NAPHIRE, of course, because it accepts that its new technology is going to have bugs and uses a cut-down version of learning selection to find and correct them. It does this by using its customers' experiences, their *learning by using*, to find the bugs for it but prevents them fixing them themselves – in our terms, generating novelties – by denying them the source code required to do so. In other words, because the firm sells 'cars with the hoods welded shut', the key stakeholders, its customers, can participate only as consultants. They can never become co-developers and can never gain ownership of the technology. Microsoft's Valloppillil is worried by this. 'Linux could win', he wrote in his leaked memorandum. 'The ability of the open-source software process to collect and harness the collective IQ of thousands of individuals across the Internet is simply amazing.'[38]

One reason why open-source projects can muster more creative talent than a company as wealthy as Microsoft is that money does not necessarily motivate people to be inventive, a fact that has vital implications for the learning selection model. Theresa Amabile, associate professor of psychology at Brandeis University in the USA, has done a great deal of work on creativity and motivation and has repeatedly found that there is an inverse relationship between creativity and external reward. 'It may be concluded', she says, 'that commissioned work will, in general, be less creative than work that is done out of pure interest. The more complex the activity, the more it is hurt by extrinsic reward.'[39] Researchers offer several explanations for this surprising finding. First, rewards encourage people to focus too narrowly on the task, to do it as quickly as possible and to take few risks. 'If they feel that this is something they have to get through to get the prize, they're going to be less creative', says Amabile. Second, people come to see themselves as being controlled by the reward. They feel less independent and this may interfere with performance and creativity. Finally, extrinsic rewards as opposed to ones coming from inside can erode intrinsic interest. People who see themselves working for money, approval or competitive success find their tasks less pleasurable, and they therefore do not do them as well.

In essence, Amabile's research suggests that computer programmers working for money are likely to be less creative than those programming as a hobby in their own time. Linus Torvalds seems to agree. He thinks that there are a lot of Microsoft programmers who love programming but do not necessarily love working for Microsoft. 'The pride is not in the products', Torvalds says, 'People inside Microsoft know [Windows 95] is a bad operating system and they still continue working on it because they want to get the next version out because they want all these new features to sell more copies of the system. Microsoft isn't interested in fixing bugs, they're interested in making money.'[40]

In 'The Cathedral and the Bazaar', Raymond suggests that open-source software developers are motivated by rewards other than money. 'The utility function Linux hackers are maximising is not classically economic, but is the intangible of their own ego satisfaction and reputation among other hackers.' He believes that they are part of a gift culture where status is determined not by what you own but by what you give away. Within this culture – Raymond calls it the Noosphere – there is no shortage of 'survival necessities' as good programmers usually have well-paid day jobs. They all have enough disk space, network bandwidth and computing power. This abundance means that the only measure of competitive success available to them is their reputation among their peers.

The gift cultures that have existed in the past, and the few remaining today, are about much more than giving to enhance your status. People can only give in an environment where they know that things will come back to them. That environment is underpinned by what sociologists call a 'common property regime', where individual members of a group have rights and duties that must be respected for the system to work. Linux is the same. The common intellectual property regime is set by copyleft, which under US law gives anyone the right to copy and modify a program protected in this way, but if they do so then the hacker has the duty to make his or her novelty available to others. This is much more of a social obligation than a legal one.

Throughout the world, gift cultures have only worked when people have fulfilled their duty to give back to the system. Many have crumbled and given way to cultures based on the private ownership of property. The culture that developed Linux could well meet a similar fate, brought about by Red Hat's August 1999 stock market flotation. Some people have become, and others are becoming, very rich from Linux, setting up social strains in the group that developed it for 'free'.[41] Even Eric Raymond made $26 million on paper from the 150,000 shares he owns in VA Linux, one of Red Hat's competitors, when it was floated on the stock market in December 1999. Raymond was on VA Linux's board and admitted that he had become 'absurdly rich'.[42] These profits accruing to a few could cost Linux its volunteers' development input, just as happened in the Danish wind turbine industry when the hobbyists and enthusiasts motivated by concerns about the environment were replaced by others fired by the 'prospect of a good investment and a reasonable rate of return'. The threat of corruption that Torvalds talks about is the threat that private property rights pose to setting up and maintaining a common intellectual property regime.

In terms of the learning selection model, the novelty generation that created Linux also created new institutions and organisational structures that then changed the commercial environment in which Linux develops. The profit motive could force Linux down an evolutionary path where fitness is no longer measured in what is best for the user, but in what is likely to make most money.

Valloppillil's halloween memorandum shows that Microsoft is aware that undermining the common property regime underpinned by copyleft is the way to fight Linux. Their strategy is to attempt to privatise the technical building blocks that make up the Linux operating system by pretending to adopt them and then 'extending' them in ways that make them proprietary. The new (Microsoft) revisions would, of course, be incompatible with the 'free' versions. Bill Gates has called this process 'embrace and extend'. In reality it is 'copy and corrupt'.[43]

The Danish wind turbine industry needed to become more commercial if the benefits of the technology were to be spread more widely; the same argument can be applied to Linux. Certainly, increased commercial interest is helping Linux by providing knowledge not available to it before. Intel, which makes most of the processors fitted in desktop PCs, wants its chips to be used by lots of operating systems, not just Windows. Consequently, although its close relationship with Microsoft in the past helped it to achieve it near-monopoly position, it is now funding a company called Cygnus to adapt Linux to enable the system to run 30–40 per cent faster than at present on the Pentium MMX and Pentium III chips.

Intel is also involved with Hewlett–Packard and IBM in the Trillian initiative to run Linux on Merced, the code name for Intel's first 64-bit chip, largely because Linux is a 64-bit operating system while Windows NT is only 32-bit. The advantage of 64-bit computing is that computers can operate on 64-bit chunks of data, which makes data processing faster and more efficient. In practice it means that the performance previously only possible from highly specialised and expensive supercomputers becomes feasible on machines more like conventional workstations. Departing from its normal development practice, Intel will give each of the four commercial Linux software vendors a prototype Merced machine. 'We'll make the systems available ... so people can actually do development across the Net', Sean Maloney, Intel's senior vice-president for sales and marketing, said during the keynote address at the Linux Conference and Expo in August 1999.[44] This will inevitably lead to additional knowledge, in the form of lines of code, being incorporated into Linux software, increasing the markets in which it can compete.

There are other similarities with the wind turbine industry. Both evolutionary processes began with simple technologies that the first adopters could understand and modify. Both were developed in educational institutions. La Cour built his wind turbine at the Askov Folk High School and Tanenbaum wrote Minix for teaching purposes at the Free University in Amsterdam. Both technologies were criticised for being backward and not 'breakthrough'. However, if they had been highly advanced there might not have been enough people with a common skill set to modify them, and the evolutionary process might not have begun. In both cases, the evolution of the technologies through learning selection meant they could make up for the 'slow start' and overtake the competition. Once users participate in the development, the iterations are 'potentially an order of magnitude faster'[45] than when users are treated merely as consultants.

Conclusions

When I started writing this book I knew very little about Linux and the open-source software movement. I had not heard of Eric Raymond or Linus Torvalds and I knew nothing of the cathedral and the bazaar. I chose Linux as a case study because someone recommended it as a good example of 'grassroots' innovation that might have similarities with my experiences with agricultural equipment. So you can imagine the buzz I felt when I realised just how similar my learning selection approach was to Raymond's bazaar model for developing software. To me, the fact that Raymond and I have developed such similar models based on such dissimilar technology is overwhelming proof that the learning selection approach is applicable beyond agricultural equipment, and conversely, that the bazaar model is applicable beyond software. What the Linux case study also shows is just how powerful our learning selection approach can be under the right conditions. In addition to the conditions we have already identified – a 'plausible promise' (to borrow Raymond's phrase), novelty-generators, selection mechanisms and promulgation – the Linux case study shows the necessity of having a common intellectual property regime, in other words a sense of community among the co-developers that ensures ideas are shared. Linux has also shown us the ability of the Internet to accelerate learning selection iterations through the rapid exchange of information among people who may be separated geographically by very great distances. The ability to communicate easily over distance allows 'virtual' communities of co-developers to be built that could not exist without the Internet. Rapid learning selection iterations were also possible because modifications made to computer programs – patches – can be quickly assessed in an objective way. This is not always the case with new technology, as we will see in the next chapter. Linux has also shown us the pivotal role that a 'product champion' can play, and that for someone to do this well he or she should be 'low at the ego end' – willing to select and promulgate changes whatever the source of innovation, and whatever the consequences for their own personal stake in the technology. The next chapter will shed further light on the role product champions can play.

Uncreative accounting

Local Exchange Trading Systems

Until I began researching this chapter, I had never thought of money as an institutional innovation with an evolutionary history just like other technologies. I thought that money was simply money, full stop. Of course I had used foreign currencies like the peso, baht and dong, but these all worked the way money did at home. So, because I had only experienced one type of money in operation, I imagined that all money was essentially the same and that it must have functioned in basically the same way since the first coins were minted thousands of years ago. As a result, I never realised that we would almost certainly be using very different types of money today if currency development had followed a different path. Nor did I think about the ways in which our monetary system has affected, and been affected by, the economic system we have at present.

I was not alone in this position. Most economists think that there is only one type of money, too – that is, when they think about it at all. The profession, to quote two sociologists,[1] is 'curiously un-interested [in the topic], restricting itself to discussions of price, scarcity and resource allocation with no specific interest in money as such'. David Hume, one of the founding fathers of economics, referred[2] to money as simply 'the oil which renders the motion of the wheels smooth and easy', and his attitude persists to this day. Certainly, very few economists have examined the different types of money that are possible to establish the effects that each would have on the economic system and on people's lives.

A brief history of money

This chapter is about some of those alternative currencies, particularly Local Exchange Trading Systems, or LETS as they are known. However, before we can discuss the way grassroots movements around the world have established LETS and other currency systems, we need to examine the dominant technology – the money we have in our pockets today. This is called *fiat* money, from the Latin 'to command', and the surprising thing about it is that nearly all of it has been commanded into existence by commercial banks, in a practice that began as fraud, rather than by the government or a central bank.

The easiest way of explaining this is to follow money's development path through time. In his book *Money: Whence It Came, Where It Went*, the well-known Canadian economist John Kenneth Galbraith states that people have used one or more of three metals – gold, silver and copper – to facilitate trade with each other for four thousand years. Their use of these substances was not, in general, the result of a ruler's decree. Instead, people seem to have felt that the metals had value, although whether they did so because of their usefulness or their inherent beauty is a matter of debate. Scarcity was certainly a factor in their value, though – had they been lying around in vast quantities for anyone to pick up, they would have been worth no more than the pebbles beside them. The fact that gold did not tarnish or corrode was a factor too, and it generally seems to have been considered worth more than the equivalent amount of copper or silver.

Whatever it was that gave these metals their appeal, people were prepared to accept them in exchange for things that were clearly valuable like food and labour. Their willingness to trade in this way was a major innovation because, under the barter system which had been used previously, each participant had to have not just something the other person wanted, which was hard enough to arrange, but in the appropriate quantity and quality too. 'Is my horse worth your ox, or do I have to throw in my dog as well? Ah, you don't want the dog but you will take that knife…' and so on.

Not that the use of metals for making exchanges was entirely problem-free. For perhaps a thousand years, until, between 2250 and 2150 BC, the rulers of Cappadocia started to guarantee the weight and purity of silver ingots to help their acceptance as money,[3] traders had to check that the lumps of precious metal they were using hadn't been adulterated and hack them up to get the right weight. Then, about a thousand years later, standardised lumps of metal – coins bearing the head of the ruler as a guarantee of weight and quality – began to be produced. Where this happened first is not clear; China, India and the Aegean island of Lydia all have competing claims. However, the innovation spread to the Greek cities and then to Italy, from where it was propagated widely by the Roman Empire.

But even then exchange technology was not perfect. Rulers who owned the mints were continually tempted to reduce the weight of precious metal in the coins they produced. For example, in 1542 Henry VIII of England was sorely in need of funds to fight the French and, in order to make the amount of silver he had go further, he told his mint to add 6 ounces of copper to every 10 ounces of the sterling silver (which was itself only 92.5 per cent pure silver) it used to make pennies. A few months later the amount of copper was increased to 7 ounces per pound, then to 10, then to 12 and finally under Edward VI, to 13. Prices doubled and Kett's Rebellion broke out in 1549 in protest against the domestic inflation. On the foreign exchanges, the English pound lost over half its value. A proclamation that a shilling (12d) would henceforward be only worth 9d set off a national monetary panic. It was left to Elizabeth I to call in all the debased coins, refine out the copper and reissue them as 100 per cent sterling silver.[4]

As dishonest merchants also debased coins by filing off some of their metal to sell, confusion and doubt over the value of the money in use in Amsterdam, one of Europe's main trading centres in the seventeenth century, became so bad that it seriously affected business. This is not surprising since, in 1606, the Dutch parliament listed no fewer than 341 different types of silver coins and 505 different types of gold ones in circulation there. Moreover, the confusion was compounded because fourteen mints in the Netherlands alone were churning out their own monies.

An innovation was required to bring about some order, and in 1609 the Bank of Amsterdam, the first public bank, was set up under the guarantee of the City.[5] This took in foreign and local coins, assessed what they were worth on the basis of the precious metal they actually contained, and then marked this up as a credit to the depositor. Because the bank was guaranteed, depositors quickly learned to trust it and found it safer and more convenient to trade with each other using the receipts it had issued for the precious metal in the coins they had handed in rather than with the coins themselves.

As Galbraith wryly remarks, 'where reward is waiting, men have a natural instinct for innovation'.[6] Unfortunately, however, a less beneficial one followed. Once many of its customers were trading with receipts rather than coins, the bank realised that it had coins in its vaults that were never taken out. For about one hundred years the bank resisted the temptation to lend out these, the property of its depositors. Consequently, when the armies of Louis XIV were marching towards Amsterdam in 1672 and the depositors panicked and demanded their money, the bank was able to supply coins to everyone who asked. Then, gradually, self-interest became stronger and 'corrupted' the bank. Some of its directors were also directors of the Dutch East India Company, which needed short-term loans to cover its costs until its ships returned home. These loans were, naturally, agreed. The funds were advanced by giving the East India Company receipts for coins it had never deposited. This caused few problems because the bank found that most of its existing stock of coins stayed in its vaults as the false receipts were rarely exchanged for the coins they represented. People were happier to trade with the receipts instead.

Problems with these loans would arise, however, if too many of the borrowers and the genuine depositors presented their receipts and demanded cash at the same time, as there would be insufficient coins in the vaults to pay them. But the chances of this happening seemed remote, and, in any case, the bank was earning interest. This created wealth which gave it the resources to lend out even more money. In short, the Bank of Amsterdam had adopted the profitable yet fraudulent way to create money that London goldsmiths had discovered several decades previously.[7]

The bank's volume of lending gradually grew until, in 1780, the Dutch East India Company, its biggest debtor, ran into trouble when many of its ships and their cargoes were lost during the war with England. Confidence in the bank was shattered and merchants who had previously given a better price on transactions paid in the bank's receipts rather than coins now began to favour cash, fearing that the bank might not have enough gold and silver coins on hand to pay them. These fears caused a run on the bank in 1819. The bank closed its doors and many depositors lost their money.

Despite this dismal end, the Bank of Amsterdam laid the foundations of our current monetary system. Banks still create money in the way the Bank of Amsterdam did by making loans which would require them to pay out far more notes and cash than they have in their vaults if ever everyone with an account in credit or a partially unused loan facility simultaneously wanted to draw it out as money, rather than as a credit note or cheque. In fact things are worse today in the sense that banks no longer pretend that their receipts entitle the bearer to any quantity of gold, silver or, indeed, anything at all. Until 1971, the US dollar was convertible into gold at a fixed rate and most other major currencies were convertible into dollars, so paper money and bank receipts – the balance in a bank account – did, in theory at least, represent something. However, the USA, which, as the world's banker, held a huge stockpile of gold at Fort Knox to guarantee the currency, did what the Bank of Amsterdam had done two centuries previously. It failed to observe a sufficiently cautious ratio between the number of dollars it allowed to go into circulation around the world and the amount of gold it held in Fort Knox. After confidence in the ability of the USA to maintain the exchange rate with gold was finally destroyed by the flood of dollars America released to cover the costs of fighting the Vietnam war, there was a run on the dollar. On Sunday, 15 August 1971, President Nixon cracked. He took the United States off the gold standard and removed the last fixed link between the world's money and anything real. As a result the value of every currency has been based on nothing but confidence ever since and has fluctuated in response to the whims of the market to an unprecedented extent. The monetary world was left with no foundation, no fixed point – 'a floating non-system', the then German Chancellor Helmut Schmidt called it.[8]

The reason why banks were allowed to continue to create money in this fraudulent way is simple: there was no political will to stop them. Business people prosper in periods in which there is plenty of money about, even if that money has to be borrowed from the banks by those who spend it into circulation. Ordinary people benefit too – more jobs become available and it is easier for them to borrow if they want to. However, if the amount of goods and services available for purchase increases less rapidly than the total amount of money in circulation during a period of buoyant bank lending, prices go up and an inflation occurs.

This can alter the structure of the economy. According to Galbraith, inflation eased the path of the industrial revolution by undermining the 'steady-state economics' that existed at that time. It did this by gradually reducing the value of peoples' wages in real terms – their money bought less and less – while simultaneously increasing their employers' profits. The higher profits created capital surpluses that had to be invested in other money-making schemes because if they were just deposited in a bank, inflation would eat them away as well. Inflation therefore encouraged people to be innovative and provided them with the necessary capital to do so. It also created a forgiving environment by reducing the real cost of their loans, and hence their inevitable mistakes, over time. It rescued 'traders from their errors of optimism and stupidity,'[9] as Galbraith says. More positively, the expanding market it brought about, as well as creating opportunities for profit, gave businesses the chance to learn and correct past errors. In terms of our model, inflation created an environment that fostered learning selection.

There is a downside to inflation, of course. It impoverishes those people who are least able to adapt and change – the poor and the elderly. There is also an extremely serious drawback to allowing banks to create the money that causes the inflation: it makes the economy fundamentally unstable. One reason for this is that the national money supply – the money available to be spent – is not just the notes and coins in circulation. It also includes each bank's liabilities – the amount its customers have in their accounts plus the money it has agreed to lend but which the borrowers have not yet drawn down. These liabilities amount to many times more than the sum available as cash. In Britain in October 1999, the cash in circulation amounted to £29.3 billion while the amount that people could draw without notice from their bank accounts was £389 billion.

This means that 93 per cent of money in use in Britain was created by people going into debt, which means, in turn, that if the amount they borrow falls, the amount of money in circulation shrinks. If this happens, there is less in peoples' pockets for them to spend. This hits business profits. Lay-offs result and, as the newly unemployed have less to spend, business profits fall further and some firms go bust. The deteriorating economic climate makes potential borrowers much more cautious about getting into debt and causes the rate at which new loans are being taken out to decline, thus contracting the money supply further still. A very damaging deflationary spiral develops, especially after firms in difficulties and desperate for money start reducing their prices. Once the fact that they are doing so becomes clear, anyone who can delays making purchases, confident that they will be able to buy more cheaply later on. This puts more pressure on the struggling firms. Bad debts build up. If depositors come to feel that the number of bankruptcies threatens the banks themselves and rush to withdraw their money, the whole system collapses.

Thousands of American banks failed in this manner during the Great Depression that began in 1929 and did not really end until the huge spending on arms during the Second World War reflated the economy eleven years later. Indeed, economic history since the birth of the modern banking system has been one of boom and bust. The record shows that once a deflationary spiral begins it is very hard to stop because people who have burned their fingers lack the confidence to begin to borrow again. 'Neither a lender nor a borrower be' becomes a popular adage and, without huge and coordinated government spending, the depression will not lift until memories fade.

Alternative currencies

Alternative currency systems have been invented and used whenever *fiat* money has become scarce because people have been unwilling or unable to borrow enough of it from the banks to prevent the amount in circulation from falling. This happens in all depressions and a great many alternative currencies were launched in the last major depression – that in the 1930s. All were intended to be media of exchange that allowed people to escape from poverty by using their skills and resources to trade and thus meet each other's needs without using the scarce national currency.

The most successful alternative currency system started at this time is the Swiss Wirtschaftsring (Economic Circle) co-operative – or WIR, as it is called. It was launched in October 1934 by a group of businesspeople led by Dr Werner Zimmermann and Paul Enz and has since grown into a massive organisation turning over 2,521 million Swiss francs ($1,800 million) in 1993 among its 60,000 account holders.

The founders' idea was simply that traders who knew and trusted each other would extend each other credit for purchases within their group, cutting down their need to borrow from banks. According to a 1971 report[10] on the system, 'they thought they could transact business among themselves with a system of chits similar to IOUs that would cover at least part of the price of any transaction, the balance being settled in the conventional way. [However,] it was soon found that in order to bring about wider acceptance of these chits, and also to comply with existing banking laws and avoid financial losses, collateral was essential.'

This insistence on collateral might partially explain why WIR has survived and similar systems established at the same time in England, Germany, France and Austria have disappeared without trace. However, an official history of WIR produced in 1984 for its fiftieth anniversary suggests that WIR is the sole survivor because the other circles did not realise the significance of what they were doing and wound themselves up when the financial crisis was past. But opposition from vested interests played a part in some cases too. Zimmermann and Enz visited circles in Norway and Denmark before starting WIR; when they returned to Denmark for a second visit, they found that the circle there had been closed by the government after pressure from the banks.

Essentially, WIR is an independent currency system for small and medium-sized businesses. A company wishing to join contacts the head office in Basle or one of the six regional offices and sets up a meeting at which the firm's credit requirements and the collateral it is able to offer are discussed, just as they would be if the business sought a loan from its bank. The collateral most frequently offered is a second mortgage on a house or business premises: in recent years, over 80 per cent of WIR's loans have been secured this way. If the meeting is successful, a loan application is sent to the WIR credit approval committee which checks the security and obtains a report on the applicant from a credit-checking agency. If the report and the security are in order, the new participant is given a WIR chequebook, a plastic charge card and a fat catalogue listing other participants with whom the loan has to be spent.

Although the sums in WIR accounts are denominated in Swiss francs they are not Swiss francs at all since, unless one breaks the rules, they cannot be turned into normal currency, paid into ordinary banks or given to non-members. We will therefore call the system's units 'Wir'. Even when someone wishes to leave the organisation, he or she cannot exchange Wir for national currency. As a result, the purchasing power created when the credit committee authorises a loan stays entirely within the 'ring', generating increased business for all participants. Secured loans of this type are cheap. In 1994 Wir mortgages carried a service charge of 1.75 per cent and relatively long repayment terms could be negotiated; the charge for ordinary current-account loans was 2.5 per cent.

The credit committee has a policy of restricting the total value of the loans it authorises to one-third of the system's annual turnover in order to maintain the Wir's value. All repayments are made in Wir which participants earn by selling his or her goods and services to other members. Only service charges have to be paid in Swiss francs, since the co-op itself cannot function without some national currency.

Almost every conceivable product and service was listed in WIR's summer 1994 catalogue which included 167 lawyers, 16 undertakers, 1,853 architects and 18 chimney sweeps. 'The main areas are gastronomy and the building trade while the odder categories are astrologers, piano tuners, matrimonial agencies, genealogical researchers and magicians. There's even a circus', Claudia Horny from WIR's public relations office said.

Not all suppliers take 100 per cent payment in Wir, but, with several sources listed for most products and services, it is generally possible to find at least one who will, particularly at slack times of year or during sales. Prices and payment terms for transactions in Wir are just the same as they would be for cash and, until recently, if a supplier insisted on getting a proportion of his invoice paid in national currency, two cheques, one in Wir, one in Swiss francs, were handed over at the same time. However, since the beginning of 1995, it has been possible to make combined payments of cash and Wir using a single plastic charge card.

The percentage of the Swiss franc price of the goods and services that participants will supply for Wir is discussed with each member when he or she joins, and the service charges mentioned so far only apply to 'official' members who have agreed to accept at least 30 per cent of the payment in the system's unit. Members unable to give such an undertaking are called 'unofficial' and pay higher charges –

3.5 per cent for current-account loans and a 1.2 per cent rather than 0.6 per cent levy on the value of each cheque.

Another interesting alternative currency that rose to prominence during the Great Depression was launched by the Freiwirtschaft (Free Economy) movement in Germany, which took its inspiration from the writings of Silvio Gesell. This currency was called the Wära, a combination of the words *Ware* (commodity) and *Währung* (a currency unit which preserves its value). It was worth exactly a Reichsmark and could be exchanged for one in emergencies since the entire proceeds from the sale of Wära notes was lodged in a redemption fund.

The key difference between the Wära and the Reichsmark lay in the fact that the former were costly to hoard since anyone holding some at the end of a month had to buy special stamps costing 2 per cent of each note's face value to revalidate them for use during the following month. Naturally, this meant that anyone who received Wära tried their best to spend them before they needed to be stamped again and the new currency began to circulate rapidly among Freiwirtschaft enthusiasts throughout Germany. The 2 per cent monthly levy was used for promotional purposes.

Gesell got the idea for this innovation from bracteates, the thin silver-alloy coins issued by the rulers of dozens of small independent states in the Holy Roman Empire from the twelfth to the fifteenth centuries. Holding bracteates was risky because they could lose up to a quarter of their value overnight because whenever a ruler who had issued a batch died, all the coins bearing his head became invalid and had to be exchanged at a 20–25 per cent discount for ones bearing his successor's features. Rulers also recalled them as a useful way of raising taxes. In the fourteenth century Duke Johann II of Saxony changed his currency no fewer than eighty-six times in thirty-six years.

Because bracteates might lose so much of their value overnight, there was a strong incentive for people to spend them as quickly as possible on things of lasting value like house improvements and good clothes. The devaluation of the bracteates and today's loss in the value of one's money as a result of inflation had quite different effects, because with bracteates the level of prices did not change. So long as you spent your money quickly – and the poor always do – you lost nothing, and because everyone wanted to spend their money as soon as they could your labour was always in demand. The devaluation of bracteates therefore tended to favour the poor.

Nobody in authority took much notice of the Freiwirtschaft currency until 1931 when the purchaser of a defunct coal mine at Schwanenkirchen, a village with a population of five hundred in Bavaria, was able to reopen the mine by paying the miners in Wära, which he had arranged they could spend in the village shops. In their turn, the shopkeepers forced their wholesalers to accept Wära and the wholesalers passed them back to their suppliers, who spent most of the notes they received on buying Schwanenkirchen coal, since there were few other ways in which Wära could be used. According to an account published in August 1932 in an American magazine, *New Republic*, the effects on the village were dramatic: 'One would not have recognised Schwanenkirchen a few months after work had been resumed at the mine. The village was on a prosperity basis, workers and merchants were free from debts and a new spirit of life and freedom pervaded the town. Reporters came from all over Germany to write about the "Miracle."'[11] The article pointed out that if Reichsmarks had been used in place of Wära, they would have been hoarded because of the uncertain times and the venture would have failed. Moreover, even if they had not been hoarded they would have dispersed all over Germany and there would have been little likelihood of their returning to Schwanenkirchen and increasing demand at the mine.

Although only 20,000 Wära were ever issued, some 2.5 million people handled them in 1930–31 as a result of their high rate of circulation. Their success in Schwanenkirchen terrified the German government, which feared they would cause inflation, and, after an unsuccessful court action on the grounds that Wära infringed the state's sole right to issue money, it passed emergency legislation in November 1931 to bring their use to an end. The mine in Schwanenkirchen closed and its workers were plunged back into unemployment.

Local Exchange Trading Systems (LETS)

Development and start-up phase

Most of the alternative currencies in use today are issued by Local Exchange Trading Systems, or LETS as they are usually called. A

Scots-born Canadian, Michael Linton, is usually credited with their invention but David Boyle suggests in his book *Funny Money* that David Weston, an academic, thought the system up in the late 1970s. Weston did not push the innovation, however, just as Andrew Tanenbaum did not promote Minix, the inspiration for Linux. Linton himself admits that 'all the components of LETSystems were drawn from other sources.' (A LETSystem is run strictly according to Linton's five principles – see below. A LETS system is the generic term and covers a wide range of variants. All Linton claims is that 'the precise arrangement of them seems to [have been] unprecedented'.[12]

Linton says he spent a year researching alternative currency schemes before coining the phrase 'Local Economic Trading System' and setting up the first LETSystem in the Comox Valley near Vancouver in British Columbia in 1983.[13] He started the system when an air base in the valley closed, putting a lot of people out of work and reducing the amount of money in circulation in the area. Linton defines a LETS as 'a self-regulating network which allows its users to issue and manage their own money supply within the boundaries of the network'.[14] In other words, it is a user-created currency, just like the Native Americans' wampum shells, with the major advantage that people do not need to spend time and effort finding shells, drilling holes in them and threading them onto strings.

These networks can do wonders for the quality of people's lives. One young couple, she unemployed, he temporarily disabled after an accident, used their local system to transform the garden of a semi-derelict cottage they had just rented: rank grass and scrub was cut, a 200-tree shelterbelt planted and a rockery and herb-garden built and stocked. 'If we had been paid in real money rather than LETS, we'd never have felt able to spend it this way. Other things would have seemed more important', the man told me. 'But it's had a wonderful effect on the house and how we feel about living here.'

When a LETSystem begins, none of its members has anything in their account. As with *fiat* currencies, money is created by people going into debt when they buy goods or a service from someone else in the system. Their trading partner's account is credited with the amount by which their account goes into the red. When members go into debt, they are implicitly making a promise to the other members to pay it off at some time. In many systems, though, the word 'debt' is never used. Instead, the term is 'commitment' –

members 'in commitment' are committed to working off their commitment to the others.

According to Linton, a community currency is only a LETSystem if it holds to five principles.[15] First, LETSystems should be set up and run professionally rather than on a voluntary basis. The 'cost of service' should be born by the community benefiting from the LETSystem and paid in the LETSystem's currency. Second, the principle of consent is enshrined to the extent that 'there is never any obligation to trade'. In other words, even if I have a very large debt there is nothing compelling me to provide services to others to pay it off other than peer group pressure. This peer group pressure is supposed to arise from the third principle, that of the full disclosure of every member's account balance so that people can see who is not pulling their weight. Ultimately, however, if a member refuses to fulfil his or her 'commitment' the only sanction they face is the disapproval of their former trading partners. The fourth principle is that the unit of currency created by going into debt should be equivalent to the national currency. Finally, no interest or commission should be charged on debt.

Before setting up the Comox Valley LETS, Linton, a systems analyst by training, founded Landsman Community Services Ltd, which describes itself as a 'company which propagates LETSystem development on a global basis'. This indicates that Linton and Landsman see themselves as playing what our model calls the promulgation role. But Linton does much more than this. Like Torvalds with Linux, he is also a novelty-generator and a selector of what constitutes a LETSystem and what does not.

As we saw in the Wind and Linux chapters, personal motivations critically influence the novelties people generate and the selection decisions they make. In both case histories, the early efforts of people unmotivated by financial reward were the reason the core innovation developed and was later able to become commercial. With Linux, Torvalds began the project as a hobby while he was a student on a grant. The hobby clearly became his primary interest but he continued on his Master's course for four years and lived on his student income. As we saw, he recognises that if he had had a commercial interest in Linux, he would have become 'corrupt' and this would have damaged his ability to play the selector role.

With LETS, the motivation was different and some people believe that Linton's attempts to make money from LETSystems has damaged the evolution of the technology. Jan Wyllie, managing director of the magazine *Trend Monitor*, who is working to set up a knowledge-based LETS, seems to agree. 'Please beware of anything to do with Michael Linton's LETSystem, e.g. LETSgo Manchester', he writes. '[These] have never succeeded anywhere because they try to work on an unaccountable "get rich quick" business franchise model.'[16] This criticism is harsh. After all, to adapt a principle from the free software movement, 'even LETS designers have to eat' and Linton and other LETS designers have not generally had lucrative day jobs. They might therefore have needed to behave more commercially than well-paid computer programmers.

Adaptation phase

Whatever their motives, Linton and Landsman have been very active in promoting LETSystems around the world. Linton has written and travelled extensively since 1983 and in 1985 began distributing diskettes with the full specification of a LETSystem, administration materials and accounting software. Landsman has received $300,000 in donations, mainly from individuals, and has used the Internet since 1986. As a result, by 1999 there were over a thousand LETS-type community currencies around the world, more than four hundred of which were in the UK,[17] thanks mainly to another organisation called LetsLink UK.

The UK was a particularly fertile ground for LETS, possibly because the breakdown in community life there helped to give the UK a lower quality of life than that in almost every other western European country.[18] High unemployment rates in the early 1990s, combined with an ungenerous social security system, have also helped to generate a substantial need for the innovation. The idea arrived in 1984, when Linton spoke in London at the first TOES (The Other Economic Summit), a conference held to raise awareness about economic alternatives, at the same time as the ministers of finance of the G7 countries were discussing the conventional solutions at their summit about 200 metres away. The first British LETS was set up in Norwich in 1985, but it was not until the economic recession in the early 1990s that the adoption rate soared. 'One in six UK households is experiencing severe debt problems because of high interest rates and recession', Liz Shephard said in February 1993.[19] In 1990 there were 6 LETS in the UK; by 1993 there were 45; and in 1999 LetsLink estimated there were 450.

Shephard, inspired by Linton's ideas and the principles espoused by E.F. Schumacher in his book *Small is Beautiful*, set up LetsLink UK with two friends in 1991. It was the world's first LETS development agency. Its web page says that it 'has been dedicated to testing, researching and developing sustainable models for local and community-based LETS and complementary currencies. LetsLink's national advice line has serviced 50,000 enquiries and developed the model rules, materials, back-up and 'best practice' guidelines used by its 450 UK LETS schemes and subscribers.'[20] In other words, LetsLink says it is fulfilling all the functions of learning selection – novelty generation, selection and promulgation – exactly the role that Linton and Landsman Ltd say they are playing too.

In spite of the large number of LETS systems established around the world, the technology has not yet moved into the mainstream. One of the stumbling blocks has been the cost of setting up and managing them. This is partly because the volume of trading in many systems has been low, especially at the beginning, and hence the scope for charging fees to cover development and administration expenses has been limited. Landsman recognises this problem and recommends an organisational innovation to overcome it, LETShare, a 'sweat equity' arrangement under which people run their system for nothing or very cheaply during its early stages but keep a record of their time and expenses. Then, when it has taken off, those who worked to set it up can gradually receive their back pay.

LETShare does not seem to have worked in Linton's own Comox Valley system. This ground to a halt in 1988 'when a lack of trading determined that the administration be suspended until the community woke up again'.[21] Outsiders suggest that the system wound down because Linton had run up a huge deficit by purchasing goods and services and not supplying other members of the system with enough goods and services of his own to pay them off. Linton rejects this charge. 'During those three years [1985 to 1988] there was no appropriate way within the system to pay me for my more than full-time work. My function was design, development, promotion, and training, and it was related to longer-term issues and required wider resources than the local network could possibly provide. Since I couldn't be paid I ran up my own commitment.'[22] Linton's debt stood at the equivalent of $17,000 out of a total debt of $60,000 when the system suspended trading. The total amount of business done by the Comox Valley LETSystem beforehand was $300,000.[23]

If people run up large debts in a LETS system and fail to pay them off, the average balance of the other members becomes positive, signalling that they should spend their units rather than earn any more. They therefore become reluctant to provide more goods and services through the system, which effectively devalues the currency because the range of things that the LETS unit can buy is reduced. This means that members in credit have to spend more time and effort persuading others to do business with them; if they agree, they might well put their prices up. A downward spiral starts which can be difficult to reverse.

Because some over-idealistic LETS designers dismiss the problem of excess credit as trivial in comparison with other types of debt, they have failed to examine its consequences. The attitude of Graeme Taylor, a leading LETS activist in Australia, is typical. 'Should the occasional member not fulfil their obligation, everyone who provided goods and services to this naughty person has been credited for their stuff anyway', he explained in an article in *Community Quarterly*. 'The debt ... can be absorbed by the local community. Compared to the debts that we have to absorb as a result of our nation's entrepreneurs, this is chicken feed.'[24] All this is true, but Taylor fails to suggest ways the debt can be absorbed before it damages the system in the way we discussed above.

Mark Jackson, when he was a student at Latrobe University, Victoria, Australia, concluded that such people need to have a much clearer and more realistic view of what LETS currencies are and are not. Jackson surveyed three LETS in Australia (1996) and New Zealand (1993) and found that the average balance was positive in all three.[25] In the Whangarei Exchange and Barter System (WEBS), the first New Zealand LETS, set up in 1986, the average balance was one hundred times the average monthly turnover. In other words, at the rate they are currently spending, it would take an average member more than eight years to bring his or her account to zero if they stopped providing any further goods or services. The accounts of the defunct Baytown LETS (not its real name) in Australia displayed a similar overaccumulation. Jackson also found evidence that it was only newer, less jaundiced members who tended to be net providers of goods and services. The main concern of more experienced members was to unload the stock of units they had built up when they were new and keen.

Jackson believes that LETS have much to offer and stresses in his article that he is not trying to undermine the idea but rather point out a common cause of problems so that it can be corrected. An innovation some LETS systems have adopted to try to solve it is to set limits on how much people can go into debt. Other systems have rejected this solution, however, on the grounds that the imposition of limits would imply a lack of trust and so damage the LETS ethos. In practice it seems that LETS systems can work reasonably well without formal limits if they remain small – up to two hunred members – and have an energetic co-ordinator to help members who are persistently in debt or who have problems spending the credits in their account.

If LETS systems are to become economically significant like the WIR or commercial barter circles, then overdraft limits alone will probably not be enough to prevent bad debts causing them to collapse. The collateral that the WIR requires its members to post for their loans can be forfeited legally if they renege. So far this innovation has not been tried in LETS systems because it appears to many LETS members to have too much in common with the conventional banking system, something from which they are often trying to escape. In other words, they reject the potential innovation not because it won't work but because it is ideologically unacceptable.

Evolutionary theory can help us understand another LETS stumbling block. LETS activists readily admit that their ideas are on the fringe. In biological evolution, competition can be most severe on the fringes because the necessities of life are most limited there. For organisations like LetsLink or Landsman, the necessities of life are people who subscribe to their ideas, pay subscription fees and provide the justification for National Lottery and local authority grants. So long as LetsLink and Landsman see things in much the same way and are therefore promoting essentially the same species of LETS then they can co-operate and complement each other. However, if they begin to see things differently – if 'forking' starts – then we would expect competition for the limited number of followers to become extreme unless there was some higher selection process that brought recombination about. As we saw in the last chapter, Linux has a two-tier selection process, while its competitor BSD does not. The development of LETS appears to be following the BSD forking model rather than the Linux recombination one because of the characters of the people involved.

Dr Gill Seyfang concluded as early as 1994 in the first piece of academic research into LETS in the UK that the disagreement between Landsman and LetsLink stems from a fundamental difference in opinion as to whether LETS should become more professional and mainstream, or be more community-oriented.[26] The rift is clear. The first key to success that LetsLink stresses is to stay local because 'there is much more trading where members are geographically close, and abuse is easily prevented'. This makes sense because the worth of a system's currency is completely dependent on the strength of its members' commitment to pay off their debts in the future and almost everyone feels more obligation to fulfil commitments to their neighbours than to people who live further away. The peer group pressure which is the only sanction a LETS system has to make people discharge their debts in a reasonable time is generally more effective in a geographically close community.

The second principle in LetsLink UK's mission statement makes it clear the organisation sees LETS primarily as a way to build communities and to tackle social exclusion, and only secondly as an economic tool. The objective reads as follows: 'To promote the appropriate, ethical and sustainable development of LETS or local exchange in practice, and in accordance with co-operative principles, especially for the purposes of building community, alleviating social hardship, promoting equality of opportunity, supporting the local economy and protecting the environment.'[27] This community scale obviously limits each system's size and, consequently, its ability to support the paid managers that Linton wants. The Wära, on the other hand, was conceived of as a national currency and caused the 'system' so much alarm that the German government had to pass an emergency law to kill it. Its proponents had similar motives to those in the open-source software movement who wish to see Linux challenge Microsoft Windows. Linton and many other LETS activists have a similar dream. They want LETS to move from the fringe to challenge the mainstream. 'The very pattern of conventional money trading is destroying our world', Linton says. 'LETSystems must become mainstream very soon if we are to have any hope of leaving to future generations a world in which they can even survive, much less thrive.'[28] Accordingly, Linton and Landsman have put a lot of innovative effort into developing ways of interlinking LETS so that people can spend currency earned in one system in another. They argue that this is to give members more choice and allow them to meet more of their needs through their own currency.

On the face of it, the easiest way to link LETSystems would be to make their individual currencies equivalent in value to the national currency. One Bobbin earned in Manchester would have the same value as one Stroud earned in Stroud. But there is a problem. If, as a member of the Stroud LETS, I drove to Manchester and was able to persuade Cristina to accept Strouds for a jar of honey, then I would have committed Stroud LETS as a whole, and not me personally, to provide goods and services equal in value to the jar of honey. My only personal obligation would be to discharge the debt I have just run up by providing goods or services to other members of the Stroud system.

At present, Cristina would only be able to spend her Strouds in Stroud, two hundred miles away. Even if she did make the journey and wanted a Shiatsu massage, she might have problems getting one. For example, she might find the masseuse suspicious of her, having never met her before. Even if her long explanation that Stroud LETS had an obligation to her was convincing, she might find that the masseuse did not feel like giving a massage on that particular day. After all, the LETS ethos is that no one has any obligation to do anything. If she lived in Stroud this might not matter because she could arrange to walk around for a massage another day, but the need to travel from Manchester might make a later date completely impractical. In practice, then, Cristina is likely to find Strouds of little or no value to her.

MultiLETS is the innovation Linton and two other LETSystem designers, Richard Kay and Ernie Yacub, have developed to solve some of these problems. People wishing to trade beyond the confines of their own LETS open a second account in a meta or umbrella currency. We'll call its units Umbrellas. Once I have my account, if I want to buy a jar of honey in Manchester I pay for them in Umbrellas and, if the transaction means that my account becomes negative, I have a personal commitment to provide goods and services to anyone else with an Umbrella account to make up the shortfall. Umbrella accounts are maintained by a registry using a software program that can also administer accounts for individual LETS systems.

According to its inventors, a multiLETS exists when two or more LETS systems agree to recognise an umbrella currency and to hand over their local account administration to a central registry, a move they claim would reduce administration costs. However, when Jeff Powell and Menno Salverda, two employees of the Thai Community Currency Systems project, surveyed LETS systems in the UK, they found that the only working multiLETS was East Kent LETS, with which Richard Kay is associated. East Kent LETS is made up of four local LETS systems, but the survey found that its existence was of little benefit because over 95 per cent of all trading was within each local LETS where people knew and trusted each other. Powell and Salverda concluded that the multiLETS innovation was being pushed prematurely, before people had reached the limits of what was possible within their local LETS and wanted to move into a multiLETS. They also thought that the people who had set up the individual LETS saw multiLETS as a threat to their ownership and control.

Manchester shows the strengths of local LETS and some of the problems of multiLETS particularly well. Manchester LETS, one of the most successful in the UK, was set up by Andy Rickford and his partner after they had learned about LETS at a conference in Scotland. They linked up with others who had read about LETS and formed a core group of eight people during the summer of 1992. That November, they launched a pilot LETS with thirty members but over 120 others attended the launch and many of these signed up too. The new recruits then brought in others and the system grew rapidly over the next few months.

Peter North, who did his Ph.D. research on Manchester LETS, believes that this early growth occurred because word spread among interconnected networks that shared similar ideas and principles such as the Quakers, the Labour Party and the Manchester Green Party. Sidonie Seron, who also studied Manchester LETS for an academic thesis, thinks that coverage in the local and national press, including articles in the *Guardian* and the *Sunday Telegraph,* was also important, as was a feature on BBC2's *The Money Programme.*

The media coverage might have encouraged individuals to join, but it did little to attract business members. This was because the business community saw the system as being motivated and shaped by people with strong political views it did not share. This was a serious drawback because without business involvement there was only a limited number of ways the system's currency, the Bobbin, could be spent. The system therefore set up the Small Business Network (SBN) in 1994, which purposely tried to cultivate a professional image to bring businesses into the fold. By 1996, SBN had eighty-five small businesses as members. Most of these were sole traders but six were high street shops. Interestingly, Noppes, the Amsterdam LETS system, followed exactly the same strategy. 'Noppes was seen as too alternative for most business people to be connected with directly',[29] says Werner Barendrecht who worked with Noppes for two years before helping to set up Amstelnet, its equivalent of SBN.

One SBN member, Misty's Café, run by Phil Hardy, was clearly benefiting from LETS when Peter North interviewed him in 1996. 'Without LETS, we couldn't have opened on time', Hardy said. 'One thousand bobbins were paid out to people who came to help with painting the premises and chairs, distributing flyers and generally giving their support.'[30] After opening, Hardy linked up with a grocery store called Unicorn, which began to supply him with the ingredients to make cakes, which it bought back to sell to its customers. Both sales were made in bobbins. Since the café opened, a tenth of Hardy's customers have paid in bobbins. He uses these to hire musicians to play on Sunday afternoons.

Perhaps because the literature generally tries to paint LETS in a good light, it is hard to find stories of businesses or individuals who have had unfavourable experiences with it. Nevertheless, of the eight hundred people who had registered with Manchester LETS, only half were actually trading in 1999, so it is possible that many of these had dropped out because the system was not working satisfactorily for them. Alternatively, it could be that the system had served its purpose and they no longer needed it. This could have been either because they had found a well-paid job in the conventional economy or because they had built up a network of friends with whom they exchanged favours outside the LETS system. Certainly, the economic benefit of belonging to the system – as opposed to its social ones

– was not high. According to another academic researcher, Colin Williams, the average member's monthly trading was only £11. This is much the same as the £15 average monthly turnover in Stroud LETS, which is generally seen as one of the most successful in England. Richard Douthwaite estimates that this was less than 5 per cent of the average participant's income.[31]

Williams's survey of Manchester LETS also found that the most popular type of transaction fell under a category of 'therapies and health' and included massages, acupuncture, healing, reflexology, homeopathy, reiki and counselling sessions. 'I wouldn't normally be able to pay for a massage out of my weekly wages but on LETS it becomes an affordable treat', one member said. This is quite typical. Many LETS systems make luxuries like original paintings and stained-glass work affordable for their participants but fail to provide them with the opportunity to buy basic necessities. LETS systems can therefore appear to be of fringe importance to a fringe group of idealists.

Liz Shephard argues that to evaluate LETS purely in economic terms misses the point. 'There is something wonderful about LETS in the sense of rebuilding communities, bringing people together in a way that nothing else does', she says. LETS forges friendships and builds social networks that can add greatly to the quality of peoples' lives but whose value is difficult to measure in purely monetary terms.

Mark Jackson also sees LETS as a community-building technology rather than a way in which people can make as much money as they want and solve all their economic problems. He believes that thinking of LETS as some sort of magic money that breaks conventional economic rules would be to take it down a path leading to over-accumulation, devaluation and stagnation. Instead, its ethos of reciprocity, which is fundamental to community building and crucial to any system's success, needs to be stressed. Richard Douthwaite, who has written extensively on LETS, believes that anyone setting up a community currency system has to decide what its objectives are. If they are primarily social and the system can stay small, an ordinary LETS is ideal. If, on the other hand, they are mainly economic, then relying on group pressure to get members to discharge their debts within a reasonable time will prove grossly inadequate, especially as the system grows. In this case, he thinks, the WIR model with its legally enforceable agreements would be a better one to adopt.

Expansion phase

Some LETS designers and champions become frustrated when people dismiss their 'baby' as alternative or fringe and hope for an event to propel the technology into the mainstream, just as the 1979 oil price increase did for wind turbines. Some, indeed, long for nothing less than the collapse of the world money system, which they think will happen quite soon. Landsman and Linton have not been content to wait for such a crash, however, and since 1984 Landsman has been trying to mount a large, successful showcase project that would be hailed as a 'breakthrough' and launch LETS into its expansion phase by leading to its rapid adoption elsewhere. The firm's first attempt in Vancouver failed in 1984, as did its second in Toronto. LETSgo Manchester was its third. It was launched in 1994 and can be seen in some respects as the flash dryer of the LETS world.

Explaining at the time why LETSgo Manchester was being launched, Linton wrote:

> So far, the development of LETSystems around the world has been extraordinary; it has been under-funded, incoherent and generally erratic. If we are to continue to move in this manner, there is every likelihood that such under-funded initiatives [will] be overwhelmed – at least temporarily – by others who might see the potential for substantial profit and jump to take advantage of it.[32]

He therefore proposed a pre-emptive strike. LETSgo would use the incentive of large profits to create a 'high profile and high energy initiative' that would generate the tools and innovations to propel LETS into the mainstream. Once this had been done, Linton and Landsman would place this knowledge gained in the public domain to prevent anyone gaining a monopoly on LETS in future. 'This project ... will make a speculative profit for the participants,' he wrote.

The projected profits were huge – £20 million – and would go to 'the initial risk-takers, those active in the current LETSgo Manchester project, and those who have contributed to the process up to this point.' Linton and Landsman would qualify under all three headings and stood to make millions. For example, Landsman was to receive £500,000 for LETS development from 1984,[33] indirectly rewarding Linton for the years of 'more than full-time work' for which he considers he has not been paid. Perhaps this was reasonable, but our learning selection model has alerted us to the extent to which peoples' actions as novelty-generators, selectors and promulgators are shaped by their motivations. We therefore have to ask whether the desire to make large profits left Linton completely free to act in the best interests of the LETS technology.

The budget projections for LETSgo Manchester were wholly unrealistic. Landsman assumed that all the estimated 200,000 businesses in the Greater Manchester area would open an average of ten accounts each with LETSgo. Quite why they would want to open so many is unclear, particularly as most firms don't have this many bank accounts and they were to be charged £50 sterling plus 50 of the LETSgo currency units, gm pounds, for every account. Anyway, the assumption was that as the average business would contribute £500 to LETSgo, a total of £100 million would come from the corporate sector. Of this, £18 million would be spent on LETS promotion throughout the world and £2 million would go to the LETSgo developers, including the £500,000 for Landsman.

Other details of the LETSgo plan read more like a pyramid-selling scam, in which participants commit their own resources in order to earn the right to 'get rich quick' by persuading others to join too, than what it was – an honest attempt by an idealistic and ethical, if grossly over-optimistic, company to put LETS on the map. Angus Soutar, an engineer, systems analyst and management consultant, provided £80,000 in seed money and the rest of the development funds were to have been in the form of LETShare sweat equity – people would work for free at the beginning and be paid when the registration fees started rolling in. It was hoped to train two hundred people, who would then go out and sign up businesses at, it was thought, an average rate of two a day each. During the training course, which was scheduled to take fifty days, the participants, attracted by the promise of their share in the £1.5 million, would cover their own living expenses and be paid nothing. Another incentive was a trust fund, which it was thought would have grown to £20 million in time to be shared out as a Millennium bonus.

The project began in April 1994 and by June offices had been rented and twenty-one full- and part-time staff were employed. However, although a television advertisement was screened to recruit two hundred people for the first training course, only fifty participated. According to Soutar, many of these were 'rebels and revolutionaries' with attitudes that made it difficult for them to work with other people. The level of dissension was so serious that a rival LETSgo organisation was even set up for a short time. Soutar also accuses LetsLink UK of mounting a sustained campaign of mis-information against them that cut the project off from a previously supportive network. This is perhaps not surprising given that LETSgo Manchester had little if anything to do with building communities. A year after the first training course there were only twenty business accounts and turnover was very small, and by 1999 LETSgo Manchester was effectively dead. The project did not meet any of its objectives and the confusion and division it caused damaged Manchester LETS, which saw its membership fall drastically, although it later recovered.[34]

Linton says that LETSgo failed from lack of funding, some external opposition and much internal confusion and contention. He admits they were far too optimistic and brought in people who were 'more cost than benefit'. The project tried to 'start a fire with wet wood'. The experience has taught him to start on a smaller scale with people who are committed and qualified to do the work, he says.

LETSgo Manchester has striking similarities with the introduction of the flash dryer into the Philippines. Both initiatives began with wildly optimistic predictions about adoption levels and the benefits the technology would bring. This created the momentum for both to begin. Then, when it became clear that the expected benefits and adoption rates were not being achieved, in both cases the implementing agency, which included the designers and project champions, reacted by blaming the skills and motivation of adopters and trainers. As a result, the agencies stifled a learning selection process that could have salvaged something. In both cases, too, well-intentioned attempts to bring the advantages of a new technology to people as quickly as possible backfired and damaged the reputation of the innovation. The striking thing is that these similarities exist even though the technologies, the implementing agencies and the geographic locations were very different. This leads me to think that a similar fate could befall other top-down projects designed to achieve a 'breakthrough'.

Linton still believes that LETSystems have 'breakthrough' potential because of the success of commercial barter schemes, which now turn over billions of dollars per annum. These companies act as brokers and enable member businesses to trade their surplus stock, perishable assets, time, space and skills with each other without paying hard cash. John McLennan, the Director of Operations of Capital Barter Corporation International (CBCI), gives this example of how commercial barter works. [35] A Central London hotel has an unfilled room costing £200. Rather than losing this money by allowing the room to remain empty, the hotel sells it for 200 trade pounds (the CBCI's currency unit) and uses the proceeds to buy something from one of the other 250 other companies in the barter ring. The cost to the hotel of this transaction in sterling is the money spent to clean and heat the room (£20) plus the commission charged by the barter company (14 per cent or £28), a total of £48. The hotel is therefore able to buy something worth £200 for £48, effectively at a 76 per cent discount. Moreover, the people staying in the room are likely to buy meals and drinks at the bar.

While LETS systems and commercial barter rings both allow the use of resources that would otherwise be wasted or under-utilised, the rings differ from LETS in that they are entirely profits-driven and have no interest at all in building local communities. Linton, too, has little interest in building communities. He believes that using LETS to do so in a way 'requiring substantial central bureaucracies and deserving of grant funding' is a 'recipe that has so far led to nothing but contrived incompetence and marginalisation'. LETSystem development should be self-financing, he thinks, and once a large project has broken through and shown that this is possible, LETSystems will take off, just as commercial barter operations have done. 'It is extremely important that the [LETS] development group base their operational style on the clear assumption that they are … financially viable, and not in need of grant funding', he wrote in the LETSystem design manual.

Linton told me in 1999 that his work since LETSgo Manchester has been directed towards demonstrating the Community Way approach. He claims this is another LETSystem,[36] although this stretches the definition in the LETSystem design manual. One defining characteristic the manual mentions is a 'flat start', which means that when a system commences to trade everyone begins with a balance of zero, and the money is created by people going into debt. With Community Way (CW), however, the currency is created when a business gives a donation to a charity or social organisation. Instead of receiving cash or goods from the donor directly, the good cause gets community currency notes printed by the CW development group instead. These can be spent with the donor or with other donors in the system. However, donors can impose restrictions if they wish. For example, they might agree to accept the community currency units only at off-peak times or for a portion of the purchase price. The charity then exchanges the notes with the general public for cash, something Linton believes it ought to be able to do because the people it approaches will know they are giving to a good cause and that all the donor businesses in the community will accept the notes they are getting.

One of the scheme's advantages is that the businesses involved get public recognition for their donations, which ought to lead to their being more generous to local good causes. A second is that their willingness to accept the community currency brings them customers that they might otherwise not have. And a third is that the notes printed by the organisers are effectively an injection of cash into the local economy, which boosts its trade.

A problem with CW, however, is that once a business has taken enough CW notes to cover its donations, it may no longer want to accept them. This would make them harder to spend. A second problem is that CW notes do not circulate unless people are prepared to take them in change, something they become increasingly unlikely to do if the businesses they use reach their quotas and refuse to accept more.

According to Powell and Salverda, Landsman has launched four Community Way programmes – in Manchester, Victoria (BC), Hawaii and Vancouver – which all failed.[37] Late in 1999, however, it had two ongoing projects, one in Comox Valley and the other in Santa Cruz in California, although the one in Comox Valley was said to be running into problems because businesses there had become suspicious of LETS-like schemes, which they saw 'as discounts with no particular benefit to business'.[38]

Powell and Salverda believe that the four failures happened because Landsman took a controlling, top-down approach to the introduction and adoption of 'its' technologies. If so, then Landsman says one thing and does another because its website states that organising a CW system is 'a matter of putting the pieces together in a way that really works. We don't have either the time or the space to operate on the old hierarchical models, to compete on territorial issues, to seek control by withholding information. The more we deal with chaos, the more it is essential to have good information management processes. Design is crucial.'[39]

Although Linton told me[40] that he believes that Landsman has played a very similar role in the development of LETS to that played by Linus Torvalds in developing Linux, there are major differences. Torvalds did not design Linux, as Wayne Sennett's comment that 'Linux has a mind of its own' shows. Instead, he acted as a meta-selector, skimming off the ideas that rose to the top as a result of learning selection. Nearly all the creativity that enabled Linux to evolve from an embryo operating system with just 10,000 lines of code to something 150 times bigger came from people other than Torvalds. In contrast, Linton sees LETSystems as something that he alone has developed and says that none of the 'earnest adjusters' has contributed anything of value to the basic innovation outlined in the LETSystem design manual, most of which he wrote.[41] Linton's claim that the Community Way is also a LETSystem, and hence something that Landsman has sole authority over, speaks volumes about how reluctant he is to let go and to accept that others might have something to offer.

Another key difference between Linton and Torvalds is that Linton hopes to profit from his innovation while Torvalds does not. The last page of the LETSystem Design Manual says:

> Any persons or organisations active in LETSystem development are encouraged to submit, to Landsman, accounts of their contributions. If these accounts are indeed considered to reflect actual and substantial furtherance of the directions Landsman is proposing, then the accounts are accepted as a record showing that person or organisation's contribution to the effort, and their entitlement to a share of the proceeds.

In light of this, Linton's refusal to give credit to other people's innovations could be seen as a way of avoiding sharing the proceeds of any eventual commercial success.

The knowledge that others are seeking to claim proprietary rights to innovations makes people more territorial and closed with their ideas and experiences. Landsman is therefore not only hindering the free flow of information, and hence learning selection, by asking people to submit their ideas for commercial appraisal but erecting an almost impenetrable barrier to new thoughts when it says, as it does, that it would prefer that contracts about how the spoils from intellectual property are carved up to be negotiated with it before the innovation is divulged.

Linton's failure to relinquish control and acknowledge other people's innovations could explain two of the difficulties LETSgo encountered in Manchester. As we have seen, if people are not allowed to contribute to the development of an idea, they never take ownership of it and lose motivation and interest. Was this the problem with the sales force? Second, forking takes place when people become frustrated because their ideas are being ignored. It often leads to their setting up a rival system in competition, exactly as happened in Manchester.

This closed, territorial behaviour is almost certainly damaging the evolution of LETS. For example, what Richard Douthwaite considers to be one of the best systems for keeping LETS accounts evolved in Germany in 1997. However, he only found out about it in 1999 when he met someone from the pioneering system at a conference in the Netherlands. As a result, he was able to suggest that the Westport LETS, which he had helped set up, adopt the innovation. But why, he asks, were the LETS promotional bodies not promulgating the idea? With Linux, suggestions are e-mailed in for possible dissemination within minutes.

Those LETS systems using the German innovation give each member a special printed record book in exchange for their annual membership fee. When the member goes to work for another member, or sells them something, the other member writes the details and the amount of the transaction in the first member's record book, and signs it, while the first member writes a receipt in the other's. This means that the balance of each member's account is constantly up to date. The record books are exchanged for new ones at the end of each year and are checked by the managing committee to ensure that no fraud has occurred. Besides eliminating centralised account-keeping, the books make it easier for social pressures to stir debtors into action because people can know the balance of anyone they are proposing to trade without having to search for a centrally published list – and one that might in any case be out of date. Further, the system makes it easy for the LETS committee to set overdraft limits.

Members can simply be told that they must not sell to anyone if the trade would put the other party over the system limit.

The nearest thing I could find to an independent selection mechanism in the LETS world is the e-mail discussion group econ-lets (econ-lets@jiscmail.ac.uk). I described the German innovation to the group and asked 'surely the 1000+ LETS in the world must have tried lots of different things and come up with many refinements to Linton's original idea. Even if these innovations were all location specific (which I doubt) a forum where these experiences were exchanged would help LETS evolve, wouldn't it?' The posting generated a lot of reaction. Richard Kay, one of the leading lights in LETSystems, said that he thought the innovation disqualified the German LETS from being a LETSystem. He wrote:

> Many different approaches to community currency (CC) suitable for different situations have been discussed here on econ-lets. For example not bothering about keeping accounts, charging commissions, having debit limits, having units based on time, etc. etc. Many of these variations are useful and effective in their different contexts.... I do not however consider that it is as useful to describe all of these many variations of CC as being LETS. There are plenty of other useful CC descriptors such as Time Dollar Exchanges, Business Trade Exchanges etc.... As far as I have been able to evaluate, all of the most effective implementations of CC which can fairly be described as LETS without debasing this term have operated around the design of the Linton core accounting model with relatively minor changes.[42]

What Kay is saying, in effect, is that Linton's LETSystem doesn't need a forum to evaluate modifications to LETSystems because LETSystems are already fairly much 'perfected.'

Other people, however, felt differently. Lorne White, the treasurer of the Niagara LETS in Canada wrote: 'This [a forum to exchange LETS experiences] is a great idea, and what I have been slowly finding on <econ-lets> and <lets onelist> is a place to compare what people have done in LETSystems around the world, versus the "official" LETS Guidebook [the one written by Linton and Landsman].'[43] Nick Mack wrote: 'As someone heavily immersed in "monitoring and evaluation"' for active learning and research I fully agree with your suggestion – but how to do it productively? Perhaps an "observatory" model ... may be of value – the observatory collects patterns and trends in LETS innovations, synthesises them, and produces updates on potential best practice.'[44]

Our understanding of the innovation process developed in the previous chapters suggests what might be happening in the LETS world. A particular type of LETS, the LETSystem, is being championed by Linton, Landsman and a few 'lieutenants'. They believe that Linton's design, in the words of Nigel Leach, 'has the best chance of being widely adopted because it is the least directive and/or intrusive (and therefore lightest in management).'[45] They realise from experience that modifications to the design can reduce the 'fitness' of the technology and so they have come to see adaptations as a threat. Linton believes that rather than advancing the basic LETSystem model 'earnest adjusters' have propagated obscurity and nonsense.[46] However, Linux and our learning selection model show that if the product champion squashes novelty generation then the technology does not evolve and the chance to capture the 'power of the bazaar' and grow an innovation to challenge the mainstream orthodoxy is lost. In these conditions forking is likely, and has clearly happened among people involved with LETS.

Disappearance phase

Unlike wind turbines and Linux, LETS systems have not been accepted into the mainstream – they are not seen as standard practice. The technology therefore has not reached the disappearance phase. In my view, this is largely because they have lacked good selection and promulgation mechanisms to encourage and capitalise on user learning selection. However, there is a very important difference that makes learning selection much, much harder with LETS than with Linux. This is the speed and objectivity with which systems can assess novelties. With Linux, changes can be assessed in minutes. The new code is copied in, the computer is rebooted and the modification either works or it does not. It takes longer to test for unforeseen interactions but this can still be done quickly if many people get involved in the debugging. (Bugs are unexpected interactions but they are not things that could not have been predicted with enough time and effort. The fact that computer programmers do not spend this time is simply that it is much quicker and cheaper to find bugs when they cause a problem than to struggle to write perfect code.)

In contrast LETS is an innovation that works in the social environment. This is fundamentally unpredictable and tests are often unrepeatable. Testing an innovation, such as whether the imposition of overdraft limits is beneficial, for example, can take years and the result may still not be clear-cut. Moreover, it is impossible to run a control because, as no two LETS systems are the same, the failure of one and the success of another might be due to another factor for which the researcher had not controlled. Even if you do test something then peoples' evaluation of the outcome is often subjective and might tend to confirm their existing beliefs. Linton says that differences in peoples' political opinions has made Landsman's selector and promulgator role very difficult.

In some respects LETS systems are at the stage wind turbines had reached in Denmark at the end of the 1970s. They have an alternative image as the turbines had then, which means people don't take them seriously. By paying a high price for electricity the turbines generated, making earnings from them tax-free and providing a subsidy for their installation, the Danish government took wind power out of the 'alternative' ghetto. LETS developers like Richard Kay want the British government to do something similar for LETS, like allowing some taxes to be paid in local currencies. If this happened, they say, then businesses would take LETS much more seriously and the first step to the widespread acceptance of the technology would have been taken.

In 1999 LetsLink UK was working to change the policy environment in another direction: it was trying to persuade the then Department of Health and Social Security (DHSS) to change its rules so that someone's involvement in LETS does not jeopardise their social security payments. It had also lobbied Members of Parliament and government ministers.[47] Although campaigners in Australia have already had similar rules changed there, those who, like Richard Kay, think that LETS has a large potential as an economic tool, have misgivings because they feel that if LETS is granted special-case treatment, it will reinforce its image as something for the unemployed and marginalised, and not for mainstream businesses. Either way, both groups agree on the importance of a favourable environment for a new technology and have recognised the importance of government policy in creating that environment.

Conclusions

LETS, like most other alternative currency schemes launched in the past hundred years, is an innovation to alleviate some of the problems caused by imperfections in the national and international economic system. People are most highly motivated to adopt and adapt it during times of economic depression or in areas which are economically marginalised. It is undoubtedly a successful innovation – in the course of seventeen years the number of LETS systems has grown from one to over a thousand and it has spread to at least seventeen countries. However, it is still viewed by mainstream opinion as a hobby for a 'bunch of motley hippies'.

The motivations that drive LETS developers are similar to those that drove the Linux and wind turbine pioneers. They range from wanting to leave a better world for one's grandchildren to a desire to save the world from the 'evil empire' created by globalisation. Many people in the latter group who want to use it to revitalise local and regional economies are upset about the way that others are developing the community-building aspects of the technology. This, they think, is embedding it even more deeply in its fringe position and will make businesses more suspicious of it. The community-builders, however, point out that for LETS to vault to economic significance it will need to become more like the conventional money and banking system and thus move away from its community roots. In other words, the technology is moving into exactly the same transition that the wind turbine industry went through in Denmark, and that Linux is now confronting.

Differences of philosophy between the 'jumpstarters' and the community builders have led to a split in the LETS world which has hampered learning selection. One of the consequences is that there is no universally respected selection and promulgation mechanism that picks and publicises successful innovations. Unlike adopters of Danish wind turbines, adopters of LETS do not have something like *Naturlig Energi* to provide them with information about new innovations and objective evaluation data of what works and what does not. There is no forum for a dispassionate discussion of best practice based on what actually works. Nor does LETS have a single, respected and 'uncorrupted' meta-selector like Linux has with Torvalds.

In their haste to spread the technology, the jumpstarters have adopted top-down approaches, just like the Department of Agriculture in the Philippines and the governments who tried to push the development of wind turbines. All these programmes failed in terms of their original objectives, while grassroots initiatives achieved more with less.

LETS systems reinforce a lesson from the wind turbine chapter about the advantages of an iterative approach based on user learning selection. User learning selection leads to local ownership of the idea, and this in turn leads to attempts to improve the policy environment for the technology. So, when Linton discounts the contributions made by 'earnest adjusters', he ignores the fact that, thanks to learning selection, the 400-odd LETS in the UK have spawned a movement that is lobbying for reforms in the government's social security rules that will improve the environment for the technology LETS.

7

Food for thought

Aftermath of the Green Revolution

Karl Popper, the philosopher best known for his theory of scientific falsification, would have had a big problem with this book so far. He would have said that I have proposed a hypothesis – that user innovation is crucial to the successful early adoption of new technologies – and then tried to prove it with case studies carefully chosen to demonstrate what I wanted to prove. He would have argued that the proper test is to look for circumstances where the model does not hold. So, in deference to Popper, this chapter examines a hugely successful raft of technologies developed with little or no user innovation – the Green Revolution – which *Compton's Encyclopaedia* defines as a 'spectacular world development ... producing high-yielding strains of wheat, rice, corn, potatoes, and other crops.'[1] As we haven't space to discuss all these crops, I am going to concentrate on rice, the one with which I am most familiar.

Rice production increased spectacularly after the International Rice Research Institute (IRRI) introduced its first high-yielding variety (HYV), IR8, in 1966; a quarter of a century later, the new strains had replaced traditional varieties in much of Asia. Average rice yields went up by 83 per cent and total production in South and Southeast Asia rose by 120 per cent while the area cultivated only increased by 21 per cent.[2] Because the population of the area doubled over the same period and famine was frequent before the new varieties arrived, IRRI believes this increase saved many people from starvation. In fact, as we will see, IRRI was set up specifically to halt the spread of communism by improving the food supply, since left-wing movements were seen as following in famine's footsteps. The Green Revolution was brought about to prevent a Red one.

The Green Revolution was certainly a triumph of Big Science. Doug Horton and Gordon Prain, two social scientists working in the Consultative Group on International Agricultural Research (CGIAR) system, wrote in a paper in 1989 that, 'Stated most simply, it was believed [by those who set up IRRI and other international agricultural research centres in the 1960s and 1970s] that if a group of competent scientists were based in a developing country, were provided with excellent facilities, and were isolated from political pressure for several years, they were bound to generate useful new technologies.'[3] This is reminiscent of the words of Eric Raymond I quoted in Chapter 5 about building new technologies like cathedrals 'carefully crafted by individual wizards or small bands of mages working in splendid isolation, with no beta to be released before its time.' Both statements express the realist–positivist paradigm: the view that specialists can develop useful technologies through the application of science alone. Just as NASA scientists had put a man on the moon with no input from the public other than their taxes, IRRI scientists believed that without using part of their public, the farmers, as co-developers they could develop a technology – high-yielding rice varieties – which would solve the problems of inadequate food production. The other part of their public, the consumers, they largely ignored and hardly any attention was paid at first to the new rices' acceptability and taste. The technology would be released once it had been 'finished' and its adoption would be simply a question of spreading the message. Indeed, this seemed to be all that was necessary for several years as farmers soon saw the advantages of the 'miracle' rice and rushed to adopt it. In the few circumstances in which farmers did need to adapt the technology to their local conditions this did not seem to affect adoption rate and scientists could therefore dismiss local modification, and hence the need for farmer co-development, as unimportant and unnecessary.

So what was it about seed technology that meant that Big Science could achieve a breakthrough with it, but not with wind turbines or flash dryers? Are there other types of technology where top-down development models have produced such fast results? Could a bazaar approach have worked as well? Let us follow the pattern of previous chapters and examine the innovation history of seeds and plant breeding in terms of novelty generation, selection decisions, promulgation and motivations to see if we can come up with some answers.

The Green Revolution: buying time

Pre-development phase

Seed-based technology, the name now given to the results of modern plant-breeding programmes, is one of humankind's oldest technologies and probably the one which had the least auspicious start. The first agricultural research laboratories were latrines, spittoons and rubbish dumps in human settlements ten thousand years ago,[4] before any of the crops we know today had been domesticated. Indeed, agriculture itself had not begun and people lived by hunting animals and gathering wild foods. All the fruits and berries they ate had evolved through natural selection to be eaten by animals and birds as a way of dispersing their seeds. The mango, for example, evolved to be plucked by bats that would fly away with the fruit, dropping the seed perhaps miles from the parent tree. When our ancestors discovered mangoes they also took some of the fruit away with them and dropped the stones. Crucially, though, they were selective about the fruit they took. As a young boy in the West Indies I loved mangoes but would not climb just any mango tree to get them because there was a particularly vicious wasp, the Jack Spaniard, that sometimes built its nests there. I would only run the risk of getting badly stung if a tree had the biggest, sweetest and juiciest fruit in the area. Boys ten thousand years ago would have been the same and taken as much fruit as they could carry back home from the best trees to eat later, tossing the well-sucked stones away when they had finished.

This is how the domestication of crops started. Without knowing anything about genetics, people selected the tastiest and biggest wild fruits, the seeds from which then started to grow in the rubbish tips and latrines around their camps. Later, when they began to settle and to plant crops, it was the seeds from the plants growing around them that they used to do so.

In his book *Guns, Germs and Steel,* Jared Diamond explains that agriculture first started in the Fertile Crescent in the Middle East because its climate and indigenous flora and fauna enabled the early inhabitants to develop a package of technologies that made it feasible

to live in one place and farm. For any farming community to survive it must have crops that it can store for long periods of time to
enable it to cope with droughts or other natural calamities. The
fleshy fruit of tree crops does not usually keep for long, but because
the Fertile Crescent's warm, wet winters and long, hot and dry
summers favour annuals – plants that put nearly all their effort
into producing seed before the dry season kills them – it had
many wild plants whose seeds remained viable through the dry
season and were thus naturally adapted to be stored. These seeds
were also ideal as food, as the plant had put most of its energy and
goodness into them. Experiments by botanists have shown that
naturally occurring stands of wild cereals in the Fertile Crescent
could yield up to a tonne of seed per hectare and give the people
who gathered them fifty times more food energy than the energy
they spent harvesting.[5] It was consequently not a big step for hunter-
gatherers to start to plant these seeds rather than continuing to rely
on natural stands.

Wheat and barley were among the first crops to be domesticated.
In the wild form, the ears of both plants shatter easily when ripe,
dropping the grain to ground so it can germinate. This is good for
the plant but bad for farmers because once grain falls it is almost
impossible to retrieve to grind and eat. A single genetic mutation
prevents grain shattering, however. In the wild this mutation is lethal
to the plant because it leaves the seed in the head, suspended in the
air and unable to grow. Yet these suspended seeds are exactly the
ones most likely to be collected by farmers for planting the following
year. In other words, the cycle of harvest–sow–harvest–sow selects
unconsciously for non-shattering mutants. Today, wild rice with the
unmutated shattering gene is one of the main weeds in cultivated
rice.

The second difficulty with planting wild cereals is that they have
evolved to hedge their bets about when they germinate. The start of
the rainy season in the Fertile Crescent is unpredictable; so, if all
seeds were to germinate straight after the first rain, a subsequent
frost or drought could kill them all. Wild cereals therefore evolved
to space their germination out over several years. For a farmer,
though, this variability is a bad thing because he wants the seeds he
plants to germinate at the same time so that all the crop matures
simultaneously. The normal harvest–sow cycle automatically solves

this problem too, as farmers usually gather grain only from plants that germinated immediately from seed planted in moist soil. Grain from plants that germinated a year or more later is likely to be eaten by birds. Repeated planting and harvesting increases the proportion of the grain carrying the immediate-germination characteristic and brings the farmer higher yields.

Another advantage of the Fertile Crescent as the birthplace of agriculture was that many of the wild plants with potential for domestication were 'selfers' – plants that usually pollinated themselves, but that are sometimes cross-pollinated. Selfers are unusual because most wild plants are cross-pollinated. Cross-pollination makes domestication very difficult because if a farmer selects a plant with favourable characteristics, she cannot ensure that its offspring will inherit its desirable characteristics as she has no control over the plants with which it interbreeds. To keep beneficial characteristics in cross-pollinated plants, farmers must build up a composite population that maintains the desirable characteristics from one generation to the next. This is hard to do as frequent outcrossings with weedy relatives can erode away gains. It is therefore not surprising that three of the four main cereal crops – wheat, rice and barley – evolved from grasses that were mainly self-pollinating.[6]

The evolutionary history of these cereals and other old and important crops is a story of countless learning selection cycles carried out by millions of farmers for thousands of years. The only difference between early farmer learning selection and the learning selection we have looked at so far is that the farmer plant-breeders were not generating novelties – random gene mutations and hybridisations were doing that. All the farmers were doing was selecting and promulgating the best of these natural changes because they wanted to take home a better harvest for their families.

The story of how wheat evolved is better-researched than that of rice so I'll use it to illustrate how the interaction between farmers and plants produced the crops we know. First, though, we need to understand a little bit about genes, chromosomes and how plants reproduce themselves. The nuclei of all plant and animal cells contain chromosomes which carry the chemical 'instructions' that allow the organism to reproduce. Chromosomes are made up of strands of DNA (deoxyribonucleic acid) wrapped in a double helix around a core of proteins. A gene is an inherited arrangement of these proteins that occupies a specific location on a chromosome and determines a particular characteristic of the organism.

During sexual reproduction, germ cells from the male and female combine, each with a basic information-carrying set of chromosomes called a genome. The number of chromosomes in the genome is called the haploid number and is a characteristic of the species. Rice (*O. sativa*), for example, has 12 chromosomes while humans have 23.

If we stain the cells from a plant's root tips, where the nuclei and the chromosomes they contain are easiest to see, and look at them through a microscope, we will notice that the chromosomes are bunched together in sets. Most wild plants have two sets of chromosomes and are called diploid, while many domesticated plants have three sets (triploid), some four sets (tetraploid) and some even more. Having more than two sets of chromosomes is called polyploidy.

Back to wheat. Einkorn (*T. monococcum*), one of the ancestors of modern wheats, is still grown in mountainous parts of Turkey and Yugoslavia. If we look at its nuclei we will observe that einkorn is diploid. Cytologists, who study these things, call its configuration AA. However, if we look at the germ cells in einkorn's pollen, we will find that they have just one chromosome, A. When pollen fertilises an ovule – the female germ cell that also only has one set of chromosomes – a seed is formed with one set of chromosomes from each parent. If the plant is self-pollinating, and if the male and female chromosome sets are identical, then the seed will grow a plant genetically identical to the parent. If, however, the plant is heterogeneous, meaning that the male and female chromosome sets are not identical, then the progeny will not be carbon copies but will, in the jargon of plant breeders, segregate. This means that the progeny will exhibit different traits to their parents, depending on the genetic mix they have inherited and how those genes express themselves.

The self-pollinating grasses from which wheat, rice and barley evolved do sometimes cross-pollinate. In rice, the cross-pollination rate is about 1 per cent. Whether cross-pollination produces viable seed depends on how similar the pairing sets of chromosomes are. There is, as we would expect, complete compatibility between the pollen and ovules from cultivars of the same species, and almost always complete incompatibility between the pollen and ovules from plants of different species. In fact, if two organisms can breed and produce non-sterile progeny, they are defined as belonging to the

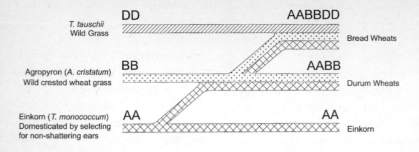

Figure 7.1 Evolutionary pathways of cultivated wheats (*Triticum spp.*)[7]

same species. However, even within species, crosses between distinct subspecies can sometimes be sterile if the differences between the chromosomes are fairly large, because these differences cause problems during the complicated process of splitting chromosome sets that occurs when the progeny attempt to form germ cells. Crosses between similar species can produce fertile progeny, but this is rare. A cross between two parents of different cultivars or different species is called a hybrid. The mingling and recombination of different genetic material generates novelty and it is this novelty that has largely led to the evolution of the world's crops.

The fertility of hybrids between different plant species often comes about thanks to a genetic mutation. Our modern wheats have arisen because of two such crosses between different grass species, as shown in Figure 7.1. The first was between einkorn (AA) and a weedy quack grass called agropyron (BB). What happened was that an einkorn plant failed to split its genomes in half and instead produced a germ cell with two genomes (AA). It then crossed with an agropyron plant suffering from the same mutation and produced a seed with AABB chromosomes in its nuclei. When the seed grew into a plant the germ cell creation did not abort because the hybrid had two genomes from einkorn, and two from agropyron, and both of these set pairs were able to go through the splitting process almost as well as the original parental species. The pollen and ovules so produced contained the AB genome and were fertile. The result was emmer wheat (*T. turgidum*) which is tetraploid, created from a diploid by chromosome doubling.

Plant breeders today need not wait many lifetimes for natural chromosome doubling to create novelties. A chemical, colchicine, which prevents chromosome splitting, allows them to design plants with the attributes they want.

When one looks at the evolutionary pathway of wheats shown in Figure 7.1 it is easy to forget that this is not like other evolutionary pathways. Wheat did not evolve simply as a result of natural selection. It evolved because of a combination of natural selection and farmers' learning selection. As we have seen, learning selection embeds knowledge into a technology. In other words, wheats, rices, barleys and nearly all the other crops in the world represent a huge wealth of farmer knowledge, embedded in the seed by thousands of years of agriculture. Modern plant breeders sometimes forget this and see themselves as the only source of innovation and intellectual property.

Recent work gives us some indication of how much knowledge the early farmers contributed to domesticating crops. Archaeological investigation by Gordon Hillman, Susan Colledge and David Harris at the edge of the Euphrates Valley in Syria revealed that the people living there between 10000 and 9000 BC gathered a prodigious range of plants. No less than 157 species were identified from their seeds.[8] Nor was this the indiscriminate collection of anything that looked remotely edible. All 157 species fell into three categories: seeds that were non-poisonous and immediately edible; seeds like pulses and mustards that contained toxins which could be easily removed; and seeds belonging to plants traditionally used as sources of dyes or medicines.

This result is in line with what ethnobiologists have found again and again – that hunter-gatherers and other people relying heavily on wild plants for food are walking encyclopaedias of knowledge about their environment, often able to name in their own language a thousand or more plant and animal species. This intimate knowledge was used by the early farmers when deciding what species to culti-vate, as two Israeli scientists, Ofer Bar-Yosef and Mordechai Kislev, showed when they analysed the wild grasses in the Jordan Valley to see which would be the best candidates for domestication[9] if they were to attempt it today. The two plants the first farmers chose, wild wheat and barley, came top of the scientists' list of twenty-three grasses with edible seeds of a size worth gathering.

Once the domestication of crops began, learning selection by farmers coupled with natural selection created great diversity in the gene pool of the major food crops. IRRI, for example, estimates that there were over 100,000 different rices growing in the world before the Green Revolution, and it now holds seed from 80,000 of these in its genebank. It was this diversity that modern plant breeders exploited when they developed their first 'miracle' crops.

Diversity increased when farmers took seeds to areas with different agro-ecological conditions and then selected seeds from the plants that did best there when they came to plant again. The introduction of maize into New England provides a good example of this. Native Americans brought maize to southern New England about a thousand years ago but the Penobscot nation only managed to adapt it to the shorter growing season in northern New England about eight hundred years later. Their farmers noticed that maize, like other members of the grass family, grew in segments with nodes in between, and that it took approximately one phase of the moon for each segment to grow, and that most plants produced about seven segments in all. They noticed that ears formed only at the nodes and that in some plants the ears formed on lower nodes than others, and hence earlier. By planting the kernels from these early maturing ears, the farmers changed the genetic composition of the south New England maize strain to favour the gene, or combination of genes, that had produced ears on the low nodes,[10] and in doing so they developed a new strain or landrace which was able to produce crops further north. (A landrace is simply a version of a species or a variety that has become locally adapted through changes to the 'average' genetic composition.)

As early as 1914, G.N. Collins described in *The Journal of Heredity* how Hopis and Navajos, Native Americans from the southwest of the USA, had developed maize varieties suitable for very dry areas through selection techniques incorporated in their culture. These varieties could be planted up to 30 cm deep and had a very long primary seminal root that could reach and absorb water from deep soil layers. 'Their work [is] not sufficiently appreciated – probably much yet to be learned from them', he wrote.[11]

Similar breeding successes by African farmers have been documented by P. Richards, working for the West Africa Rice Development Association. For many years, West Africans have been growing African rice (*O. glaberrima*) in their fields with two wild rices, *O. breviligulatai* and *O. longistaminata,* growing alongside them as weeds. From time to time, the species hybridised spontaneously and farmers selected and propagated these hybrids. 'Some of these local selections are especially significant as hardy types well adapted to low-potential environments by their early and abundant tillering capacities and greater tolerance to low phosphorus',[12] Richards says.

The fact that the Penobscot nation was able to find in the south New England landrace plants that produced ears on the low segments is evidence of a key characteristic of landraces – and wild varieties for that matter – they are genetically diverse. In Edgar Anderson's wonderful book *Plants, Man and Life* he describes a grain field in the Fertile Crescent that he believed had changed little for thousands of years and was typical of the diversity once found in traditionally farmed fields in the Old and New Worlds. 'The crop itself is a mixture of wheat and barley and rye. The wheats are a mixture, partly various tetraploids and partly hexaploids. In the field and growing around its margins are such related weed grasses as *Aegilops squarrosa*, Haynaldia, rye and the like.'[13] This mixture was a veritable hotbed of potential novelty generation because of the myriad possibilities for cross-pollination. Such a hotbed, coupled with an observant and knowledgeable farmer, would have produced, selected and nurtured the rare polyploid cross between emmer wheat and the wild grass *Agegilops* that gave us the most commercially important wheats, the bread wheats. A cross like that is a 'macro-invention', while the genetic diversity within the new species is the source of 'micro-inventions' that allow the crop to respond to the learning and natural selection pressures and adapt to become new landraces.

Genetic diversity in a crop was good for farmers because it meant that they could expect to have something to harvest even in very bad seasons and that pests or diseases were unlikely to destroy everything. This was because the landrace they were planting would have contained some plants resistant to whatever weather conditions, disease or pests the crop might encounter. In his book *Weapons of the Weak*, James Scott looked at thirty years' rice harvest figures for an area of Southeast Asia and showed that, although the indigenous varieties of rice gave smaller yields than the seed companies' strains, their crops were more reliable. Had the people depended on the imported varieties, he said, they would have starved because of the extreme fluctuations. The native landraces saw them through every year.

Little scientific work has been carried out to discover the potential of landraces to adapt over time in response to different selection pressures. One of the few experiments began in 1928 at the University of California. The researchers produced a genetically highly diverse 'landrace' by crossing different barley varieties. This was then grown under modern agricultural conditions. At first, yields were low but as successive plantings of the seed were harvested the landrace adapted to become quite productive, with exceptional yield stability and disease resistance.[14]

Traditional farmers contribute to developing the world's crops not only by selecting the best strains to plant, but also by spreading them when they exchange seed with other farmers, very much in the way that hackers in the open-source software community give and exchange software. The 'gift culture' ethos is the same in both cases: farmers give and exchange seed partly in order to build their status within their community by becoming recognised as a source of good seed. 'The traditional breeders ... treated seeds as sacred, as the critical element in the great chain of being. Seed was not bought and sold, it was exchanged as a free gift of nature', says Dr Vandana Shiva, who established Navdanya, a movement for biodiversity conservation and farmers' rights, and now directs the Research Foundation for Natural Resource Policy.[15]

Until this century, seeds were the defining grassroots technology. For over ten thousand years, millions of farmers in millions of fields carried out learning selection, first on wild seeds, and then on their increasingly domesticated progeny. This process, combined with natural selection and novelty generation resulting from crosses, produced the crops shown in Table 7.1, most of which are of great antiquity. The farmers didn't just produce the crops themselves, but also the genetic diversity within them. And it was this diversity, by allowing the evolutionary process to continue, which made traditional agriculture sustainable.

In view of the remarkable success of traditional farmers as innovators, why did modern scientists unleash the Green Revolution that has destroyed traditional agriculture in many areas? Figure 7.2 gives much of the answer. Until about two hundred years ago the

Table 7.1 The world's major crops and their probable areas of origin[16]

Andean South America	Africa	South Pacific
Potato	African rice	Sugar cane
Peanut	Sorghum	Coconut
Lima bean	Pearl millet	Breadfruit
Cotton	Finger millet	
Squash	Yam	**Southeast Asia**
	Cowpea	Asian rice
Northeast South America	Coffee	Banana
Yam		Citrus
Pineapple	**Asia Minor**	Yam
Cotton	Wheat	Mango
Sweet potato	Barley	Sugar cane
Cassava	Onion	Taro
	Pea	Tea
Meso-America	Lentil	
Maize	Chick pea	**China**
Tomato	Fig	Soybean
Cotton	Date	Cabbage
Avocado	Flax	Onion
Papaya	Pear	Peach
Cocoa	Olive	
Cassava	Grape	**Central Asia**
Sweet potato	Almond	Common millet
Common bean	Apricot	Buckwheat
		Alfalfa
North America	**Europe**	Hemp
Sunflower	Oats	Broad bean
Cotton	Rye	
Avocado	Sugar beet	**India**
	Cabbage	Pigeon pea
		Eggplant
		Cotton
		Sesame

Source: Harlan, 1976.

world's population increased gradually, allowing humankind to live in relative harmony with the environment. Then numbers started to increase very rapidly as technological developments began to break down traditional population control measures[17] while at the same time improving sanitation, health care, medicines, shelter and nutrition meant that people lived longer and had more surviving children.

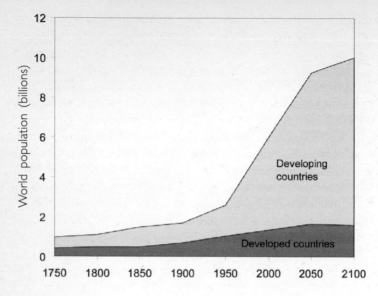

Figure 7.2   World, developed and developing country population growth from 1750 to 2100[19]

In Europe, the Industrial Revolution and the population increases that fuelled it were made possible by an agricultural revolution that had begun in the early Middle Ages. This, in turn, was built on a technological package made up of the heavy plough, or *carruca*, the horse collar and the open-field system,[18] as Box 7.1 explains.

At the beginning of the nineteenth century, a few farmers began to select the promising plants from the landraces they grew and evaluated the progeny they produced, rather like the New England Native Americans. Unlike the Native Americans, though, they set out to make money from their efforts and began producing and marketing their improved varieties, which often bore their selector's name. Two of the best-known wheat varieties from this period were Vilmorin from France and Shirreff from Scotland, both of which went on to replace the landraces, and hence reduced the genetic diversity, from which they had been selected. From its outset, then, commercial plant breeding has gone hand-in-hand with genetic erosion.

Box 7.1   The Agricultural Revolution in Europe

The heavy plough was a European development of the ancient plough, the aratrum, which was used in Asia Minor and the Mediterranean during the Roman times. The drawback with the aratrum was that it was ill-suited to the heavy and moist clays north of the Alps. As a result, vast tracts of fertile land were either uncultivated or exploited by slash-and-burn farming that could support only a small population. In its ultimate form the heavy plough moved on wheels, had a knife, the coulter, that cut the soil vertically, a flat ploughshare that cut the soil horizontally, and a mouldboard that turned the cut clods over into the deep furrow cut on the previous pass. Such an implement required a team of four to six oxen to pull it, more than one peasant could reasonably expect to own or feed by himself, so, just as with wind turbines, the full benefit of the new equipment only emerged after a social innovation had taken place as well. This was the semi-cooperative three-field system organised at the village or manorial level. In this system, each plot of arable land went though a three-year rotation between fallow, winter crops and spring crops. Animals grazed the fallow land and fertilised it with their droppings, and the fields under crops were also opened up to grazing after the harvest. Animals also grazed on the common, which was not part of the rotation system.

The three-field system increased agricultural productivity, because before its introduction fields had been left fallow every second year and were not necessarily fertilised with animal droppings. Not only did it increase cropping intensity from a half to two-thirds, but, as the second crop was often a legume which fixed nitrogen, it increased soil fertility.

When the early plant breeders found that simple selection from within their improved but inbred cultivars was no longer bringing gains,[20] they adopted a hybridisation technique first described in 1761 by Joseph Gottlieb Koelreuter of Germany. Hybridisation was important because it enabled people to generate novelty in their plants rather than waiting for it to arise naturally. In 1866 Gregor Mendel, an Austrian monk, provided a theoretical understanding of hybridisation when he published the first and second laws of genetics; with this knowledge, scientists were able to develop improved varieties much faster that had been possible with evolutionary plant breeding.

New crossing techniques emerged. For example, if a cultivar could not be crossed directly with a wild relative to obtain a desired characteristic such as pest resistance, a ' bridge cross' was made. This was an interim cross between the wild plant and an intermediate plant with which the cultivar would also cross. The wild plant was crossed with the intermediate, its progeny selected for the desired characteristic, and these were then crossed with the cultivar. Selection techniques also improved.[21]

Up until the 1950s plant breeders carried out crossing and selection in the greenhouse or in the field. Then breeders began to use tissue culture techniques, first developed in the 1930s, to give them much greater control over the crossing and to speed up selection. Tissue culture works because the chromosomes in the nucleus of every cell have the potential to produce a complete, new plant. Plant tissues are cultured in the laboratory in sterile conditions to grow clones of the plant from which the tissue was taken. The combined effect of the use of tissue culture and the improved selection techniques was to allow plant breeders to set up product lines that could create a new variety in just one generation rather than the many required using conventional techniques.[22]

This greatly improved crop yields in developed countries. In the United States, for example, maize yields have more than tripled from an average of 2.3 tonnes per hectare in the 1930s to 7.5 tonnes per hectare by the end of the 1980s. Of this increase, 60 per cent was due to the improved seeds[23] and the rest to changes in the way the crop was grown.

Agricultural extension

Everett Rogers attributes the development of hybrid maize and its almost 100 per cent adoption by farmers to agricultural research and extension, which he regards as the most successful technology generation and transfer system in the USA. The foundations of the system were laid by the Morrel Act of 1862, which established 'land-grant' universities in each state, first to teach agriculture and engineering and then, after 1887, to carry out research with federal funds. As these research findings accumulated, so did the need for a mechanism to transfer them to farmers. Accordingly, state agricultural extension services were established by the Smith–Lever Act in 1914 'to aid in diffusing among the people of the United Sates useful and practical information on subjects relating to agriculture and home economics, and to encourage application of the same.'[24]

County extension agents were appointed to spread research findings among rural people and to encourage their application. In addition, state extension specialists were appointed to work beside the university researchers to provide a two-way flow of information from researcher to grassroots, and vice versa. These extension specialists had the same professional status as the researchers, a fact that helped ensure that the scientists were responsive to farm-level concerns. This integration of research and extension has not been widely understood by people who have tried to copy the model, Rogers says.

Development and start-up phase

Europe also succeeded in applying scientific knowledge to agricultural production so well that during the second half of the twentieth century food surpluses became a problem in the European Union and farmers were paid to 'set-aside' their land and not produce anything on it. It was a different picture in the poorer countries, however, where, each year in the 1950s, there were 54 million more mouths to be fed in countries which had not gone through an agricultural revolution. Experts forecast that Asia would suffer from chronic and widespread famine by 1975,[25] a prediction which alarmed the US government because hungry rural populations had already proved to be fertile breeding grounds for communism.[26] Asian countries would 'fall like dominoes' unless something was done. So the Rockefeller Foundation (RF) established the International Rice Research Institute in the Philippines in 1960.

The Rockefeller Foundation got involved because of its success with maize breeding in Mexico. In the Depression years of the 1930s, Henry A. Wallace, the US vice-president, had travelled in Central America and Mexico and subsequently proposed to RF that it consider setting up an agricultural programme to raise the yield of Mexico's food crops. Accordingly, RF inaugurated a programme in

1943 in co-operation with the Mexican Department of Agriculture. It proved successful, and in 1956 Dr J. George Harrar, the architect of the Foundation's agricultural programme and later the Foundation's president, could write: 'Corn [maize] production in Mexico has increased steadily since 1947. The country has been able to meet the demands of increasing population since 1947 without resorting to the importation of the basic food from abroad.'[27]

IRRI's first director-general, Dr Robert F. Chandler, recruited 'world class' scientists and set them the target of producing rice varieties with the highest possible yield, 'when growth is not limited by water or nutrients, pests, diseases or weeds.'[28] In the 1960s, traditional rice farmers were harvesting 2 to 3 tonnes per hectare for the addition of just 30–40 kilograms of nitrogen per hectare (kg N/ha). If more fertiliser than this was added, the long stems of their local varieties tended to buckle under the added weight of grain, and lodge – that is, fall down.

Some traditional varieties were adapted to produce one crop during the five- or six-month monsoon season and to ripen only at the end of the rains when harvesting was easier. This clever trick was a result of photosensitivity – the plants' growing cycles were regulated by changes in day length. However, this made the varieties somewhat latitude-specific and meant they would only grow one crop a year.

IRRI's scientists decided to increase yield potential by breeding a short-strawed 'semi-dwarf' plant type that could grow quickly irrespective of day length and respond to high fertiliser application rates without falling down. Also the plant was to have a higher harvest index. In other words, it was to produce more rice and less straw than traditional varieties. They knew where to begin. Just as Unix provided the template for Linux, previous work to increase wheat yields had given them a road map. In particular, in 1948 a land-grant university, Washington State, had begun a programme to produce wheat varieties that could respond to heavy applications of nitrogenous fertiliser without lodging. Its approach was to breed plants incorporating a dwarf gene from a Japanese wheat variety. Accordingly, IRRI found a dwarf gene in a Taiwanese rice variety called Dee-Geo-Woo-Gen and crossed it with a long-stemmed but vigorous Indonesian variety called Pea. The result – IR8 – remained standing when 150 kg N/ha was added and produced up to 11 tonnes per hectare in four months rather than two or three tonnes in five or six.

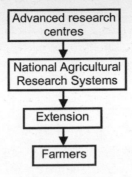

Figure 7.3   The transfer of technology
(TOT) model[29]

The new strain produced four times the rice for four times the fertiliser and in less time. Equally importantly, IR8 was photoperiod insensitive, which meant that farmers could grow it at any time of the year. They could therefore grow two or more crops per annum if they wished. As a result, IR8 and later IRRI cultivars were hailed as 'miracle' seeds representing a major breakthrough. IR8 was released in 1966 as a 'finished' cultivar – in other words, one which was not expected to require any further adaptations.

As the driving force behind IRRI was the Rockefeller Foundation and the Institute's first director-general was also American, it is scarcely surprising that the extension model IRRI used to transfer its technology to farmers was similar to that used by the US land-grant universities. The IRRI version has been called the Transfer of Technology (TOT) model by two early champions of the participatory technology development, Janice Jiggins and Robert Chambers.[30] It is shown schematically in Figure 7.3. In the diagram, IRRI is an advanced research centre generating new breeding lines at the beginning of a knowledge pipeline. The seeds are then sent to National Agricultural Research Systems (NARS), who can release them directly, as happened with IR8 and the IR cultivars that followed shortly afterwards. Later, however, after training at IRRI, NARS scientists were able to 'finish' the breeding lines themselves by adapting the plants to local conditions. But whether they 'finish' a new cultivar or not, the NARS hand the seed over to the local extension services to multiply.

Adaptation and expansion phase

Hans Ruthenberg, one of the most respected agricultural economists of the Green Revolution, described the ideal role of extension in the TOT model as follows: 'The starting point is a technical innovation that has become available and that has been tested under conditions as similar as possible to those of the smallholder. The task then is spreading the message to achieve diffusion and adoption of the innovation by as many smallholders as possible.'[31] This makes it clear that the TOT model implicitly assumes that by the time the seed reaches the extension service it is 'finished' – that is, farmers are either going to adopt it or not but they are not going to adapt it. In other words, the TOT model does not have an adaptation phase, which in turn means that there is no provision for the 'cathedral-building' plant breeders to descend to the 'bazaar' of farmers' fields and take part in learning selection. This, together with the lack of high-status extension specialists stationed at IRRI to link the research scientists with the grassroots extensionists in the national agricultural extension systems, meant that IRRI's plant breeders received little feedback about how farmers were trying to adapt the 'miracle' rice.

The feedback that IRRI did receive was that IR8 was susceptible to seven serious diseases and pests. These were grassy stunt virus, tungro virus, blast (a fungal disease) and bacterial blight; from insects there were stem borer, green leaf hopper and three types of brown plant hopper. Accordingly, they looked for genes in the rice gene pool to give resistance against these and in 1969 released IR20, which had at least moderate resistance to everything but brown plant hoppers and grassy stunt. To find resistance to grassy stunt virus IRRI screened seventeen thousand varieties and landraces it had collected in its genebank, as well as more than a hundred ecotypes of wild species. Finally the breeders found the resistance gene they were looking for in one ecotype of an annual wild rice (*O. nivara* – the immediate progenitor of *O. sativa*) from Uttar Pradesh, but only three plants out of thirty tested contained the gene.[32] This is a very good illustration of the genetic diversity that exists naturally in ecotypes and landraces, and of what can be lost through genetic erosion. Somewhat ironically, IR36, which was resistant to everything that had plagued IR8 when it was released in 1976, went on to become the most widely planted rice cultivar ever, thus causing untold erosion to the genetic diversity which had made it possible. In 1982 it was planted on 11 million hectares[33] which had been growing a huge diversity of landraces a few years earlier.

Disappearance phase

How and why were IRRI's high-yielding varieties so quickly and widely adopted? One answer lies in the characteristics of the technology itself. Unlike rice dryers or wind turbines, IRRI's seeds were not a new technology to the farmers who adopted them because even HYVs were still varieties of rice, and farmers had been growing rice for thousands of years. In the main grain-growing areas of Asia, many farmers had reasonable control of irrigation water and were already using some inorganic fertiliser before IR8 came along. It was therefore possible for them to adopt HYVs without having to make any change to their farming systems, except perhaps to their planting or harvest dates. And, as the addition of some extra fertiliser and the switch to growing two or three crops a year allowed farmers to double or treble their yields, the new seeds were very attractive to them, particularly as they could get them cheaply or for free from government programmes. Moreover, they didn't have to commit themselves to adopt them. They could experiment first on a small area and go back to their traditional varieties if they wished.

Contrast this with early wind turbine adoption in Denmark. When Flemming TrTranæs and his co-operative were deciding whether to buy a wind turbine it was such a big decision, with such serious financial consequences, that they sent one of their members to visit all the wind turbine factories to collect information. In economic jargon a wind turbine is non-divisible – the co-operative could not adopt a small bit of a wind turbine to see if the new technology was going to work for them. Moreover, few of the co-operative members had any previous experience with wind turbines so they had to spend time and effort to learn something new, which is a cost in itself.

A second reason why high-yielding rice varieties were adopted so quickly was that IRRI's director-general had (and has) an international status equivalent to that of an ambassador and so was able to champion promising new technologies at high levels in governments in Asia. My experience with stripper-harvesters in Burma, where only days elapsed between the Minister of Agriculture seeing video of the prototype for the first time and the government's decision to commit millions of dollars to building it, is typical of how fast things can move when someone powerful finds out about a new technology that promises to tackle a pressing problem. Certainly, no bottom-up approach in Burma would ever have been able to mobilise as many resources as quickly as the top-down one was able to do by getting the Ministry of Agriculture, the Ministry of Railways and the Ministry of Heavy Industry working together within three months to build twelve machines per day.

Seed is therefore a very easy technology to transfer using a top-down hierarchical system with little or no feedback, particularly if governments promote irrigation schemes, subsidise fertiliser and other inputs, and adopt other policies to help bring the benefits of the new technology to as many farmers as possible.

The TOT approach and the changing policy environment in Asia was so effective at encouraging adoption and production increases that rice prices halved in real terms between 1980 and 1994.[34] This meant that farmers who had not adopted the new varieties and increased their yields found that every year they earned less and less when they took their surplus to market. This effectively forced many either to grow HYVs or to cease production. In other words, the HYVs that created the Green Revolution had the same effect as the invention of *fiat* money did when the inflation it caused reduced the purchasing power of the money held by people who did not change. It forced change and thus caused the loss of skills and landraces in Asia that farmers had used to feed a growing population for thousands of years. Moreover the Green Revolution has taken away the responsibility for plant breeding from farmers themselves and given it to breeders in public research institutes and private companies.

The only things that farmers needed to learn to grow HYVs well was how much fertiliser to apply and when, so, from the early 1980s, IRRI's only fertiliser recommendation was to spread two-thirds of it during land preparation and the final third when the seeds began to form. NARES (National Agricultural Research and Extension Systems) usually worked out their own recommendations but these were at a regional level and thus not tailored to the soil farmers actually had in their fields. For example, the Rice Research and Development Institute in Ibbagamuwa, Sri Lanka, posts fertiliser recommendations on the Internet for seven agro-ecological zones including low-country dry zone, mid-country intermediate zone, and upcountry wet zone.[35]

In the early 1990s IRRI's anthropologist, Dr Sam Fujisaka, found that Philippine rice farmers had largely ignored the fertiliser recommendation of their extension service,[36] which was based on the IRRI recommendation. Instead, they had developed their own fertiliser application strategies through learning selection. Later research by IRRI[37] showed that its 1982 fertiliser recommendation was wrong to say that farmers should apply most of their fertiliser just before the rice crop was planted, because if they did the nitrogen in the fertiliser only stayed in the soil for fifteen to twenty days. Rice plants need relatively little nitrogen just after planting, and all they do need can be supplied by a fertile soil. Instead, the fertiliser is required about fifty days after transplanting, which was roughly what Philippine rice farmers, through learning selection, had worked out themselves to be the best time to apply.

There was nothing sloppy about the science that IRRI used to work out its 1982 fertiliser recommendation. Its advice was based on the rate at which inorganic nitrogen is lost from the soil as a result of volatilisation and denitrification. IRRI researchers knew that fertiliser stayed around longer if it was incorporated into the soil when the latter was being prepared for planting than if the chemical was just broadcast into the flooded field later on, which is the usual method of applying it. What the researchers failed to consider, however, was whether the young rice crop needed that much fertiliser so early. This is not surprising because it is the nature of conventional science to be reductionist and not look at systems as a whole. However, reality for farmers is different, as Fujisaka points out. Farmers are not interested in minimising volatilisation and denitrification losses *per se*. They are interested in seeing the most efficient conversion of their time and money (in terms of the fertiliser bought) into extra rice yield.

While farmers have been able to adapt fertiliser recommendations, they have had little success modifying the HYVs they fertilise
because of the cultivars' lack of genetic diversity. Harold C. Conklin,
an anthropologist who has worked for many years in the Philippines,
found in 1957 that the Hanunoo people, an ethnic people in Mindoro
in the Philippines, were planting ninety-two distinguishable (by them)
rice varieties.[38] The farmers interacted with their seed technology
and could tweak it, albeit sometimes unconsciously, to do things they
wanted. Farmers who have adopted HYVs and abandoned their
traditional varieties can no longer do this. They have become dependent on outsiders – plant breeders in research institutes or in
commercial seed companies – to provide them with new cultivars.

The reason farmers growing genetically homogenous HYVs need
new cultivars is that pest and disease populations, which are genetically diverse as a result of many thousands of years of an evolutionary 'arms race' with farmers' landraces, can evolve to break down
whatever resistance was bred into the HYV in the first place. The
evolutionary pressure placed on disease and pest species faced by a
single HYV grown on millions of hectares two or three times a year
is huge. Te-Tzu Chang, who was part of the IRRI team that created
IR8, says that resistance to brown plant hoppers can be broken down
within three to five years[39] and resistance to the fungal disease blast
can be overcome even more quickly.[40] When resistance does break
down, pest infestations and disease epidemics of previously unknown
proportions occur. For example, in 1990, 76 per cent of Thailand's
rice area was planted to HYVs, with just four varieties accounting
for half of the total area. The following year a strain of brown plant
hoppers had evolved that had overcome the bred-in resistance.
Because so much of Thailand's crop was so similar, these insects
completely destroyed over half a million hectares of rice that if
harvested would have yielded at least 2.5 million tonnes, worth $400
million.[41]

The resistance bred into HYVs is particularly short-lived because
it is conferred by a single gene or a very limited number of them.
This makes it easy for a pest to develop to overcome it. An ancient
Indian proverb sums things up perfectly: 'If you sweep nature out
of the door with a broom she will come through the window with
a pitch-fork.' Plant breeders are therefore engaged in a permanent
struggle which they cannot win, and which they cannot quit without

nature coming though the window with a very large pitchfork. Not only do they need to find new resistance genes every three to five years just to maintain yield levels; they also need to find ways to increase yield to feed a burgeoning population. Gurdev Khush, IRRI's principal plant breeder and winner of the World Food Prize, once explained the problem to Lynne Malcolm during an interview on an Australian Broadcasting Company television programme.

> [By 2020] the world population will be 8 billion and out of that 5 billion will be rice consumers. Now we have 3 billion rice consumers so we have to increase rice production by 60% ... and this has to be increases from the existing lands. There are no new lands to open up for new cultivation, so we have to develop the technologies that can give this production from the existing land resources.[42]

Indeed, not only is there no new land; some of the best existing agricultural land is being lost as cities grow. Shaobing Peng and Dharmawansa Senadhira, two IRRI scientists, conclude that the only option available to avoid a Malthusian crisis is to double rice yields again in what would amount to a second Green Revolution.

What makes this conclusion frightening to some people is the growing evidence of problems with the first Green Revolution. Dr Vandana Shiva, author of the influential book *The Violence of the Green Revolution,* wrote in 1991 that

> The Green Revolution has been a failure. It has led to reduced genetic diversity, increased vulnerability to pests, soil erosion, water shortages, reduced soil fertility, micronutrient deficiencies, soil contamination, re-duced availability of nutritious food crops for the local population, the displacement of vast numbers of small farmers from their land, rural impoverishment and increased tensions and conflicts. The beneficiaries have been the agrochemical industry, large petrochemical companies, manufacturers of agricultural machinery, dam builders and large land-owners.[43]

Many NGOs agree, as do some people working for the NARES. For example, Nguyen Ngoc Hai, a spokesman from the Vietnamese Ministry of Agriculture, is on record as saying: 'The Green Revolution in Vietnam has led to monocultures of preferred and constantly used varieties, which in turn has led to pests and diseases.'[44]

Another criticism of the Green Revolution is that it is based on using high levels of external inputs and on controlling growing conditions for the HYVs, both of which require large amounts of energy, nearly all of which comes from fossil fuel. Agriculture in the USA, which employs all the Green Revolution technologies, uses fifty times more energy than traditional agriculture; when processing and transportation is taken into account as well, as much as one quarter of all energy used in developed countries goes into putting food onto peoples' plates.[45]

As fossil fuels are running out, an agriculture based on their use is fundamentally unsustainable. World oil production is likely to peak at around 2008[46] and then decline rapidly, and gas production will start contracting within the next twenty to twenty-five years. Unless coal takes up the slack, or renewable energy sources can be developed, food production will collapse.

Until the Industrial Revolution 150 years ago, agriculture was solar-powered because the energy used came from the farmer or his animals, both of which ate the products of photosynthesis. Traditional agriculture was therefore sustainable in terms of its energy source and, because the supply was limited, farmers developed technologies honed to work with relatively little energy input compared to that used in agriculture today. For example, without boreholes and diesel pumps, Native Americans could not irrigate their maize so they developed varieties that would yield in dry conditions. But such farmers cannot compete against a system of agriculture powered by cheap fossil fuels. Consider this. A small engine fitted on a pump will produce about 9 kWh of energy from 4.5 litres of petrol, which is enough energy to pump 3,300 tonnes of water up one metre. It would take one man three weeks to pump that amount of water by hand instead.[47] In the Philippines in 1999 three weeks' labour cost $75 while a gallon of gasoline costs about $1.50. It is no coincidence that the ratio between the two costs – 50:1 – is the same as the ratio between the amount of energy used in US agriculture compared to traditional agriculture.

As well as being unsustainable in themselves, high levels of inputs to agriculture cause soil erosion, reduce the diversity of flora and fauna, contaminate the environment with fertilisers and pesticides, and deplete groundwater reserves.[48] They therefore destroy the eco-systems on which agriculture depends. Indeed, this destruction has gone frighteningly far already. According to a UN report, by 1990 poor agricultural practices had contributed to the degradation of 562 million hectares, about 38 per cent of the roughly 1.5 billion hectares in cropland world-wide. Some of this land was only slightly degraded, but an appreciable amount was damaged severely enough to impair its productive capacity or to take it out of production completely. Since 1990, losses have continued to mount year by year, with an additional 5–6 million hectares lost to severe soil degradation.[49] If ecosystems are destroyed, technology alone cannot produce food because technology needs to have a resource base to work with, and that base has limits beyond which it cannot be pushed. For example, the world fish catch is already close to 100 million tonnes, which is thought to be the maximum possible figure. As a result, improving fishing-vessel technologies actually reduces the fishery stock unless fishing effort is reduced. A switch-over point has been reached where more technology can actually mean less food.[50]

IRRI defends the Green Revolution from these criticisms by pointing out that without HYVs, yields could not have been increased fast enough to feed the world's rapidly growing population. It is nevertheless researching the problems that have emerged. High on the list is a common complaint from farmers that if they adopt the whole HYV package of growing two or three crops a year and adding fertiliser, over time they find they have to add more and more fertiliser to get the same yield. This, together with falling rice prices, has meant the profitability, and hence some of the attraction, of rice farming has been falling, further fuelling urban drift and the loss of agricultural land. In IRRI's own long-term yield experiment, which occupies a field right outside the director-general's office, dry season harvests have fallen from around 9 tonnes per hectare to between 6 and 7 tonnes over a period of about twenty-five years.[51] Research at IRRI reported in 1996 suggests that similar falls in farmers' fields are at least partly because mistaken fertiliser recommendations have meant that farmers have not put everything back into their soils that intensive rice cultivation has been taking out.[52]

Improved nutrient management is therefore one plank of what IRRI hopes will be Green Revolution II. The other main plank is the development of a 'super rice' which will break through the 10 tonne-per-hectare dry season yield ceiling at which Green Revolution I HYVs appear to be stuck. This involves breeding a 'new plant type' (NPT) that, because it has fewer and thicker stems holding up larger panicles, should theoretically be more efficient at converting solar radiation into grain. The head of the breeding programme, Gurdev Khush, says that NPT should raise the yield ceiling by 20 per cent to 12 tonnes per hectare. However, in November 1999, nearly twelve years after work on the project began and twice as long as it took IRRI to produce IR8, the 'super rice' had not been released in spite of advances in tissue culture that had greatly speeded up the breeding process.

The main problem is that while NPT produces enough grain heads per square metre to break the yield ceiling, the heads are not filling properly with grain. Dr Khush says that it will be another five years before NPT is ready for widescale on-farm production, although IRRI has already released NPT lines to several NARES and one line has been released as a variety in Yunnan province in China.[53] This would seem to be an example of the 80:20 rule – you get 80 per cent of the results from the first 20 per cent of effort, while it takes 80 per cent of the effort to achieve the last 20 per cent of gain.

Biotechnology: Big Science's technical fix?

The problems that IRRI faces in attempting to break the 10 tonne yield ceiling underscore a general truth: we live in a world that has limits. This means that all attempts to expand output by using more and more of the same inputs eventually produce diminishing, and then zero, and then negative returns. The standard way of getting round this problem is to find another input, and as far as plant breeding is concerned the great white hope is biotechnology. As Vernon Ruttan, a professor emeritus in the departments of Economics and Applied Economics at the University of Minnesota, writes, 'biotechnology is poised to become the most important new general-purpose technology in the first half of the twenty-first century.'[54] Many scientists hope that the novelty generation that biotechnology offers will produce the breakthroughs needed to carry on producing more and more rice from a shrinking resource base. *Let the Harvest Begin*, a public relations document published by Monsanto, a leading biotechnology company, puts it this way: 'agricultural biotechnology will play a major role in realising the hope we all share. Accepting this, science can make a dramatic difference to millions of lives.'[55]

For rice breeders, biotechnology offers three key tools: tissue culture, which we have already explored, DNA probes and genetic engineering. DNA probes make the selection of desired traits such as disease resistance much easier. With other techniques, breeders have to rely on 'phenotyping' – identifying the desired gene from the traits it produces in plants growing in the field or the greenhouse. With DNA probes, however, they can identify the desired gene chemically, which is more reliable and makes the selection process much faster, particularly as it is possible to screen for a number of genes at the same time. The ability to do several screenings simultaneously is very important because features such as high yields and the most stable resistance to pests and diseases come from the interaction of a number of genes, rather than the presence of just one.[56]

The tool that gets scientists most excited, however, is the most controversial: genetic engineering, the manipulation of an organism's genetic information by introducing or eliminating a specific gene. Whereas in conventional plant breeding, breeders are tied to using genes from the same species, genetic engineering allows them to look almost anywhere for genes with the traits they desire. For example, scientists have transferred a gene from fish into strawberries so that they can be frozen without turning to pulp on defrosting.[57] In rice, the main interest is in transferring the poison-producing genes of a bacterium that lives in the soil, *Bacillus thureingiensis* (*Bt*), into the plant in order to protect it from insects.

Another major benefit of genetic engineering is that it allows, say, a gene conferring resistance to brown plant hoppers to be transferred from a wild species into an already 'fit' cultivar without also transferring other genes that would reduce the cultivar's yield. When such a cross is made in conventional plant breeding, a long and often difficult process of back-crossing is needed to eliminate the unwanted effects of the genes from the wild species.

Biotechnology can, then, greatly increase the rate at which plant breeders can generate and select novelty. Even so, many plant breeders, including Khush and most of the IRRI group, adopted a 'wait and see' attitude to genetic engineering, believing that conventional breeding techniques can produce the same results more slowly but with fewer political problems.[58]

Our learning selection model helps us see the attraction of biotechnology. If you can increase the rate at which you are generating novelties and selecting the best of them, you ought to increase the evolutionary rate – provided, that is, that the novelties generated and the selection decisions made actually increase the fitness of the technology. Biotechnology certainly promises to speed up novelty generation and selection, but many plant breeders are waiting to see if it will really increase the fitness of seeds by enough to bring about Green Revolution II. Their caution may well prove wise, as we will see.

The learning selection model also explains why genetic engineering is controversial. The nature of the products that emerge from the genetic engineering process depends on who is doing the novelty generation and selection, and on the environment in which they work. US companies like Monsanto are the world leaders in biotechnology. Accordingly, the US government put pressure on the World Trade Organisation (WTO) to make it possible to patent plants that have been genetically modified using biotechnology, or even changed through conventional breeding techniques. Its request was granted. The biotech companies argue, just as Bill Gates did in his open letter to hackers, that they have invested millions in research and need some protection from copying to give them time to recoup their costs. This excerpt from a speech made by the then US Secretary of Agriculture, Daniel Glickman, to the Indian Institute of Agricultural Research, in which Glickman argues for Indian compliance with the WTO, shows how effective the lobbying of multinational seed companies has been.

> I hope your new legislation will provide a responsible and reasonable protection to seed companies, which will encourage them to provide the best seeds available for your farmers. There would be very few innovations of anything, particularly in agriculture, without patent protection because it is the fundamental fact of human nature that people will not go through the expense of development of new ideas for the altruistic benefit of the human race.[59]

The case studies we have looked at so far all show this to be propaganda. People do develop new ideas without thinking of their own personal profit. They may do it for altruistic reasons, but more likely they do it because it interests them and they gain peer group recognition. Either way, if enough people are doing it, and they can share information among themselves, ideas are developed of benefit to the human race – viz. wind turbines, Linux, LETS, rice dryers, and all the world's crops. However, this reality is not one that bene-

Box 7.2   WTO and TRIPs[60]

The agreement on Trade-Related Aspects of Intellectual Property Rights (TRIPs) was signed at the end of the GATT Uruguay Round on 1994. It came into force in 1995 and the World Trade Organisation, the successor body to GATT, was given the task of ensuring that it, and other international trade agreements, were implemented.

The TRIPs agreement sets out compulsory uniform standards for legal mechanisms such as patents, copyrights and trademarks that provide protection for intellectual property. One TRIPs requirement is that all signatory countries give the 'inventors' of micro-organisms, micro-biological processes and products, and plant varieties title to an intellectual monopoly over them. Plant varieties must either be patentable or subject to an effective *sui generis* system, which many governments interpret to mean plant variety protection, a special kind of patent developed in Europe for the corporate breeding industry. In principle, developing countries must implement this provision or face sanctions from the WTO.

TRIPs has been strongly resisted in the South partly because farmers' traditional landraces are not genetically homogenous enough to qualify as distinct cultivars and so do not qualify for a patent. This leaves the door open to companies to take a traditional landrace, modify it using biotechnology and then claim intellectual property rights over it, a procedure objectors term 'biopiracy'. The companies can then earn revenues from their 'inventions' while the farmers who maintained and developed the landrace receive nothing.

fits the shareholders of multinational biotech companies. Biotech firms see the possibility of making billions of dollars in sales of genetically modified (GM) seed to Third World farmers if, through the use of patents, they can take over the intellectual property embedded in the seeds.

Proponents of *laissez-faire* capitalism say that the patenting of life is a good thing because it means millions of dollars is spent on research to improve crops. However, the learning selection model leads us to question the types of novelty generation, selection and promulgation this money will produce. As the comparison between Linux and Microsoft showed, a company motivated by profit will modify a technology to suit its own market requirements rather than to benefit the end user, and this can lead to the development of an inferior technology. The frustration felt when Microsoft Windows crashes is intense, but it is not usually a matter of life or death, whereas an equivalent failure with Third World farmers' seeds could be. In India, the combination of hybrid cotton seeds and pesticides foisted on farmers by seed companies and the Indian government led to 103 farmers in the state of Andhra Pradesh committing suicide in 1998 by drinking insecticide after their cotton crop failed completely.[61]

What has happened with seed is directly comparable with what happened to computer software in the 1970s. For millennia farmers exchanged seed and allowed others to grow and reproduce it, albeit often within closed social groups, in just the way that computer programmers once freely exchanged code among themselves. Then, in both areas, private companies motivated by profit 'corrupted' things by seeking to appropriate for themselves what had previously been in the public domain. In other words they sought to replace a public property regime with a private one. With software, Richard Stallman and the open-source software movement fought back with copyleft, a copyright that made it impossible for anyone to take someone else's program, change it, and then prevent others copying and changing it too. With seeds, however, it is unfortunate that nothing as simple or effective exists to protect Third World farmers from finding that modified versions of the crops they helped evolve for millennia are being sold back to them as the patented property of a multinational corporation. As Dr Shiva said in a BBC *Newsnight* interview on 4 October 1999: 'We cannot afford to have ... crops that originated in India (cotton, soybean and mustard), [that] have been evolved by millions of farmers over thousands of years of farmer breeding, owned as private property by Monsanto.' Some seed patents make it illegal for farmers to save seed and plant it the next year, just as it is illegal to copy a Microsoft program. And if farmers can no longer save their best seed and share it with their neighbours, then this halts the farmer learning selection that produced the crop in the first place.

The clearest evidence that biotech companies are using genetic modification to align seed technology in their own interests rather than those of the farmers is the so-called Terminator gene, which makes the seed the farmers harvest infertile and thus forces them to buy a new supply the following year. Genetic engineers produced the Terminator by inserting a gene from another plant that produces a seed-killing toxin into the genome of the crop plant. However, so that their companies could grow fertile seed themselves, they also inserted bacterial DNA that is a 'genetic switch' for the production of the toxin. Before the seeds are sold they are immersed in a solution that induces the production of an enzyme that turns on the seed-killing gene. This means that the toxin is produced when the next generation of seeds starts to grow and kills them.[62] Monsanto paid a very large sum to purchase the company that developed the Terminator, and other seed companies have equivalent technologies.

Another Monsanto innovation is to alter crops genetically to make them resistant to its broad spectrum herbicide, Roundup. This is good for Monsanto, as it can sell more of its GM seed and its herbicide. It is also attractive to farmers as they can achieve effective weed control with a chemical that, as it binds tightly to soil molecules, is not toxic to wild life. However, the widespread use of a chemical that kills all plants except the crop will reduce the biodiversity, particularly of microorganisms, in farmers' fields. And because microbial activity is essential for the nutrient cycle, this could lead to a loss of soil fertility.

Another disadvantage is that the weeds will eventually evolve to become Roundup-resistant themselves, so Monsanto will have to develop a nastier herbicide and find a resistance gene to that. And when the weeds overcome this one too, it will have to find another. The company is on a treadmill that will spin and spin until, like the hospitals with superbugs that have developed resistance to all known antibiotics, it runs out of solutions. Its approach is simply not sustainable and will produce a crisis when it finally breaks down. As the *Newsnight* programme concluded, 'the promises of the next revolution [the GM revolution] may be as hollow as the last.'

To be fair to the new biotech companies, the idea of encouraging farmers to buy fresh seed each year is not new. The maize varieties that contributed to the threefold increase in US yields were all F1 hybrids, the term used for seed produced by crossing unrelated parents. Hybrids possess 'hybrid vigour', which can increase yields by 20 per cent, but which is progressively lost with subsequent generations (F2, F3, etc.). Farmers were prepared to buy F1 hybrid seed each year to obtain this vigour and today all maize seed planted in the USA is hybrid produced by private companies.

Because there is very little potential for making a profit by improving non-hybrid maize, much less research effort has gone into doing so than into developing hybrids. As a result, US farmers now have little choice but to buy their seed from private seed companies. In some ways farmers in the Third World are better off because IRRI's sister agency CIMMYT (International Maize and Wheat Improvement Center) has deliberately bred composite maize populations which allow farmers to save their own seed from year to year and which also have some capacity to adapt to changing local conditions.

Large seed companies would naturally like seed-saving to end, and it was their influence that led to the clauses in TRIPs which force all WTO members to allow patenting of plant varieties. Many people are deeply alarmed by this. Dr Shiva once remarked: 'If we don't keep up the active campaigns that have been launched in the last two years then ten years down the line what we'll see is India not a colony of the UK but a colony of the Monsanto empire. This is a future I do not want to see for my myself, for my personal family or for the larger family of India.'[63] Monsanto and its Terminator technology has become a focal point of the campaign against TRIPs and bio-technology.[64] Kent Whealy, director of the Seed Savers Exchange in Decorah, Iowa, says: '[Terminator technology] is really a vicious, anti-farmer technology. Using genetic engineering to break that chain of seed that has always fed us just for a corporation's profit is wrong. If this technology were to become widespread, it would essentially end anything except what genetic engineering gives us.'[65]

Another reason for the campaigners' concern is that if the biotech companies take over the food chain and actually use their technologies to increase the food supply, the extra food won't find its way onto the plates of the people living in absolute poverty simply because they will be too poor to buy the food they need, let alone new seeds every year. Even today, the world produces enough food to provide everyone with a nutritious and adequate diet, but nevertheless one-seventh of the world's population – 800 million people, many of whom live in India – go hungry as a result of their poverty. The conclusion we reached in Chapter 3 is valid here – private companies are most likely to benefit rich farmers by providing complex technologies developed in other countries (see Table 3.2). Jules Pretty summed up the situation neatly in the magazine *Red Pepper*. 'It is possible that GM crops could make a contribution to food production in the South – but only if the technologies are produced by public-interest bodies which make them available to poor farmers. Organisations seeking a quick and large return on a technology cannot possibly argue that they are working directly to benefit 800 million hungry people in the world.'[66]

In October 1999 the news broke that Monsanto was considering selling off its GM business under intense pressure from Wall Street analysts and professional investors. [67] This was an amazing development for a company that, only a year before, had been described as standing 'on the brink of engineering a massive transformation of world-wide agricultural practices.'[68] The reason for the abrupt change in the company's fortunes was that protest campaigns and critical media coverage had turned public opinion firmly against GM food in Europe. They had also, in the words of the US Secretary of Agriculture, Dan Glickman, spread across the Atlantic like 'an infectious disease'. Monsanto's shares fell by 25 per cent in six months. The company was particularly hard hit because it was seen as the most aggressive of the biotech companies. 'New York's financial community is now convinced that successful protests ... have hurt Monsanto's growth prospects and its stock market rating so badly that the only option to realise some value for its investors would be some kind of sell-off', one journalist wrote.[69] One result of these protests was that Monsanto said it would not use its Terminator technology in 'recognition that we need some level of public acceptance to do our business.'[70] Part of the pressure on Monsanto came from other biotech companies who felt that its aggressive promotion of biotech had damaged the public image of the technology.

In January 2000 Robert Shapiro, Monsanto's chief executive, announced that the company was merging with the US–Swiss drugs group Pharmacia & Upjohn.[71] The group, headed by Shapiro, was to be called Pharmacia, using the names Searle, Pharmacia and Upjohn for its three sales divisions, retaining the name Monsanto only for an autonomous subsidiary. Hendrik Verfaillie became the chief executive of the new, smaller Monsanto and immediately admitted past errors. 'Even our friends told us we could be arrogant and insensitive', Mr Verfaillie said, reflecting the pressure on Monsanto from other biotech companies. 'We missed the fact that this technology raises major issues for people – of ethics, of choice, of trust, even of democracy and globalisation.'[72] In an attempt to change the company image Verfaillie published a five-point pledge of new commitments: respect, transparency, dialogue, sharing and benefits.

However, despite the best efforts of biotech companies, the 'infectious disease' of public suspicion about GM crops has continued to spread in the USA. An ABC poll in June 2001 found that 52 per cent of consumers thought that GM foods were 'not safe to eat', and only 35 per cent expressed total confidence. A year earlier a Gallup poll found the opposite, with 51 per cent seeing no health hazard.[73]

Unlike the biotech companies, IRRI and the other institutes in the CGIAR system are funded by governments, so that they can bring the benefits of biotechnology to poor farmers. IRRI's work with the new plant type is a case in point. While multinationals were carrying out research on innovations like Terminator technology that helped their bottom line, IRRI was attempting to break the physiological yield barrier, which promises to be of direct benefit to farmers. Even so, Dr Shiva and many others working in NGOs, community groups and other third-sector organisations see IRRI and the CGIAR system as being on the same side as Monsanto. For example, Genetic Resources Action International (GRAIN), an international NGO, says the Green Revolution 'prime[d] the pump for genetic engineering'.[74]

GRAIN has a point. The realist–positivist paradigm on which the Green Revolution was built is the same paradigm that is now used in biotechnology. 'Biotechnology is being developed with the same vision that promoted chemicals to meet the single, short-term goals of enhanced yields and profit margins', Jane Rissler of the Union of Concerned Scientists said. 'This is based on the view that nature should be dominated, exploited and forced to yield more. The preference is for simple, immediately profitable "solutions" to complex ecological problems, using reductionist thinking that analyses complex systems like farming in terms of their component parts, rather than as an integrated whole. [A]gricultural success [is defined] according to short-term productivity, rather than long-term sustainability.'[75]

Another reason that IRRI gets lumped together with Big Science and the biotech multinationals is the fact that IRRI has genetically engineered rice by adding the *Bt* gene. Greenpeace got extensive press publicity in spring 1995 when it hijacked a parcel containing the gene on its way to the Philippines from the Institute of Plant Sciences in Zurich.

Our learning selection model helps us see that the controversy about biotechnology is also a debate on the pros and cons of the two development models we have been looking at in this book. It is part of the struggle between the Big Science, 'breakthrough', cathedral paradigm based on a realist–positivist road map, and the more iterative, grassroots, bazaar paradigm based on a constructivist view. Unfortunately the debate has become polarised and the result is '"two-value thinking" – the assumption, frequently unexamined, that every question has two sides, and only two sides',[76] and that organisations and individuals are either on one side or the other.

A result of this is that many third-sector organisations maintain their critical view of CGIAR centres even though the centres have been trying to chart a third way since the appointment of Dr Ismail Serageldin as CGIAR chairman from 1994 to 2000. IRRI, for example, actively campaigns for integrated natural resource management. This is 'the responsible and broad-based management of the land, water, forest and biological resources base – including genes – needed to sustain agricultural productivity and avert degradation of potential productivity.'[77] This is all part of a realisation at IRRI that in future rice will have to be grown with less water, less labour, less pollution, and on much less land. Accordingly, it is now trying to develop technologies that enable farmers[78] to substitute knowledge for external inputs, very much as they did when agriculture was solar-powered and they had control of their technologies. A very good example of this is IRRI's and FAO's work on integrated pest management (IPM) and the farmer field schools described in Box 7.3.

Box 7.3 Learning selection in action: Integrated Pest Management in Indonesia

In the 1960s, the USA was worried that several Asian countries would fall to communism. One of these was Indonesia, which was not able to match its rice production to its burgeoning population. Accordingly, the Indonesian armed forces were funded by the World Bank to carry out a massive programme. Irrigation systems were to be built and a Green Revolution package made up of IRRI's high-yielding rice varieties and subsidised chemical inputs was to be imposed.

'Farmers who still cultivated the old varieties were sometimes forced by the army to pull up their plants', says Jan Oudejans, who worked in Indonesia for the pesticide manufacturer Ciba Geigy until 1975. 'Then they had to replant, using the shorter-stemmed variety.'[79]

The campaign did increase rice yields but then disaster struck. In 1985 and 1986 a fifth of farmers lost their entire crop to plagues of brown plant hoppers (BPH). This were caused in part by excessive pesticide use, which had killed the natural predators that usually kept the hoppers in check. In some cases, spraying was carried out as often as fifty times a season. Other crop losses arose because, since just a few rice varieties were planted over very large areas, there was tremendous selection pressure on pests and diseases. Whatever resistance had been bred into the few rice varieties broke down quickly and the incidence of pest and disease attack soared, just as had happened in Thailand and the Philippines in 1985–86. The Indonesian government was forced to import rice again.

It was only in the late 1970s that IRRI realised that chemical spraying was helping to cause outbreaks of the very pests the farmers were trying to control. This came about largely because one of its entomologists, Peter Kenmore, had shown that natural predators allowed less than 4 per cent of brown plant hoppers to reach the adult stage in unsprayed fields. Kenmore's work helped lay the foundations of Integrated Pest Management (IPM) for rice. IPM is an approach to pest management based on an understanding of pest and predator ecology rather than blanket spraying recommendations.

Kenmore moved from IRRI to FAO to become director of its South and Southeast Asia IPM programme, a position that required him to champion the technique's use. 'Kenmore is a very political animal', states Jan Oudejans, who did a Ph.D. on IPM in Indonesia after leaving Ciba-Geigy. 'He introduced [IPM] to FAO.'

At the time of the BPH plagues, Indonesia was suffering from the slump in world oil prices and wanted to borrow money. Kenmore lobbied the Indonesian government and USAID (the United States Agency for International Development),[80] and was able to convince the Minister of Finance, Mr Sumarlin, that IPM made sense. 'Sumarlin only had to look at his budget to see that hardly any agricultural revenues had come in, while the government had spent 130 million dollars on pesticide subsidies' Oudejans says.[81]

Accordingly, in November 1986, a presidential decree (INPRES 3/86) banned fifty-seven broad-spectrum pesticides and declared IPM as the national pest control strategy.[82] Shortly afterwards, the subsidy on pesticides, which had been running at 85 per cent, was dropped. USAID was happy, but, according to Oudejans, the Minister of Agriculture was so furious that the cabinet decided to implement the rice IPM programme through the National Planning Board (BAPPENAS) to avoid possible obstruction by the Ministry of Agriculture. Nevertheless, IPM beat the brown plant hopper. Within five years, pesticide use in rice had fallen by 60 per cent while rice yields had increased by 13 per cent.[83]

Initially the falls in pesticide use came from the increase in price and the successful transmission of the message by the extension service: 'spray less pesticide'. Government research institutes developed blanket spraying recommendations for the extension workers to take out to the field. However, it quite quickly became clear that this top-down approach was not helping farmers make decisions based on the conditions in their own fields about how to manage their pest problems. As a result the Indonesian government, with help from FAO, set up the National IPM Programme in May 1989 to teach farmers rice-pest ecology. This was done in 'farmer field schools'. The World Bank describes them as follows:

> The farmer field school training approach represents a move away from conventional packet technologies in agricultural extension toward empowering farmers with knowledge and skills, using non-formal education methods and a field-based, experiential learning process. Farmers make their own decisions about crop management based on their experience, on local field and market conditions, and on basic IPM principles learned in farmer field school training. These principles include weekly monitoring of pest levels, conserving the natural enemies of pests, sharing information and co-ordinating control strategy with neighbouring farmers.[84]

In other words, farmer fields schools are all about getting farmers to do learning selection. The schools set out to give farmers the knowledge they need to generate novelties and make selection decisions while interacting with their neighbours. They have been very successful. Between January 1990 and May 1993 the National IPM Programme had trained over 200,000 farmers. FAO data show that these farmers had slightly higher yields despite using 36 per cent less pesticide than farmers who had not been trained.[85]

Some important lessons have been learned in the process of implementing IPM in Indonesia. First, the success of the programme was only possible because of strong support at the government level, bolstered by the World Bank. In part this came about because of successful lobbying by a product champion, Peter Kenmore, who was able to help create and nurture a favourable environment for the technology, as well as promulgate it. Second, the Indonesian experience tallied with experiences in the Philippines and the Netherlands in finding that traditionally trained extension workers did not make good facilitators in the farmer field schools. Many extensionists found that the paradigm shift required of them, to go from being an instructor who knows more than the farmer to a facilitator who assists the farmers in a learning process, was too great.[86] In addition, some extension workers sold pesticides as a private sideline and so were not necessarily motivated to help farmers reduce spraying.

People at IRRI are increasingly realising that new technologies can no longer be crafted like cathedrals and transferred to farmers as finished products. They have to be constructed by farmers in their fields. Professor Niels Röling of Wageningen Agricultural University says all agricultural scientists must enlarge their realist–positivist outlook to include the idea that reality, and hence technologies, are socially constructed.[87] IRRI's staff are trying to do this; if they are successful, their activities will become indistinguishable from those of many of the NGOs that now criticise IRRI so fiercely.

By 2000, IRRI's main attempt to develop farmer-controlled, reduced-input, site-specific technologies involved helping farmers choose how much fertiliser to add to achieve sustainable and economic yields.[88] Dr Christian Witt, a soil scientist working at IRRI, described their project 'Reaching Toward Optimal Productivity' to me in December 2000.

Our thinking has evolved a long way from the Green Revolution days. After the introduction of modern high-yielding varieties in the 1960s it was easy to increase rice yields by simply adding nitrogen fertiliser. However, we've since found that optimising fertiliser use or increasing yields above an average of 5 tonnes of grain per hectare needs farmers to use more site-specific knowledge than the current blanket fertiliser recommendations given to them by extension services. Simply telling a farmer to add x kilograms of fertiliser to a rice crop is not taking account of local differences in soils and hence differences in the amount, type and timing of fertiliser that a farmer should add to harvest a given yield. Moreover the blanket recommendations, mostly based on 'best rates' worked out by researchers from a few fertiliser response experiments conducted by researchers on experimental stations, don't take into account the fact that not all farmers want to harvest the same amount from their fields. Some farmers may want to harvest more, while others may want to minimise their risk of losing money and harvest less. It's not surprising, then, that farmers rarely follow official recommendations.

In our project we've set out to do better and to understand better the local constraints to growing more rice with less fertiliser. In 1994, IRRI, together with our NARS partners, started field trials in more than two hundred farmers' fields in six Asian countries, developing and testing a new site-specific nutrient management approach. We found we could increase yields by about 10 per cent at most sites simply by better matching the plants' requirement for nutrients with the fertiliser application. We did this by changing the timing and number of times fertiliser was added in a season, as well as adding a more balanced mix of nitrogen, phosphorus and potassium. IRRI also successfully developed and tested a simple leaf colour chart based on Japanese prototypes. This is a simple field tool that further helps farmers decide whether or not to apply nitrogen fertiliser because the greenness of rice leaves, which is what the chart measures, is a good indicator of the plant nitrogen status. What we've done is summarise all these results into a comprehensive field handbook called *Rice: Nutrient Disorders and Nutrient Management*[89] and we are now distilling this information to develop a practical pocket guide that could help extension workers or educated farmers to develop better nutrient management strategies. We realise, however, that so far we have only really looked at the technical side. We are in the position to offer solutions to site-specific nutrient management problems, but we also have to find ways of making sure these solutions match farmers' individual expectations and their ability to make changes. Choosing the right strategy involves working with the farmer in a stepwise refinement process. We're going to develop this iterative approach in pilot villages starting in 2001, before we think of larger scale extension thereafter.

From Christian Witt's description of this project it is clear that IRRI has begun to adopt a learning selection approach. The project has already realised that the knowledge it is generating is too complex, too location specific and in need of too much local adaptation to be transferred to farmers using conventional Green Revolution extension methods. Through world-class research the project has developed a 'plausible promise' of bringing real benefit to farmers. Now they need to work with farmers as first adopters, and extension staff, NGOs or representatives from co-operatives as crop consultants to learn how to adapt and improve the tools. It appears that IRRI has realised its need to change, and that its researchers have to work alongside farmers as colleagues, to ensure that excellent research does not end up on the shelf. Alternatively, it could encourage its NARES partners or NGOs to fill the role of the R&D team in our learning selection model, a course that would give them the kudos of working with a promising technology based on world-class research.

Participatory plant breeding: a sustainable solution?

Participatory plant breeding (PPB) is another area in which the CGIAR institutions might be able to combine good science with farm-level learning selection. It is also one in which NGOs could get involved. PPB is one of the main interests of the CGIAR's system-wide initiative on Participatory Research and Gender Analysis (PRGA), launched in 1996, but, as Gigi Manicad and Volker Lehmann wrote in *Biotechnology and Development Monitor*, 'it [PRGA] remains unclear if this will set a serious trend within the CGIAR. At the moment [1997] it is a marginalised activity with a budget of US$1 million.'[90] The year after they wrote this, however, PRGA received a 50 per cent budget increase.[91]

In PPB, scientists encourage farmers to resume breeding crop varieties in their fields in much the same way as they did for millennia before the Green Revolution. This time, however, the scientists add their own skills, knowledge and resources to the process. As the PRGA programme coordinator Louise Sperling points out, researchers have access to 'exotic materials' and knowledge and can screen plants for basic adaptation as well as for their response to stresses that may not be visible to farmers. This may sound straightforward but it requires the scientists involved to make a paradigm shift and expand their conventional realist-positivist outlook to include constructivism. This is a big change. As Vandana Shiva said in her book *Monocultures of the Mind*, 'uniformity and diversity are not just patterns of land use, they are ways of thinking and ways of living.'[92]

The story of MASIPAG, one of the best examples of PPB, has been told in a paper by David Frossard.[93] MASIPAG was formed in 1985 in Los Baños in the Philippines as a partnership between a group of farmers dissatisfied with the economic and environmental cost of growing HYVs with high levels of chemical inputs; a group of 'dissident, nationalist, crop scientists from the University of the Philippines'; and some social scientists from an NGO. All three groups were from the fringes of their respective professions. After meeting for a week at the University of the Philippines in Los Baños (UPLB), Frossard says the UPLB scientists were at a loss. 'How could their knowledge – intimately tied to their own scientific education and work in the Green Revolution paradigm – help farmers?' Apparently the farmers replied: 'Teach us to do what the crop institutes do. Teach us to hybridise rice.'

And so MASIPAG was born. The word, which means industrious, is an acronym for 'Farmer–Scientist Partnership for Agricultural Development' in Tagalog. The farmers involved in it appear similar to those who became innovative adopters of the SG harvester in that they were interested in experimenting with new technology and rich enough to be able to do so. The organisation began by collecting rice varieties and by 1992 it had 210 in its breeding stock, of which 87 were HYVs. At the same time, the scientists trained the farmers in the basics of hybridisation, selection and record-keeping. The learning curve was long, but eventually the farmers became competent.

Frossard writes that some 'conventional' plant breeders treated MASIPAG's claims that farmers were doing their own hybridisations with disbelief. 'You are wrong', Mang Marciano, a farmer who had given some of his land to MASIPAG for use as its research station, told them. 'You are underestimating the ability of small farmers. Scientists are limiting the capabilities of farmers. Because they are learned and studied, they belittle small farmers. Now the little farmers are trying to prove they can do the work. They are encouraged by the example of MASIPAG in producing varieties. If farmers are really interested, they can easily learn.'[94]

The tools Marciano and other MASIPAG farmer–breeders use are simple: small, sharp scissors, a pair of tweezers, a paper bag and a piece of cardboard. Using the same process that IRRI used to create the first HYVs, a farmer–breeder snips off the male parts of the rice flower with scissors to stop self-pollination and instead takes pollen from the other parent and sprinkles it on the unsnipped ovary. The paper bag is used to cover the emasculated flower to stop stray pollen fertilising the flower instead. This process is called sexual hybridisation and the resulting seed will grow to produce a hybrid with one set of chromosomes from each parent. The results of MASIPAG crosses between HYVs and traditional varieties have become popular: they taste good, are pest-resistant, and yield well with low fertiliser application rates.

Interestingly, J.V. Dennis, Jr, who carried out similar research to Frossard but in Thailand, found that some innovative farmers continued to grow traditional varieties long after the majority had discarded them in favour of HYVs. Dennis's conclusion was that the innovative farmers saw the benefits of retaining diversity. One benefit was to allow them, like the MASIPAG farmers, to give up growing HYVs in favour of alternatives, which, although Dennis does not say, could well have been HYV and traditional variety crosses.[95]

H. Brammer reported in 1980 another example of farmers continuing their age-old tradition of plant breeding by selection. He found that some farmers in Bangladesh, whose fields flooded quite deeply, had developed a taller version of IR8 by selection.[96] Although Brammer does not say how this novelty – taller IR8 plants – was generated, it must have come about either by mutation or by natural hybridisations with local landraces, given that the other alternative – diversity within IR8 itself – is unlikely.

Frossard's, Dennis's and Brammer's findings all point to the conclusion that the introduction of HYVs has not stopped farmers breeding better seeds, and in some circumstances may even have contributed to greater experimentation and biodiversity. In addition, MASIPAG shows that they can learn new techniques and become more effective breeders.

All this is very exciting because of its parallels with the open-source software movement that created Linux. For software read seed. Some farmers at least are seed 'hackers'. Although their source code – the DNA coding – is closed to them, nature itself or human intervention generates new 'hacks' by crosses and mutation, and farmers select hacks that they judge beneficial. The tantalising prospect opens up that PPB might be able to capture the power of the 'bazaar' development model in the same way that the open-source software movement has. Remember, Microsoft, the richest company in the world, with revenues nearly three times greater than all the money[97] spent every year on public-sector agricultural research in the Third World, has admitted that the bazaar model has captured more creative talent than it can afford to employ. If PPB can harness the creativity of farmer 'hackers', wouldn't this be a better and safer way of trying to double rice production in the next twenty years than relying on Big Science to pull off a second Green Revolution?

PPB is already capturing the power of the bazaar with some success. Louise Sperling reports that Rwandan bean farmers were invited to the country's central research station to evaluate finished or nearly finished conventionally produced cultivars.[98] They then chose the ones they wanted to take home with them. Subsequent research found that these farmers' choices performed better in the conditions they had been selected for than plant breeders' choices for general release as part of a national extension programme.

Sperling calls this co-operation PVS, for participatory varietal selection. It is lower down the participatory scale than the MASIPAG's approach because farmers only select novelty and don't generate it. John Witcombe, a plant breeder from the University of Bangor in Wales who has written extensively on participatory plant breeding, says that PVS is the appropriate choice where conventional breeding has produced cultivars that are suitable, and it is just a matter of farmers finding out which fit their local conditions. He adds that PPB should be used after PVS has exhausted the choice of conventionally bred varieties because PPB takes up more resources, as researchers have to interact more with farmers and spend more time to train them. PVS, in contrast, requires very few resources. In its simplest form researchers can just disseminate an assortment of seed to farmers and then rely on farmer selection and promulgation to take it from there.

PVS is becoming popular because it is a cheap way for plant-breeding institutes to gain higher rates of adoption for their cultivars among poor farmers in marginal areas. By contrast, PPB has barely begun. It is 'poorly demonstrated, and there are few examples in the literature',[99] Witcombe says, listing only three examples himself. In none of these were farmers given the tools and the breeding material to take over the whole breeding process. This allows Witcombe to conclude, 'in all [PPB] methods, plant breeders are the facilitators of the research since they have the essential understanding of the underlying genetics of parental selection and subsequent genetic segregation.'

The importance of MASIPAG is that it shows that this is wrong and that farmers can understand enough about genetics and crossing techniques to allow them to become independent of plant breeders. To paraphrase the well-known adage: 'If you give a farmer a new cultivar, you have to keep giving him cultivars every three or five years, but if you teach him to breed his own varieties he can always feed himself.' The MASIPAG type of PPB should not only be highly cost-effective in narrow economic terms but, besides making farmers more self-reliant, should help increase biodiversity,[100] two important development objectives in themselves.

Our learning selection model gives us a good chance of designing an effective PPB programme. First, it needs a meta-selection and promulgation mechanism, for, although PVS shows that farmers do not need to be trained or motivated to select and spread the best new seeds for their local conditions, the wind turbine and Linux case studies showed the value of having a way of assessing improvements and passing them on to a wider group. So, just as Netscape created mozzila.org to play this role, agricultural research institutes could consider establishing their equivalents.

Second, it needs a new source of novelty. As we noted earlier, farmers have historically relied on natural hybridisations or mutations to create novelty for them to select. However, since Asia needs to double rice production on its good land over the next twenty years, ways need to be found of speeding up the novelty generation process. Drawing on the University of California's research with a genetically diverse population of barley, Tryvge Berg from the Agricultural University of Norway suggests that plant breeders should create breeding populations with a very high evolutionary potential and grow them in farmers' fields. He writes:

> The immediate outcome … will be unadapted everywhere and is likely to yield poorly. With time, however, recombinations and natural sorting will improve the adaptation, and, according to the Californian experience,

narrow the [yield] gap with commercial varieties. The long term outcome will be populations that outperform commercial varieties in disease resistance and yield stability and that may be used as a source of artificial selection for high-yield.[101]

I imagine that Berg thought that researchers would be in control of growing the diverse breeding populations and subsequent artificial crosses and selection. But what if farmers were given these populations and taught how to make artificial crosses at any stage? If this were possible there could be thousands of 'barefoot' plant breeders working in thousands of locations producing a huge amount of novelty. Research institutes could then concentrate on producing the breeding material for the novelty generation. Designer plants, like IRRI's new plant type, could be part of this. Another role for formal research centres could be to facilitate an information exchange network on novelty generation and selection.

Some plant breeders are already thinking along these lines. Jean-Louis Pham, who works for IRD (Institut de Recherche pour le Développement) in France, but is seconded to IRRI, is seeking funding for a project that would give farmers composite rice populations that have been specially doctored so that they hybridise, and therefore create novelty, at a much higher rate than would happen normally. The way this is done is by introducing a gene for male sterility into some of the plants in the composite population, either by manual hybridisation or by genetic engineering. (Genetic engineering has the advantage that it allows the male sterility gene to be inserted into an elite line without introducing unwanted genetic material that would occur with a traditional cross.) Male sterility automates the breeding process because it means no one has manually to snip off the male parts of the flower. The male sterile flowers are naturally cross-pollinated and produce hybrid seed. The male sterile gene is introduced in such a way that the progeny are fertile and hence fertilise themselves, thus preventing the novelty from being diluted away by further cross-pollination. Farmers can then select seed from the plants showing desirable characteristics and continue to plant and select until they have a population in which the novelty is fixed.

CAMBIA, the Centre for the Application of Molecular Biology to International Agriculture, is working on similar lines. It is a not-for-profit research institute in Canberra, Australia, which was set up by

Richard Jefferson, its executive director, in 1991 to develop and package the novelty generation and selection tools that biotechnology is making possible so that farmers and local researchers can use them and not just scientists working for multinational companies like Monsanto. For example, under Jefferson's leadership CAMBIA is trying to create composite populations of rice plants, but with a difference. As Paul Keese, a virologist and molecular biologist working at CAMBIA explained to me, much of the genetic variability in the plant world comes not from the presence or absence of genes, but from gene regulation, the technical term that describes the extent to which genes are 'turned on' and in which plant tissues. He and Andrzej Kilian, the head of CAMBIA's functional genomics unit, are modifying a technology developed by Jim Haseloff from Cambridge University to create a composite population of rice plants with genes that have been turned on, or made functional, that would not normally be. 'In Berg's composite barley populations and Pham's composite rice populations, the plants are still barley and rice plants', Keese says. 'However, the genome of rice has 25,000 genes, nearly all of which are the same as for an oak tree or any other plant for that matter. We could grow a tree from a rice seed if we knew which genes to turn on.'

There will not be any trees in the composite population that Jefferson and Keese envision but some of the rice plants will look very different. 'If we were designing a rice plant from scratch then we might want to have broad leaves on the lower nodes that quickly cover the ground and suppress weeds. Using our technique we can randomly turn on genes in this part of the plant and, as rice has the genes to grow broad leaves, sooner or later we should get lucky.' Rather than do selection themselves, Kilian and Keese want to provide breeders and farmers with populations of these 'turned on' plants to allow them to select the novelties they want. The power of this approach, says Keese, is that it allows farmers and breeders to scan the evolutionary history of a crop like rice and re-create a vast range of novelty that might have existed at some point but died out almost immediately through natural selection. Such novelty might be of huge benefit because what a farmer requires from a crop can be the opposite of what a plant needs to survive in nature.

Transactivation, the technical term for the technology that creates such novelty, is just one of the tools that CAMBIA is developing.

The ethos of the institute is built around an awareness of the need for local involvement in achieving lasting solutions to agricultural problems. Importantly, CAMBIA's ethos is based on a problem and solution identification that reads like a summary of some of the conclusions of this chapter, as Box 7.4 shows. Rather than top-down approaches to biotechnology applied to agriculture, CAMBIA envisions a situation that empowers local researchers and producers to

---

Box 7.4 CAMBIA – an organisation set up to democratise novelty generation and selection in plant breeding using the tools of biotechnology

The Symptoms
- Food shortages
- Crop failures
- Population growth
- Environmental degradation
- Loss of biodiversity

These are often perceived as the real problems facing the world today. In fact, these are only symptoms of the real problem.

The Problem
- The real problem lies with our way of interacting with the natural world.
- Agriculture has been uncoupled from the environment. Farming practice has tried to homogenise the environment rather than embracing biodiversity.
- Local communities no longer have an active role in stewardship of the land and are excluded from a proactive role in agricultural research and development.
- New agricultural improvement technology is increasingly centralised and access to this technology is greatly restricted.
- Local communities are increasingly dependent on external technical and financial support
- This is not sustainable for environments or societies in the long-term.

Source: www.cambia.org/main/about.htm.

develop diverse, decentralised and sustainable solutions to agricultural problems. By working with CGIAR centres like the International Institute of Tropical Agriculture (IITA), where Jefferson was a director, it is co-developing and delivering its tools through links with farmers and NARES in developing countries.

Obviously, evolutionary plant breeding would be too much effort for most farmers, just as hacking is too much trouble for most computer users. However, in all the technologies we have looked at, and in the MASIPAG research, there have been 'hackers' who enjoy experimenting and are motivated by challenges rather than by money. It would be around these people that a scientist-assisted type of PPB could be built. And if their potential could be tapped, they would add *métis*, to use James C. Scott's term, to the mix, which ought to make the programme very successful. *Métis* comes from the Greek and means knowledge that can only come from practical experience.[102] After all, according to Donald Duvick of Pioneer Hybrid International, a large US seed company, yield improvements have been due at least as much to the 'tacit knowledge' of experienced breeders as the application of the principles of Mendelian genetics.[103] And what is tacit knowledge but *métis* by another name?

Conclusions

We can now answer the three questions about the Green Revolution and seed technology that we asked ourselves at the start of the chapter. The questions were:

- What is it about HYVs that Big Science could achieve such a breakthrough with seed, but not with wind turbines or flash dryers?
- What are the other types of technology where top-down development models produce such fast results?
- Could a bazaar approach have achieved such rapid rates of adoption?

First, Big Science was able to produce a breakthrough with seed-based technology because its benefits were obvious and farmers needed to be taught very little in order to benefit from it. The technology lent itself to a top-down approach because refinement, based on user knowledge and innovation that would require bottom-up feedback, was not necessary. Wind turbines and flash dryers, on the other hand, were new technologies which required their users to learn how to use them. Moreover, because they were new, the researchers who developed them did not know enough about the climatic and socio-economic conditions in which they were to be used to develop a 'finished' technology straight off, particularly as the users needed to come up with organisational innovations and cultural changes to take full advantage of them. It took wind turbine manufacturers fifteen years or so of learning from their customers' machines before they had gathered and codified enough knowledge to move from experiential learning to 'learning by modelling' in which selection decisions could be reliably made on the basis of a computer model rather than real-life experience. This time span was also required to allow the socio-economic environment for the technology to coevolve.

Second, the sorts of technologies where top-down development and transfer approaches will work are either ones where consumers do not need to use the technology, like moon rockets or nuclear power, or where consumers have little to learn or to adapt to make it work, like pharmaceuticals.

Third, the Green Revolution clearly shows that a top-down approach that can gain political support from governments can achieve much faster adoption rates than a more disparate bazaar-type development model.

The decision about which R&D paradigm to use should not, however, be based purely on the question of which model can produce the highest number of adopters in the shortest period of time. Instead the decision should be determined according to which model is likely to produce the more beneficial impact in terms of peoples' quality of life, sustainability and the protection of the natural environment.

Big Science strives for 'breakthroughs' and is good at meeting clearly defined goals like putting a man on the moon or increasing rice production by 120 per cent. However, the breakthrough did nothing to tackle the underlying problem that required the increase in food production in the first place – population growth. In fact some people argue that the Green Revolution has made things worse because it has now run out of steam and a second Green Revolution is needed to avoid the Malthusian crisis the world sidestepped thirty years ago. Big Science, with its 'miracle', merely delayed the onset of the crisis and thus delayed our finding a sustainable response to it. It therefore lost us time and, because huge environmental damage has been done in the time that was wasted, has made the crisis more acute. Moreover, a significant part of this damage was done by the 'breakthrough' itself, as it destroyed a lot of the biodiversity on which our future food supply depends.

Biotechnology is Big Science's latest breakthrough, another technical fix to enable us to continue to dominate nature and squeeze more and more from it. However, public opinion is beginning to see that we cannot continue to make larger and larger demands from the natural world forever. The increased incidence of severe storms as a result of human-induced global warming has convinced the insurance industry at least that nature is coming in through the window with a pitchfork.

Biotech companies have been able to convince governments to allow them to patent seeds by arguing that their research is necessary to feed a hungry world. If they are to invest millions, they say, they need to be able to stop others copying their results to ensure they can get a reasonable return on their capital. However, as we saw with computer software, when private companies appropriate technology in the public domain by making alterations to it and then patenting it, this 'corrupts' the technology generation systems that produced that technology in the first place. The technology generation system still practised by many farmers in developing countries is the oldest and arguably the most important one in the world since it has given us all our major food crops. Yet the biotech companies are threatening it with their anti-copying ploys like the Terminator gene.

The learning selection model suggests that if there is any hope of developing a sustainable form of agriculture that can produce more with less, it rests on nurturing farmer experimentation and innovation rather than killing it. Producing more with less means adapting technologies to the local environment rather than the other way around, and local adaptation means local learning selection. Top-down technology transfer systems where novelty generation and selection are centrally controlled cannot meet the needs of every farmer in every field. Local adaptation on a wide enough scale to have an impact requires a bazaar-type development model, as these can generate better technologies much faster than development models where learning selection is centrally controlled. This is true, as the Linux example showed, even when the company controlling the innovation has revenues larger than the GNP of some developing countries.

Paul Ehrlich, author of the book *The Population Bomb* that sold over 3 million copies, a Stanford University professor and one of the United States' most influential ecologists, developed an equation in the 1970s to describe the impact of human population on the environment. A version of this equation, called the population–resource equation, says that

$$\text{(Natural resource use)} \times \text{(technology)} = \text{(population)} \times \text{(per capita consumption).}[104]$$

Given that our natural resource base is deteriorating and world population is increasing, new technologies are needed to balance the equation if per capita consumption is not to fall. The danger is that the debate over Big Science 'solutions' like biotechnology may cause the pendulum to swing too far against science generally for this to come about. I believe that public-sector and not-for-profit research institutes like IRRI, CAMBIA and IITA have an essential contribution to make in the generation of new agricultural technologies. They can make this contribution either by generating novelties that plausibly promise to bring benefits to farmers, or by allowing farmers to generate and select novelties themselves in ways they could not do in the past. In either case the institution's R&D team would need to help keep the promise by co-developing the technology with the intended users during the adaptation phase. Private companies' R&D departments won't do this type of novelty generation and nurturing because, as this type of work creates public goods rather than private ones, there is no profit in it. But perhaps more important than generating the new technologies themselves is developing the processes and approaches that build up a synthesis of scientific and indigenous knowledge. As Jeffrey W. Bentley, a well-respected and published anthropologist put it: 'Neither green revolution technologies nor traditional agriculture are capable of feeding the world for much longer. We desperately need alternative styles of generating new technology before we eat the Earth bare.'[105]

Learning selection may be part of the answer. It offers the prospect of an exciting future in which agricultural scientists work to nurture technological development by farmers themselves. Giving farmers back control over the crops they grow and technologies they use will, I hope, also give back to farmers and their communities a feeling of responsibility for the natural resource base they rely on. And empowering farming communities may also lead to their regaining a sense of stewardship of their resources and hence limiting their population to what their land can support. Such social controls certainly existed in traditional societies when they had this responsibility.[106]

A bazaar-type evolutionary development model offers greater hope of solving the problems facing the planet – environmental degradation, hunger and population growth – than a simple centrally controlled one because it gives local people back control over their agriculture. It will therefore influence the real problem, which is the way they see and interact with the natural world. And if this is true, then the answer to the fourth question – is a bazaar-type model likely to develop technologies that are 'better'? – is clearly 'Yes'. We will explore the answer further in the next chapter.

8

How to catalyse innovation
A practical guide to learning selection

If you have read this far, I don't think I need to spend much more time arguing that the learning selection model is applicable beyond agricultural engineering. Indeed, the uncanny similarity between the learning selection approach developed for agricultural equipment and the bazaar approach developed for computer software makes a paraphrasing of Eric von Hippel's remark that 'when a model fits reality well, data fall easily and naturally into the patterns predicted' seem appropriate. How about 'when you develop a model that fits reality well you'll probably find that someone has already developed a version of it'?

In this chapter we will pull together the ideas and the findings from the case studies by answering the five questions that a journalist would ask:

1. What is learning selection?
2. Why use it?
3. When can it be used?
4. Where?
5. How do we do it?

Finally we'll look at the implications that the learning selection has for intellectual property rights.

The learning selection approach to understanding and catalysing technological change

We began the book by recognising that people have mental maps that guide their attempts to manage innovation and hence bring about technological change. We also established in the first three chapters that these maps are often faulty and as a result the management of some innovation attempts have failed and wasted millions of dollars. The wind turbine and Linux chapters in particular showed that learning selection can provide a better way both of understanding the research, development and early adoption process and of managing it. The map of the innovation process that is core to the learning selection approach is shown in Figure 8.1. The figure shows an innovation process beginning with a bright idea that individuals or small teams of researchers then develop in 'a cathedral-like' manner. While the R&D team may ask the key stakeholders – the people who will ultimately take ownership of their idea, replicate it and make it work – for some advice, they are driving the process. Joel Mokyr believes it has to be this way because the process of inventing

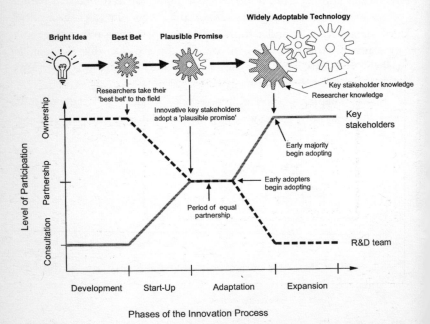

Figure 8.1 The learning selection view of the innovation process

'plausible promises' is by its nature something that 'occurs at the level of the individual'. He says that creating a plausible promise is 'an attack by an individual on a constraint that everyone else has taken for granted'.[1] It is not something that lends itself to a broad consensus approach.

At some point the R&D team crystallises the knowledge they have generated into a prototype: their 'best bet' of what the key stakeholders want. Then, in what marks the beginning of the start-up phase, they begin to demonstrate their best bet to the key stakeholders. It may take several prototype iterations before the R&D team has received and incorporated sufficient feedback for at least a few innovators to adopt it. It is this adoption, based on the belief that the new technology makes a 'plausible promise' of bringing benefit, which marks the beginning of the adaptation phase. It also marks the beginning of a period of co-development and learning selection in which the technology evolves and its fitness improves, as shown in Figure 8.2.

Learning selection is analogous to natural selection in Darwinian evolution. People make changes to a technology and then select and

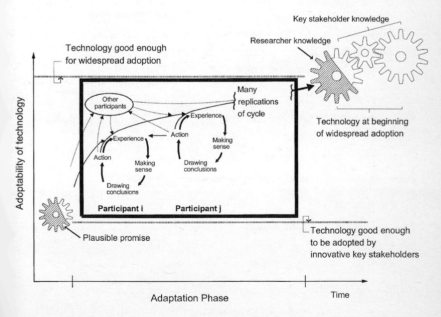

Figure 8.2 How learning selection improves the fitness, or adoptability, of a new technology during early adoption

promulgate those they find beneficial. This improves the fitness of the technology – its suitability to the environment in which it is used – and hence its market appeal. At a certain point the attributes of the technology are good enough for the second category of adopters, Rogers's early adopters, to start to show an interest. This marks the point at which the key stakeholders begin to take over ownership of the technology and market selection begins to work.

However, learning selection does not necessarily happen. It only comes about if the key stakeholders are sufficiently motivated to modify it and carry out sensible learning selection on it. They must also understand the technology well enough to do so themselves. Consequently, at least one stakeholder who understands the technology is essential as he or she must champion it and fill knowledge gaps until the other stakeholders have learned enough to take over.

The takeover also marks the beginning of the expansion phase when the technology becomes mainstream. As this happens, the people adopting the technology change from hackers (innovators) and early adopters to people who want the technology to work reliably and profitably. Increasingly in this phase, manufacturers and researchers are able to gather and codify more and more information that can be used to build predictive models. This allows them to move from 'learning by using', which requires adopters to be co-developers, to 'learning by modelling', where learning comes from virtual tests carried out on computer rather than field experience. In so doing, our learning selection model of the innovation process becomes less relevant and the conventional assumption that manufacturers or R&D departments can and do develop finished technology begins to fit better.

Advantages of the learning selection approach

To the innovators

Innovators who adopt learning selection have at least six major advantages over their counterparts who think they can develop finished technologies themselves. These are:

1. They can tap into a potentially vast pool of innovative talent 'for free'

The story of the Linux operating system showed just what is possible when inventors involve their product's users. Linus Torvalds has written only about 1.5 per cent of the coding which makes up the operating system; 98.5 per cent has been generated by hundreds of innovative adopters. The resulting program is challenging the dominance of Windows in the computer-server market, even though Microsoft was the richest company in the world by the end of 1999 with annual sales of almost $15 billion and profits outstripping those of the world's next five hundred software firms combined. Technologies that are not capable of being developed over the Internet cannot be as readily developed by their users, but, as the Danish wind turbine industry and the flat-bed dryer in Vietnam showed, user input can still make the difference between commercial success and failure.

2. They can benefit from innovations they themselves cannot develop

Some technologies require people to change their habits before they are widely adopted. Even if the design team suggests what these changes might be, the final outcome is the result of a negotiation process between the stakeholders involved and may be very different to the one the original designers had in mind. The story of the Kubota reaper in the Philippines showed that the organisational innovations that result from this negotiation process can be more important to adoption rate than almost any technical improvement.

Another example was provided by the three families in Århus who invented a co-operative wind turbine ownership structure, and then lobbied parliament for the necessary legislation and the agreement from the electric companies to make it work. Co-operatives then became the main market for wind turbines in a crucial ten-year period for the Danish industry between 1983 and 1992. Moreover, co-operative ownership has helped 10 per cent of the Danish population become shareholders in wind turbines, creating strong political support in Denmark for the technology. The importance of this public support, or rather the lack of it, is evident in the UK where a top-down development model has led to outbreaks of the not-in-my-back-yard (NIMBY) syndrome that has almost stopped new installations.

The two examples are both examples of social processes, not technical ones. Innovators who are aware of the need for this 'social construction' of their technologies through the learning selection process and seek to facilitate learning selection will be more successful then those who do not.

3. The key stakeholders work to improve the environment for the technology

When people begin to feel proprietorial towards a technology they begin to work to improve the environment for it, which is another example of the 'social construction' of a technology. One example of this was the campaign by LetsLink UK to allow people to participate in LETS without jeopardising their unemployment benefits. Another example was the campaign by the Association of Danish Wind Turbine Owners to negotiate the right for wind turbines to connect to the grid at a standard and reasonable connection fee.

4. People are more likely to adopt and recommend the technology

When users are co-developers they feel that the technology is partly theirs and are much more likely to recommend it to others. Moreover, people who are thinking about adopting an innovation find personal recommendations more convincing than scientific evaluations[2] or almost any other type of information.

5. A negative backlash of public opinion against the technology is far less likely

GM food has shown just how financially damaging consumer backlashes can be. GM food is a 'breakthrough' technology created by scientists with no input from the intended consumers, and hence no feeling of ownership. Moreover the novelties so far generated have benefited farmers, by making their crops more resistant to pest attack, not consumers. US biotech companies were able to win high-level political support for the technology by arguing that it would give the USA a lead in what is poised to be the most important new general-purpose technology in the first half of the twenty-first century. As in Denmark, the political support they won translated into regulatory changes. Now, however, the financial markets and the US government are waking up to the fact that regulations cannot make a mass market if there is no grassroots consumer support. Both GM food and the Tvind turbine in Denmark make the point that it is not technical performance that creates a successful innovation but whether people are prepared to use it. Technologies developed using learning selection, on the other hand, will not create the same shocks to the social fabric as do 'breakthrough' technologies coming from outside.

6. Research is kept relevant and rooted in practicalities

With learning selection, the R&D team does not leave the downstream, adaptive research to others. Instead it co-develops the technology with the people who are going to reproduce and use it. In so doing it gains the sort of knowledge which can only come from practical experience but which is an essential component of a successful innovation. In turn the researchers, with their own unique knowledge set, can help the key stakeholders gain the knowledge necessary to adapt and adopt the technology.

To the users

Users of the innovations developed with the learning selection approach also benefit in at least three major ways:

1. More people benefit, faster

When people understand a new technology and can adapt it to their own needs then these needs may well be met faster than if people have to wait for outsiders to do it for them. The innovation history of the flatbed dryer in Phu Tam village provided a clear example of this. Before Dr Hien introduced the dryer the villagers had no way of saving their grain from spoilage in the wet season if it rained during harvest. Hien's dryer went some way to meeting their need. Local artisans adapted and improved the dryer to make it a better match between their needs and their local resources. If the technology had not been simple enough for local people to do this no large company would have done it for them. This was clearly shown in the Philippines where international agricultural machinery manufacturers have shown themselves interested only in providing new technology for rich customers who can afford to pay for the long supply chain and the dealership network. Moreover, the Monsanto and Microsoft case histories both show that companies innovate primarily to boost their profits rather than to benefit the consumer. In addition, by seeking to restrict others from innovating, these companies have restricted the rate at which technology evolves.

2. People are empowered

People prefer to understand the changes that are taking place around them and to have some influence over them. One indicator of poverty

Box 8.1 A socially responsible framework for the application of technology developed by workers at Lucas

Essential for a successful learning selection approach

1. The product and processes should be such that they can be controlled by human beings rather than the reverse.
2. Simple, safe, robust design should be regarded as a virtue rather than complex 'brittle' systems.
3. The nature of the product should be such as to render it as visible and understandable as possible and compatible with its performance requirements.
4. In the manufacture of products, and in their use and repair, one should be concerned not merely with production but with the reproduction of knowledge and competence.
5. The production should assist co-operation between people such as producers and consumers … rather than induce primitive competition.
6. The product should be designed in such a way as to make it reparable.

Desirable characteristics of a learning selection approach

7. The nature of the products and their means of production should be such as to help and liberate human beings rather than constrain, control and physically or mentally damage them.
8. The means by which it is produced, used and repaired is non-alienating.
9. The product and processes should be regarded as important more in respect of their use value than their exchange value.
10. Products and processes should be regarded as part of culture, and as such meet the cultural, historical and other requirements of those who will build and use them.
11. Products should be considered for their long-term characteristics rather than short-term ones.
12. The products should be such as to assist minorities, disadvantaged groups and those materially and otherwise deprived.
13. The process by which the product is identified and designed is itself an important part of the process.

14. Products for the Third World which provide for mutually non-exploitive relationships with the developed countries are to be advocated.
15. The process of manufacture, use and repair should be such as to conserve energy and materials.
16. The manufacturing process, the manner in which the product is used and the form of its repair and final disposal should be ecologically desirable and sustainable.

Source: Adapted from Cooley, 1995.

is the degree of control people have over their lives. Empowerment leads to people enjoying a higher quality of life.

3. The solutions found are more ethical

Lucas Aerospace makes components for warplanes among other things. In his article 'The Myth of the Moral Neutrality of Technology'[3] Mike Cooley, a former Lucas employee, tells how he and his fellow workers tried to get the company to adopt a socially responsible, ethical framework within which technology generally, and new technologies in particular, might be applied. They created a framework with twenty guidelines, most of which are shown in Box 8.1. When I first read the list I was amazed at just how relevant the guidelines are to the learning selection approach. I have divided the relevant guidelines into those that are essential to a successful learning selection approach and those that are desirable. The fact that the Lucas workers' charter identifies some of the key requirements of the learning selection approach suggests that the learning selection approach ought to produce ethical results. More directly, if research scientists have to work with the people affected by their technology, as learning selection requires them to do, they are less likely to behave in the way described by Albert Speer in his book *Inside the Third Reich*: 'Basically, I exploited the phenomenon of the technician's often blind devotion to his task. Because of what appeared to be the moral neutrality of technology, these people were without any scruples about their activities.'[4]

Lucas Aerospace rejected the proposals for the ethical framework because they thought it would damage the company commercially, and Mike Cooley was sacked. Learning selection runs the risk of being rejected for similar reasons even though Linux and the Danish wind turbine industry both show that a co-operative, open-technology development model can out-compete a competitive and closed one. Linux in particular shows that companies can do well without having to patent or appropriate a technology – Red Hat, a company selling Linux software, had a market capitalisation of $6 billion in August 1999. McDonald's, the hamburger chain, shows this too. It sells a simple and easily copied product and yet has made a great deal of money by becoming well known for consistency and affordability.

When does the learning selection approach work?

The learning selection approach will work and provide the advantages listed above if the following three conditions can be met:

1. Early adopters are motivated to modify the innovation

There are two reasons why people might attempt to modify innovations: either they want to, or they have to.

Most people do not want to have to modify their corkscrews, cars, computers or computer operating systems to make them work. Few people bother to learn to operate their video recorders to their full potential: they simply are not interested in investing the time and the effort. However, within any adopter population is a small group of innovators who are interested in new things and get a kick out of experimenting with them. Whether these innovators actually become co-developers and make real improvements to the technology depends on how well they understand it.

You or I do not have to modify our corkscrews because if they work on one cork they will work on the next because, by and large, one cork is very much like the next. Farmers would very much like to be in the same situation with the technologies they use. They would like to plant the same seed every year and receive the same high price from it for the same yield. However, they operate in a changing and unpredictable world. Changing pest populations and market fluctuations mean that they have to change their practices and technologies over time. They will therefore want to be able to understand, control and adapt them, and are consequently likely to be responsive to a learning selection approach. Learning selection is therefore applicable to innovations in areas where technologies and practices need to evolve over time.

2. Adopters are able to modify the innovation

As we have seen, there are two reasons why the key stakeholders may not be able to modify an innovation: (1) it is protected by a patent that prevents them modifying it, or (2) it is protected by a 'natural patent' – that is, it is too complex, difficult to understand, or requires tools and skills that the key stakeholders do not possess. Technologies that fall into the latter category tend to be mature, like the current generations of wind turbines, motor cars or nuclear power. Pharmaceutical drugs provide another example. They require hundreds of millions of dollars to develop and bring to the market, and users have little scope to understand or interact with the knowledge embodied in the pills they take.

3. Evaluation of novelty is possible

Selection decisions based on open, agreed and objective criteria are necessary for learning selection to work. This is much easier with some types of technology than others. With computer software, for example, a patch can be tested within a matter of minutes. With LETS, on the other hand, the introduction of an innovation like a maximum overdraft limit may take months or years to establish, and then the results may not be determinable by objective means. Whether the innovation worked or not will depend on whether the members of that LETS thought it did. In other words, selection decisions will be made by reaching consensus among the group. This means that learning selection approaches will be harder to implement and take longer when applied to social innovations in comparison with technical ones.

The scope of learning selection

Learning selection seems to be more suitable for technical innovations than for organisational ones: LETS was the only organisational innovation we considered. However, since organisational innovations operate in social settings that are indeterminate and erratic, the people who interact with them will almost certainly need to modify them to achieve best results. It is therefore not surprising that a recent report from the European Bank for Reconstruction and Development (EBRD) shows that learning selection has worked better than top-down methods in countries adopting and adapting democratic institutions.[5] In the study, EBRD's researchers set out to correlate the results of democratic reform in eastern Europe and the states of the former Soviet Union with the nature of the governments that were established in each country after 1989. They found that, contrary to the conventional wisdom that the successful adoption of reform required strong governments with the power to act wisely and decisively against opponents, governments which went slowly and sought consensus achieved much more. Estonia, Hungary and Latvia all made significant progress in reform with relatively weak prime ministers, while Russia, Belarus and Azerbaijan, which have strong presidential systems, largely failed. The moral is that you have to take the public with you. You cannot succeed, in the EBRD's words, 'if you concentrate political power in the hands of committed reformers and insulate them from the constraints of political competition'.[6]

EBRD's finding is exciting because, when taken together with the LETS chapter, it suggests that our learning selection approach may be applicable beyond what one normally considers as the technological world (machines, seeds, computer software). Learning selection may also be a useful tool for inducing changes in organisations ranging in complexity from small companies to whole countries. However, although this is an area for further elaboration, it is clearly beyond the scope of this book.

How to launch a learning selection innovation process

This section is written for a R&D manager working in the public or private sector.

1. Start with a plausible promise

The first step towards inducing change through learning selection is to produce a prototype that convinces potential stakeholders that it can evolve into something that they really want. A prototype is necessary because experience shows that it is difficult for the product champion to enlist co-developers if the whole project is abstract and up in the air. The researchers' 'best bet' prototype may have to go through several iterations before potential stakeholders are really convinced it makes a 'plausible promise' of being of benefit to them. It is this plausible promise that motivates the key stakeholder participation crucial to learning selection.

The plausible promise does not need to be refined or polished: it can be buggy and incomplete. In fact, the less finished it is, the more scope there is for the stakeholders to innovate and thus gain ownership of the technology. Yet the more problems there are, the greater are the chances that the key stakeholders will give up in frustration. A delicate balance must be found.

2. Find a product champion

The second step is to find a product champion. He or she needs to be highly motivated and have the knowledge and resources to sort problems out. Someone from the R&D team that developed the plausible promise is likely to be suitable because they are likely to have both the necessary technical knowledge and the motivation, as they already have a stake in the technology. He or she must also have good people and communication skills as, in order to build a development community, they will need to attract people, interest them in what they are doing, and keep them happy working for the common cause. Their personality is therefore crucial.

3. Keep it simple, stupid (KISS)

Don't attempt to dazzle people with the cleverness and ingenuity of the prototype's design. As the Danish wind turbine story showed, a plausible promise should be simple, flexible enough to allow revision, and robust enough to work well even when not perfectly optimised. The contemptuous comments of your colleagues don't matter. Your potential co-developers' needs and knowledge levels do. For example, if you are designing a combine harvester and you know the manufacturers and farmers you'll be working with are familiar with a certain type of thresher, then use that in your design, even if it is not the most elegant solution technically. As someone once said: 'A complex system that works is invariably found to have evolved from a simple system that worked.'[7]

4. Work with innovative and motivated partners

Allow the participants in your learning selection process to select themselves through the amount of resources they are prepared to commit. Advertise or write about your plausible promise in the media, on the Internet, or by doing field demonstrations, and then wait for people to make the effort to contact you. Don't give enquirers anything with a resale value for free. For example, if your prototype has an engine, then charge the market value for it. Otherwise people may be motivated to adopt in order to get something for nothing. In addition, people generally value something more highly if they have paid for it and they will be more committed to sort out the problems that emerge.

On the other hand you must make it clear to the first adopters that they are adopting an unperfected product and that they are working with you as co-developers. You need to reassure them that you will be contributing your own resources to the project and will not abandon them with a white elephant. You should be prepared to offset some, but not all, of the risk they are taking in working with you. Getting the balance right is very important here too.

5. Work in a pilot site or sites where the need for the innovation is great

Your co-developers will be influenced by their environment. Their motivation levels will be sustained for longer if they live or operate in an environment where your innovation promises to provide great benefits. In addition, they are more likely to receive encouraging feedback from members of their community.

6. Set up open and unbiased selection mechanisms

(i) *The product champion/selector*   Once you have the key stakeholders working with you and generating novelties, you need ways of selecting and promulgating the beneficial ones. Initially the product champion usually plays this role. An effective selector must be able and prepared to recognise good design ideas from others. This means that, if he or she is also the inventor, they must be 'low at the ego end' and thus able to accept that others might have better ideas.

Very few people are capable of simultaneously championing their product and selecting novelties. This is because to be good at the former they need to believe deeply in the product's benefits and able to defend it against criticism. To be effective selectors, on the other hand, they need to keep an open mind and be able to work with others to question fundamental design decisions.

Both the LETS and software chapters showed that if a product champion defends the technology too strongly, or shows bias, then 'forking' occurs and the disaffected person or group branches off on their own to do what they felt prevented from doing by the selector. It is good to have people test alternative design paths, but, if it is done in frustration or spite, cliques form, making any comparison and subsequent selection between rival branches difficult. Creative talent is split and energies can be dissipated in turf wars.

(ii) *Alternative selection mechanisms*   Even if the product champion can be open-minded and unbiased, he or she may have problems convincing others. One option is to set up a review mechanism that is well respected by your key stakeholder community. The Risø Wind Turbine Test Centre played this role very successfully in the evolution of the Danish wind industry. A complementary review mechanism which started working before Risø was the newsletter *Naturlig Energi* published by the Association of Danish Wind Turbine Owners (DV). Every month *Naturlig Energi* published data on the performance of different manufacturers' machines which allowed potential customers to select the best. This, in turn, encouraged manufacturers to improve their turbines continually to remain competitive. With Linux, Torvalds used a type of peer review. Rather than evaluate every modification himself, he based his decisions on the recommendation of people he trusted and on whether people were already using the patch (modification) successfully. He in fact played a similar role to that of an editor of an academic journal who sends submitted articles for peer review but retains final control over what is published and what is not.

7. Don't release the innovation too widely too soon

For the innovation to evolve satisfactorily, the changes the stakeholders make to it need to be beneficial. As those generating the novelties will have gaps in their knowledge, product champions should restrict the number of co-developers so that they can work with them effectively. When people show enthusiasm for a prototype it is very tempting to release it as widely as possible, but this entails jumping from the *start-up* to the *expansion* phase and missing out the *adaptation* one. This should be resisted.

However promising the technology might appear, there are many things that can and will go wrong. First adopters need to be aware of this and have ready access to the product champion. Otherwise their enthusiasm will quickly turn to frustration and the product champion will end up defending the technology against their criticisms when the problems appear. Once the product champion becomes defensive, he or she will be far less useful at sorting out problems.

8. Don't patent anything unless it is to stop someone else trying to privatise the technology

In learning selection, people co-operate with each other because they believe that all will gain if they do. The process is therefore seriously damaged if one person or group tries to gain intellectual property rights over what is emerging, as the Microsoft, Monsanto, Landsman and US wind turbine manufacturers' case histories all show.

Linus Torvalds called the attempt to make money from an innovation at the expense of other people 'corruption'. He was right for two reasons. First, by discouraging or preventing others from working on the technology, the privatisation-of-the-benefits bid immediately reduces the novelty-generation rate and thus slows down future development and the flow of ideas. Second, privatisation corrupts the way the technology develops, so that, as the Microsoft and Monsanto examples showed, novelties are generated and included that work against the interests of the user. Creative talent was turned against the interests of farmers to develop the Terminator technology.

There are two ways that a technology can be protected against privatisation. One way is to take out a Statutory Invention Registration, or SIR, under US patent law. This gives the inventor no legal rights but prevents anyone else patenting the technology by declaring it to be prior art for the purpose of future patent claims. The second way is copyleft, under which Linux is registered. This protects users' rights to use, copy and change the technology. It is better than SIR from the learning selection perspective because it requires those who use the technology and then change it to pass along to others the freedom to further copy and change their work. Because it recognises the intellectual contribution of others, copyleft is the ethically correct approach to take for any technology, like computer software or seeds, that began in the public domain.

9. Realise that culture makes a difference

Danish wind turbine manufacturers took out fewer patents than their US competitors because Danish culture places a high value on co-operation. This cultural understanding meant that the Danes did not have to resort to SIR or copyleft to create a common intellectual property rights regime necessary for learning selection to take place. American innovation culture is individualistic and favours isolated 'cathedral-building'. This meant that innovators in US wind firms were actively discouraged from talking to their counterparts in other companies. This restricted learning selection. As a result, no typical 'American-style' design emerged. Instead, individual companies were on their own, each striving for its own 'breakthrough'. When they failed to achieve one, something that has to be expected in the infancy of an industry, surviving firms generally failed to learn from the failed firms' experience and to benefit from what they had achieved which was good.

10. Know when to let go

Product champions need to become personally involved and emotionally attached to their projects to do their jobs properly. This makes it easy for them to go on flogging dead horses long after it has become clear to everyone else that the technology is not going to succeed. Equally, project champions can continue trying to nurture their babies long after they have grown up, entered the expansion phase and proper market selection has begun. It is therefore a good idea to put a time limit on the product champion's activities. If they are working as part of a team, then his or her manager should offer regular counselling.

Intellectual property rights and learning selection

Societies provide protection for intellectual property so that inventors who have invested time and money in R&D to generate 'plausible promises' have an opportunity to profit from their novelty, free from competition for a period of time. However, patent systems in general assume two things. One is that inventors are only motivated by profit. The other is that developing a non-obvious, useful and unprecedented novelty costs enough to justify preventing others copying it for seventeen years. The US patent system also assumes that the patent examiners have sufficient knowledge of 'prior art' to assess whether the application in front of them constitutes something that is really new. The European system, by contrast, allows competitors some time to demonstrate that the invention is already in use, or rather obvious.

As we have seen, by providing legal support for people seeking to appropriate ideas to themselves that nearly always build on the work of others, patenting undermines the communitarian ethos necessary for successful learning selection. This is a somewhat surprising conclusion given the widespread belief, written into the US Constitution, that patents 'promote the progress of science and the useful arts by securing for a limited time to authors and inventors the exclusive right to their respective writings and discoveries.' One reason for this discrepancy is that, as our case studies have shown, innovators are often motivated by things other than pure profit: the Linux and wind turbine case studies showed that ideology and peer-group recognition were important motivators too. Similarly, my experience with the stripper harvester showed that the first adopters of a new technology are prepared to invest a very large amount of time and effort in sorting out problems and inventing solutions which they are then happy to give away.

Patents can therefore stifle rather than encourage innovation. This is not a new problem. In 1882, the American Supreme Court, when ruling on the matter of boat-propeller technology, wrote:

> Such an indiscriminate creation of exclusive privileges tends rather to obstruct than to stimulate invention. It creates a class of speculating schemers who make it their business to watch the advancing wave of improvement, and gather its foam in the form of patented monopolies, which enable them to lay a heavy tax on the industry of the country, without contributing anything real to the advancement of the arts.[8]

Box 8.2 describes the speculative froth growing on the Internet wave.

Box 8.2   Patenting the Internet creates a 'firestorm in cyberspace'[9]

Early in 2000, a serious dispute broke out over the patenting of Internet technologies. It was centred on Amazon, the largest Internet bookseller, and its successful court case against its competitor, Barnes & Noble. Jeff Bezos, Amazon's chief executive, was granted a patent for 'one-click ordering' which allows customers to order something on-line with one click of the mouse button. Tim O'Reilly of O'Reilly Technical Books believed that the patent should never have been allowed. 'It's a completely trivial application of cookies, a technology that was introduced several years before Amazon filed for their patent' he said. 'To characterise "1–Click" as an "invention" is a parody. Like so many software patents, it is a land grab, an attempt to hoodwink a patent system that has not gotten up to speed on the state of the art in computer science.'[10]

O'Reilly wrote an open letter to Jeff Bezos on 28 February 2000 and invited Amazon's customers to sign if they felt like him. By the next morning 1,000 people had endorsed the letter and this quickly grew to 10,000. The result was that Bezos and O'Reilly met face to face to talk about the issue.

By making an analogy with farming, O'Reilly was able to convince Bezos that business patents on Internet technology would seriously obstruct innovation. 'If you take from the soil and don't give anything back, crop yields eventually decline', O'Reilly said.

> If you look at the computer industry (and in fact most industries that rely on proprietary roadblocks to innovation), they resemble slash-and-burn agriculture. You strip the soil of its nutrients and move on. A fertile new field is developed, usually by people on the fringes of commercial activity, who are building for the love of it. There is a rich soil of ideas, the shared heritage of all practitioners in the field. Innovation comes naturally, since anyone can build on what has gone before.... As commercial activity moves in, the field is fenced off. Innovations are no longer con-tributed back but are hoarded within corporations. Imitation is still possible, but requires re-implementation from scratch, which raises the barrier to entry. Companies start to see ideas as scarce resources that need to be protected (and yes, they are getting

scarcer, though no one seems to ask why), and eventually they start suing each other to keep others from copying what they've done.... In short, hoarding of ideas may lead to short-term advantage for your company, but long term, it's bad for the environment … an environment that you yourself depend on.

As a result of Bezos's conversation with O'Reilly, Bezos published an open letter on the Amazon web page in which he called for 'meaningful (perhaps even radical) patent reform'. He then went on to suggest that patent law be changed to recognise that there were fundamental differences in intellectual property in terms of the cost of R&D and this should be reflected in the length of the monopoly the patent granted. Bezos also suggested that because the 'prior art' of Internet technologies had not yet been well codified, there should be a short public comment period that would allow the Internet community to oppose any patent. This suggestion would bring US patent law more in line with European law, which does allow an opposition period.

What reforms are required to patent law to provide a more favourable environment to learning selection? Eliminating patenting completely is not an option because not all innovation can be advanced by learning selection. For example, a top-down development model with patenting is necessary for the development of modern drugs. Not even the most innovative of users wants to risk a 'suck it and see' experiential learning exercise with a new medicine that has not been all but perfected. Developing and bringing a new drug to market is now estimated to cost $1 billion. Without patent protection the pharmaceutical industry would not spend this amount of money, and consumers in developed countries would almost certainly have fewer and less-advanced drugs from which to choose.

On the other hand, we need to move away from the current situation where the only criteria for granting patents are usefulness; not being obvious; lack of 'prior art'; and who gets through the door of the patent office first. In addition, there needs to be some sort of public-good criterion. Consider the expensive research being carried out in the race to introduce apomixis – the ability that some plants like blackberries have to reproduce clones of themselves – into food crops. If a public sector organisation like the International Institute for Tropical Agriculture (IITA) wins the race then the technology could be used, for example, to allow farmers to grow hybrid maize that can be replanted the following season with the same yield potential. However, if a multinational seed company wins, which is more likely given their larger research budgets, then they will most likely use the patent to stifle the use of the technology by the public sector. After all, if farmers can save hybrid seed it would threaten the company's seed sales and revenues. Granting the commercial seed company the patent could work against the public good. In this case, it would deny poor farmers in developing countries access to better seed.

The idea that science should serve the public good was behind the joint statement made in March 2000 by President Clinton and the British Prime Minister, Tony Blair. It followed the breakdown of negotiations between a private company, the Celera Corporation, and a public-sector consortium of American and British academic centres racing to map the human genome. Clinton and Blair said that all scientists should have free access to the map of the human genome to help develop new medicines for the good of humanity, even if the private sector had paid for some of the research. The statement led to a 25 per cent fall in the shares of biotechnology companies within a few days,[11] reducing their value by billions of dollars.

Differing opinions over what can be patented and by whom has had other far-reaching consequences. In November 1999, the World Trade Organisation (WTO) talks in Seattle collapsed mainly because developing countries were unhappy about the terms of trade between rich and poor countries.[12] One of the developing countries' main concerns was the WTO's Trade Related Aspects of Intellectual Property Rights (TRIPs) provisions, which require them to recognise foreign companies' patents on inventions based on crops developed by thousands of years of communitarian farmer innovations in their own countries (see Box 7.2).

The debate over ownership of the technologies that have built the Internet is just beginning. In 1998 a US judge ruled that business methods based on communal technologies could be patented. However, a Harvard law professor, Lawrence Lessing, believes that such patents threaten to destroy the freewheeling culture that helped create the Internet. 'This is the goose', Lessing[13] said in March 2000 when he described the bazaar development model that created Linux and the Internet; 'it laid the golden egg.' He believes that corporate lawyers are trying to patent the goose, build a legal fence around it, and then will wonder what happened to the eggs. For the Internet, read any learning selection development effort.

The outcome of the current debate on intellectual property rights and patent law will have a huge impact on the degree to which technology can be democratised in the future. By giving those arguing for changes to patent law the theoretical underpinning they need to win the day, the learning selection model and the evolutionary theory on which it is based can help ensure that the golden goose stays alive, healthy and free.

Notes

Chapter 1

1. Burmese names have been changed.
2. The team I led that developed the stripper-gatherer comprised Cesar Tado, Philip Cedillo, Teody Carandang, Manny Eseo and Marichu Cabungcal. Graeme Quick was Division Head.
3. IRRI, 1993.
4. Scott, 1998, p. 3.
5. See Clark, 1995; Biggs, 1989; Chambers and Jiggins, 1986.
6. Kaimowitz et al., 1989.
7. For example, see the seminal paper 'Farmer-back-to-Farmer: A Model for Generating Acceptable Agricultural Technology' by Rhoades and Booth (1982).
8. Diamond, 1987, p. 34.
9. Diamond, 1987, p. 34.
10. Röling, 1996, p. 6.
11. Ruthenberg, 1985, p. 110.

Chapter 2

1. Collinson and Tollens, 1994.
2. Patiño et al., 1999.
3. The phases of the innovation process were suggested by Prof. Lee Sechrest as part of the analytical framework for an IAEG project, 'Factors affecting the adoption of CGIAR technologies', based on unpublished work by R.K. Yin.
4. The 'safe' moisture content of paddy in the tropics is 14 per cent (wet base) which is the equilibrium moisture content of paddy when the air is 30°C and has a relative humidity of 75 per cent.
5. All moisture contents quoted are wet base.
6. NAPHIRE, 1990a; 1990b.
7. Based on an annual utilisation rate of 51 days per year (Bulaong et al., 1992).
8. Bulaong et al., 1992.
9. NAPHIRE, 1992.
10. E-mail from Dr Arnold Elepano, 20 September 1999.
11. Andales, 1996.
12. NAPHIRE, 1994.
13. E-mail from Dr Arnold Elepano, 20 September 1999.
14. Bulaong et al., 1992.
15. Andales, 1996.
16. The break-even usage rate or break-even point is the annual

usage rate where the benefits earned exactly equal the costs of using and paying for the machine.

17. Personal communication with Eng. Salvador Albia, owner and manager of Tropics Agro-Industries, Naga City, Bicol, a major manufacturer of flash dryers.
18. Personal communication with Dr Dante de Padua, IRRI Consult-ant and dryer expert, 1998.
19. Andales, 1996
20. Calculated from my survey of ten flash dryers.
21. UNDP and UPDAE, 1970.
22. Personal communication with Dr Dante de Padua, 1998.
23. Air is typically heated to 15°C above ambient compared to 90°C above ambient in the flash dryer.
24. IRRI, 1970.
25. Manalo, 1973.
26. E-mail from Dr Dante de Padua, April 1998.
27. Flue gasses from the inclined-grate furnace are mixed with am-bient air to heat it; this is then blown straight through the grain. Rice-hull ash in the flue gasses is called fly ash.
28. The colleague was Dr Cesar Tado, Philippine Rice Research Institute, Muñoz, Nueva Ecija.
29. Personal communication with Mr A. Delicana, 1997.

Chapter 3

1. Von Hippel, 1988, p. 3.
2. Nelson, 1987; Mokyr, 1990; Clark et al., 1995.
3. Hien, 1996.
4. Dawkins, 1995, p. xi.
5. Wet patches occur because as grain dries it becomes easier for the drying air to pass through it. Differential drying rates are the result.
6. Rogers, 1995.
7. Peters and Waterman, 1982, p. 203.
8. Douthwaite, 1999.
9. Layton et al., 1972, p. 3.
10. Rogers, 1995.
11. Average farm size in the Philip-pines in 1991 was 2.17 ha (IRRI, 1993).
12. Von Hippel, 1988.
13. Rogers, 1995.
14. Mokyr, 1990.
15. Leonard, 1995, p. 84.
16. Personal communication with Dr Cristina David, Philippine Insti-tute for Development Studies and member of CGIAR Impact Assessment and Evaluation Group (IAEG) board.
17. Omerod, 1998.
18. Mongkoltanatas, 1986.
19. Krishnasreni and Kiatwat, 1998.

Chapter 4

1. Bord na Mona, 1999a.
2. McWilliams, 1991.
3. Arlidge, 1999.
4. Report by the British Govern-ment's Climate Impact Program-me, *Guardian*, 25 November 1999.
5. Calculated from 30 August 1999 e-mail to author from Paul Cullen, North West station man-ager, stating that Bellacorick is a 2 × 20 MW power station, and information from McDonald (1998) that a 120 MW peat power station produces 634,000 tonnes of carbon dioxide.
6. Calculated from 30 August 1999 e-mail to author from Paul Cullen, North West station manager stating that Bellacorick power station produces about 200 GWh per year and from Bord na Mona (1999b) stating that output of Bellacorick wind farm is 17 GWh per annum.

7. Gipe, 1996.
8. *Irish Times*, 1997.
9. Gipe, 2000.
10. Calculated from Paul Gipe's (1996) estimate that the 3,500 MW of installed wind turbine capacity in 1994 generated 6 TWh.
11. According to Bord na Mona (1999b) Ireland generated 17 TWhrs in 1995.
12. Calculations from Andersen (1998) estimate that 3.3 TWh corresponds to 2.8 million tonnes of CO_2 emissions.
13. Estimate based on figures supplied by BTM Consult and quoted in Karnøe and Garud (1998).
14. *Windkraft Journal*, 2000.
15. Karnøe and Garud, 1998.
16. British Wind Energy Association, 1999.
17. Karnøe and Garud, 1998.
18. Andersen, 1999.
19. Mokyr, 1990.
20. Tranæs, 1997.
21. Mokyr, 1990.
22. Karnøe and Garud, 1998.
23. Tranæs, 1997.
24. E-mail to the author from Eize de Vries on 14 October 1999.
25. Richard Douthwaite, 1996.
26. Karnøe, 1993.
27. Personal communication with Flemming Tranæs, 1999.
28. Personal communication with Flemming Tranæs, 1999.
29. Karnøe, 1993, p. 76.
30. Mokyr, 1990, p. 154.
31. Karnøe and Garud, 1998.
32. Personal communication with Flemming Tranæs, 1999.
33. Danish Wind Turbine Manufacturers Association, downloaded from www.windpower.dk/tour/econ/index.htm.
34. *Renewable Energy World*, May 1999.
35. McKie, 1999.
36. As quoted by Richard Douthwaite, 1996, p. 203.
37. Personal communication with Flemming Tranæs, 1999.
38. Individual turbine owners were paid less because the utilities argued that they should receive some compensation for supplying the owners' electricity when the wind was not blowing.
39. Karnøe and Garud, 1998.
40. Karnøe and Garud, 1998.
41. Stoddard as quoted by Karnøe and Garud (1998).
42. Karnøe and Garud, 1998.
43. Andersen, 1993.
44. Karnøe and Garud, 1998.
45. Vestas Wind Systems, agricultural transport equipment; Nordtank, water and oil tanks; and Bonus, irrigation equipment (Karnøe and Garud, 1998).
46. Gipe, 1996.
47. Gipe, 1996.
48. Rosenberg, 1982.
49. Andersen, 1998.
50. Based on data from an e-mail from Eize de Vries to the author on 1 November 1999.
51. Based on data from Andersen, 1998.
52. The Public Utility Regulatory Policies Act (PURPA), part of the National Energy Act of 1978, attempted to foster the adoption of renewable energy resources in the USA by compelling US electricity companies to buy electricity from independent producers at fair prices. Tax credits were a further incentive and in California they were so high that investors found they could make profits from wind turbines that hardly generated any electricity (Karnøe and Garud, 1998).
53. Gipe, 1996.
54. Gipe, 1996, p. 66.
55. Gipe, 1996.
56. Karnøe and Garud, 1998.

57. Spurgeon, 1999.
58. Tranæs, 1997.
59. US$1 = DKK6.60 (average for 1997 as calculated at pacific. commerce.ubc.ca/xr/data.html).
60. Andersen, 1998.
61. As quoted by Tranæs, 1997, p. 8.
62. Andersen, 1998.
63. *Renewable Energy World*, 1999.
64. Lund, 1999, p. 1.
65. As quoted by Gipe, 1996, p. 123.
66. Gipe, 1996, p. 31.
67. Karnøe, 1993.
68. Gipe, 1996, p. 79.
69. Karnøe, 1993.
70. Karnøe, 1993, p. 17.
71. Florida and Kenney, 1990.
72. With an upwind tower the blades pass through the "wind shadow" of the tower every rotation. When it is in the wind shadow a blade has less force on it. A wind shadow therefore causes changes in the loads on the blades that vary on each rotation. This can cause fatigue failure of the blade, just like one can break a piece of wire by bending it backwards and forwards lots of times.
73. Gipe, 1996.
74. Gipe, 1996.
75. Stoddard, as quoted by Karnøe, 1993.
76. Stoddard, as quoted by Karnøe, 1993.
77. According to Gipe (1996) a new low-maintenance short-haul jet requires 5.5 hours of maintenance for every hour of flight.
78. Harrison and Møller, 1998.
79. As quoted in Harrison and Møller, 1998, p. 22.

Chapter 5

1. Raymond, 1997.
2. Gomes, 1999.
3. Gomes, 1999.
4. Taylor, 1999.
5. McHugh, 1998.
6. Moody, 1997, p. 3.
7. Torvalds, 1992.
8. Barr, 1998.
9. Raymond, 1997.
10. Torvalds, 1992.
11. Torvalds, 1992.
12. Torvalds, 1992.
13. Quoted in Torvalds, 1992.
14. Quoted by Moody, 1997, p. 2.
15. Michael K. Johnston, quoted by Moody, 1997, p. 8.
16. As quoted by Learmonth, 1997, p. 15.
17. www.linuxbase.org/.
18. Raymond, 1997.
19. Raymond, 1997, p. 18.
20. Winberg, 1971.
21. Netscape, 1999.
22. *Software Magazine*, 1998, p. 2.
23. Radosevich, 1998.
24. Taylor, 1999.
25. Windows 95, downloaded from www.honeycomb.net/os/oses/win95.htm.
26. McHugh, 1998.
27. Gates, 1976, p. 1.
28. Torvalds, 1998.
29. Trident, 1999.
30. As quoted by *Digital Producer Magazine*, 1999, p. 1.
31. IDC, 1999.
32. Petreley, 1998.
33. As quoted by *The Economist*, 13–19 November 1999, p. 20 (emphasis added).
34. *Software Magazine*, 1998.
35. Quoted in *Software Magazine*, 1998.
36. Taylor 1999.
37. Data from www.quicken.com/investments/quotes/?symbol=RHAT on 15 December 1999.
38. Valloppillil, 1998.
39. As quoted by Kohn, 1987, p. 1.
40. From excerpts of an interview with Linus Torvalds posted at www.tamos.net/ieee/linus.html.
41. Taylor, 1999.
42. *The Economist*, 1999.

43. Naughton, 1998.
44. Downloaded from www.intel. com.sv/pressroom/archive/ speeches/cn081099.htm.
45. Valloppillil, 1998.

Chapter 6

1. Neary and Taylor, 1998.
2. Hume, 1752.
3. Davis, 1994.
4. Richard Douthwaite, 1999a.
5. Galbraith, 1975.
6. Galbraith, 1975, p. 22.
7. Richard Douthwaite, 1999a.
8. As quoted by Richard Douthwaite, 1999a, p. 60.
9. Galbraith, 1975, p. 23.
10. *Initial Results of WIR Research in Switzerland*, Erick Hansch, International Independence Institute, Ashby, Mass., Fall 1971.
11. Fisher, 1933, p. 20.
12. As quoted by Richard Douthwaite, 1996, p. 87.
13. Seron, 1995.
14. Landsman Community Services Ltd, 1994.
15. Landsman Community Services Ltd, 1994.
16. Quoted from a posting on the Local Knowledge–Global Wisdom Email List on 25 June 1997, downloaded from www.tao.ca/ earth/lk97/archive/0112.html.
17. Projects LETS List, downloaded from www.telinco.co.uk/lets/ letslist2.htm.
18. Harlow and Toyne, 1999.
19. Quoted by Raven, 1993.
20. Downloaded from www. letslinkuk.demon.co.uk/ on 2 September 1999.
21. Landsman Community Services, Ltd, 1992.
22. Quoted by Richard Douthwaite, 1996, p. 74, from e-mail communication with Linton on 27 November, 1995.

23. Richard Douthwaite, 1996, p. 74.
24. As quoted by Jackson, 1997. 'The problem of over-accumulation: examining and theorising the structural form of LETS', *International Journal of Community Currency Research*, vol. 1, downloaded from the Internet from www. geog.le.ac.uk/ijccr/volume1/ 1mj.htm p. 1.
25. Jackson, 1997.
26. Seyfang, 1994.
27. E-mail communication between the author and Liz Shephard on 12 September 1999.
28. Landsman Community Services, Ltd, 1994, Paper No. 5.1, p. 2.
29. As quoted by Douthwaite and Wagman, 1999, p. 29.
30. Quoted by Rural Forum, 1997.
31. Richard Douthwaite, 1996.
32. Linton, 1996.
33. Seron, 1996.
34. Powell and Salverda, 1998.
35. This example is borrowed from Rural Forum, 1997, Section 9, p. 2.
36. Landsman Community Services, Ltd, 1997.
37. Powell and Salverda, 1998.
38. Yacub, 1999.
39. Downloaded from www.ratical. org/communityway/organise. html.
40. E-mail communication between the author and Michael Linton on 5 September 1999.
41. E-mail communication between the author and Michael Linton on 5 September 1999.
42. E-mail communication between the author and Richard Kay on 10 September 1999 also posted on <econ-lets>.
43. E-mail communication between the author and Lorne White on 13 September 1999 also posted on <econ-lets>.
44. E-mail communication between

the author and Nick Mack on 14 September 1999 also posted on <econ-lets>.

45. E-mail communication between the author and Nigel Leach on 10 September 1999.

46. E-mail communication between the author and Michael Linton on 5 September 1999.

47. LetsLink UK, 1999.

Chapter 7

1. *Compton's Encyclopedia*, 1999. www.optonline.com/comptons/ceo/17923_Q.html.

2. IRRI, 1993.

3. Horton and Prain, 1989, p. 302.

4. Diamond, 1997.

5. Diamond, 1997.

6. Several wild rice species carrying A genome are outcrossing, including *O. rufipogon*, which is the direct ancestor of *O. sativa*, or Asian rice (personal communication with B. Courtois, 1999).

7. Based on Anderson (1967) and Holden et al. (1993).

8. Quoted by Diamond, 1997, pp. 144–5.

9. Quoted by Diamond, 1997, pp. 145–6.

10. This example comes from Prindle, 1996.

11. Collins, 1914.

12. Richards, 1993.

13. Anderson, 1967, p. 62.

14. Allard, 1988.

15. Shiva, 1996, p. 1.

16. From Harlan, 1976, and Holden et al., 1993.

17. Richard Douthwaite, 1999b.

18. Mokyr, 1990.

19. Based on data from Merrick, 1986.

20. Holden et al., 1993.

21. van Bueren et al. 1998.

22. van Bueren et al. 1998.

23. Data from a survey by Dr W.A. Russell of Iowa State University, quoted in *National Corn Handbook*. Downloaded from www.inform.umd.edu/EdRes/Topic/AgrEnv/ndd/agronomy/HYBRID_CORN_HISTORY,_DEVELOPMENT.htm.

24. Text from the Smith–Lever Act, as quoted by Rogers, 1995, p. 158.

25. Paddock and Paddock, 1967.

26. Hardin, 1994.

27. Rockefeller Foundation, 1999.

28. Kropff et al., 1994.

29. Adapted from Chambers and Jiggins, 1986.

30. Chambers and Jiggins, 1986.

31. Ruthenberg, 1985.

32. Chang, 1989.

33. Holden et al., 1993.

34. IRRI World Rice Statistics Database, 1999.

35. www.rice.ac.lk/research_disciplines5.html.

36. Fujisaka, 1993.

37. Cassman et al., 1992.

38. Conklin, 1957.

39. Chang, 1993.

40. Personal communication with B. Courtois, 1999.

41. Lianchamroon, 1992, as quoted by Anonymous, 1998a.

42. Downloaded from www.abc.net.au/science/slab/rice/story.htm.

43. Shiva, 1991.

44. Shiva, 1996.

45. Richard Douthwaite, 1996.

46. Hanson, 2000.

47. Based on an example given by Giampietro and Pimentel, 1994.

48. Giampietro and Pimentel, 1994.

49. United Nations Population Division, 1996.

50. Giampietro and Pimentel, 1994.

51. Cassman et al., 1995.

52. Reichardt et al., 1996.

53. E-mail communication with Dr Gurdev Khush on 12 October 1999.

54. Ruttan, 1999.

55. Quoted by Pretty, 1999, p. 17.
56. Peng and Senadhira, 1996.
57. Andersen, 1998.
58. Personal communication with B. Courtois. 1999.
59. *The Hindu*, 30 January 1996, as quoted by Shiva, 1996.
60. Based on Anonymous, 1998a, pp. 13–14.
61. BBC *Newsnight* (television programme), 4 October 1999.
62. Nixon, 1999.
63. Interview on BBC *Newsnight*, 4 October 1999.
64. *St Louis Post*, 23 April 1999.
65. As quoted by Nixon, 1999.
66. Pretty, 1998, p. 17.
67. Martinson, 1999.
68. Shand, 1998, p. 1.
69. Martinson, 1999.
70. Philip Angel, Monsanto's director of communications, in 1999, as quoted by *St Louis Post*, 23 April 1999.
71. Finch, 2000.
72. As quoted by Vidal, 2000.
73. Vidal, 2000.
74. Anonymous, 1998b.
75. Jane Rissler of the Union of Concerned Scientists, as quoted by Andersen, 1998, p. 19.
76. Hayakawa and Hayakawa, 1990.
77. As defined on www.inrm.cgiar.org.
78. Dobermann and White, 1999.
79. As quoted by Kesbergen, 1999.
80. Personal communication with Kevin Gallagher of the FAO-based Global IPM Facility, 2000.
81. Jan Oudejans, as quoted by Kesbergen, 1999.
82. Van de Fliert et al., 1995.
83. Dinham, 1996.
84. Downloaded from www-esd.worldbank.org/html/esd/env/publicat/dnotes/dn24069a.htm.
85. Gardner, 1996.
86. Van de Fliert et al., 1995.
87. Röling, 1996.
88. Dobermann and White, 1999.
89. Dobermann and Fairhurst. 2000.
90. Manicad and Lehmann, 1997.
91. CIAT, 1999.
92. Shiva, 1993.
93. Frossard, 1995.
94. Quoted by Frossard, 1995, p. 34.
95. Dennis, 1987.
96. Brammer, 1980.
97. Source of information on Microsoft is cgi.pathfinder.com/cgi-bin/fortune/fortune500/csnap.cgi?r96=109, which quotes the 1997–98 revenues of Microsoft at $14.48 billion. CGIAR funding for 1997 was $333 million (source: www.cgiar.org/funding.htm), which is 6 to 7 per cent of the total amount of public-sector funding for agricultural research in developing countries (Collinson and Tollens, 1994).
98. Sperling et al., 1993.
99. Witcombe et al., 1996.
100. Witcombe et al., 1996 says that PPB increases biodiversity.
101. Berg, 1997.
102. Scott, 1998.
103. Personal communicatication between Vernon Ruttan and Donald Duvick, quoted in Ruttan, 1999.
104. As quoted by Giampietro and Pimentel, 1994.
105. Bentley, 1994.
106. Carr-Saunders, 1922; Wilkinson, 1973.

Chapter 8

1. Mokyr, 1990, p. 9.
2. Rogers, 1995.
3. Cooley, 1995.
4. As quoted by Cooley, 1995 p. 10.
5. Steele, 1999.
6. As quoted by Steele, 1999, p. 12.
7. As quoted in www.di-mgt.com.au/approach.html.
8. *The Economist*, 2000, p. 17.
9. Ignatius, 2000.

10. Tim O'Reilly responds to Amazon's 1-Click and Associates Program patents in his 'Ask Tim' column. Downloaded from oreilly.com/www/oreilly/press/amazon_asktim.html.
11. Berenson and Wade, 2000.
12. Egziabher, 1999.
13. Quoted by Ignatius, 2000.

References

Allard, R.W. 1988. Genetic change associated with the evolution of adaptedness in cultivated plants and their wild progenitors. *Journal of Heredity* 79, pp. 225–38.

Andales S.C. 1996. Problems and priorities of grain drying in the Philippines. In B.R. Champ, E. Highley and G.I. Johnson (eds), *Grain Drying in Asia*. ACIAR Proceedings No. 71. Australian Centre for International Agricultural Research (ACIAR), Canberra, Australia, pp. 46–53.

Andersen, P.D. 1993. En Analyse af den tehnologiske innovation i dansk vindmolleindustri. Ph.D. thesis, Copenhagen Business School.

Andersen, P.D. (ed.). 1998. *Wind power in Denmark: technology, policy and results*. Danish Energy Agency, Information Service Department, Roskilde.

Andersen, P.D. 1999. Review of historical and modern utilisation of wind power. Wind Energy and Atmospheric Physics Department, Risø National Laboratory, Denmark. Posted on www.risoe.dk/vea-wind/history.htm

Anderson, Edgar. 1967. *Plants, Life and Man*. University of California Press, Berkeley and Los Angeles.

Anderson, Luke. 1998. Genes means…, *Red Pepper*. November, pp. 18–20.

Anonymous. 1998a. Biopiracy, TRIPs and the patenting of Asia's rice bowl: a collective NGO situationer on IPRs in rice. May 1988. Downloaded from www.grain.org/publications/reports/rice.htm.

Anonymous. 1998b. Genetech preys on the rice field. *Seedling*. Downloaded from www.grain.org/publications/jun98/jun982.htm

Arlidge, J. 1999. Meltdown in the Arctic puts the heat on all of us. *Observer*, 25 July 1999, pp. 8–9.

Barr J. 1998. Paradigm shift. *Linux Gazette* 32, September. Downloaded from www.linuxgazette.com/issue32/barr.html.

Bentley, Jeffery W. 1994. Facts, fantasies, and failures of farmer participatory research. *Agriculture and Human Values*, Spring–Summer 1994, pp. 140–50.

Berenson, Alex and Nicholas Wade. 2000. Clinton–Blair statement on genome leads to big sell-off. *New York Times.* 15 March 2000. www.nytimes.com/ learning/students/pop/articles/031500sci-human-genome.html.

Berg, T. 1997. Devolution of plant breeding. In Louise Sperling and Michael Leovinsohn (eds), *Using Diversity: Enhancing and Maintaining Genetic Resources On-farm.* International Development Research Centre, Ottawa. Downloaded from www.idrc.ca/library/document/104582/berg.html.

Biggs S.D. 1989. *A Multiple Source Model of Innovation of Agricultural Research and Technology Promotion.* ODI Agricultural Administration Network Paper No. 6. Overseas Development Institute, London.

Bord na Mona. 1999a. The peatlands of Ireland. Downloaded from www.bnm.ie/ discovering_peatlands/peatlands_of_ireland10.htm.

Bord na Mona. 1999b. Wind energy. Downloaded from www.bnm.ie/exploring/ wind_energy.htm.

Brammer, H. 1980. Some innovations don't wait for experts: a report on applied research by Bangladesh farmers. *Ceres* 13:2, pp. 24–8.

British Wind Energy Association. 1999. *The Economics of Wind Energy.* Downloaded from www.bwea.com/fs2econ.htm (in August 1999).

Bulaong M.C., R.R. Paz, T.F. Anchiboy and A.C. Rodriquez. 1992. Development and pilot testing of the NAPHIRE mobile flash dryer. *Technical Bulletin No. 14.* NAPHIRE, Muñoz, Nueva Ecija, Philippines.

Carr-Saunders, Alexander. 1922. *The Population Problem,* Oxford University Press, Oxford.

Cassman, K.G., M.J. Kropff and Z.D. Yan. 1992. A conceptual framework for nitrogen management of irrigated rice in high-yield environments. Paper presented at the International Rice Research Conference, 21–25 April 1992. IRRI, Manila, Philippines

Cassman, K.G., S.K. De Datta, D.C. Olk, J. Alcantara, M. Samson, J.P. Descalsota and M. Dizon. 1995. Yield decline and the nitrogen economy of long-term experiments on continuous, irrigated rice systems in the tropics. In R. Lal and B.A. Steward (eds), *Sustainable Management of Soils.* Lewiston Publishers, CRC Press, Michigan, pp. 181–222.

Chambers, R. and J. Jiggins. 1986. Agricultural research for resource poor farmers: A parsimonious paradigm. *Discussion Paper 220,* Institute of Development Studies, University of Sussex, Falmer.

Chang, T.T. 1989. The case for large collections. In A.D.H. Brown, O.H. Frankel, D.R. Marshall and J.T. Williams (eds). *The Use of Plant Genetic Resources.* Cambridge University Press, Cambridge, pp. 123–35.

Chang, T.T. 1993. Sustaining and expanding the 'green revolution' in rice. In Harold Brookfield and Yvonne Byron (eds). *South-East Asia's environmental future: the search for sustainability.* United Nations Press, New York and Oxford University Press, Oxford. Downloaded from www.unu.edu/hq/unupbooks/ 80815e/80815E00.htm.

CIAT (Centro Internacional de Agricultura Tropica). 1999. *Annual Report April 1998–March 1999.* CGIAR Systemwide Program on Participatory Research and Gender Analysis for Technology Development and Institutional Innovation. CIAT, Cali, Colombia.

Clark N. 1995. Interactive nature of knowledge systems: some implications for the Third World. *Science and Policy* 22, pp. 249–58.

Clark N., F. Perez-Trejo and P. Allen. 1995. *Evolutionary Dynamics and Sustainable Development.* Edward Elgar, Aldershot.

Collins, G. N. 1914. Pueblo Indian maize breeding. Varieties specially adapted to regions developed by Hopis and Navajos – their work not sufficiently appreciated – probably much yet to be learned from them. *Journal of Heredity* 5, pp. 255–68.

Collinson M.P. and E. Tollens. 1994. The impact of the International Research Centers: measurement, quantification and interpretation. *Issues in Agriculture* 6, Consultative Group on International Agricultural Research (CGIAR) Secretariat, Washington, DC.

Conklin, H.C. 1957. *Hanunoo agriculture in the Philippines.* Forestry Development Paper No. 12, Food and Agriculture Organization of the United Nations, Rome.

Cooley, Mike. 1995. The myth of the moral neutrality of technology. *AI & Society* 9, pp. 10–17.

Davis, G. 1994. *A History of Money: From Ancient Times to the Present Day.* University of Wales Press, Cardiff.

Dawkins, R. 1986. *The Blind Watchmaker.* W.W. Norton, New York.

Dawkins, R. 1995. *River Out of Eden: A Darwinian View of Life.* Science Masters series. Weidenfeld & Nicolson, London.

Dennet, D.C. 1995. *Darwin's Dangerous Idea.* Simon & Schuster, New York.

Dennis, J.V. Jr. 1987. Farmer management of rice diversity in northern Thailand. Ph.D. thesis, Cornell University, Ithaca, New York.

Diamond, J. 1987. Soft sciences are often harder than hard sciences. *Discover*, August, pp. 34–9.

Diamond, J. 1997. *Guns, Germs and Steel: A Short History of Everything for the Last 13,000 Years.* Vintage, London.

Digital Producer Magazine. 1999. Microsoft renames Windows NT 5.0 product line to Windows 2000; signals evolution of Windows NT technology into mainstream. Downloaded from www.digitalproducer.com/pages/microsoft_renames_windows_nt_t.html

Dinham, Barbara. 1996. Getting off the pesticide treadmill. Our Planet 8:4. Downloaded from www.ourplanet.com/imgversn/84/dinham.html

Dobermann, A. and T. Fairhurst. 2001. *Rice: Nutrient Disorders and Nutrient Management.* International Rice Research Institute, Los Baños, Philippines, and Potash and Phosphate Institute, Georgia.

Dobermann, A. and P.F. White. 1999. Strategies for nutrient management in irrigated and rainfed lowland rice systems. *Nutrient Cycling in Agroecosystems* 53, pp. 1–18.

Douthwaite, Boru. 1999. Equipment evolution: Case studies of changes in rice postharvest technologies in the Philippines and Vietnam. Ph.D. thesis. University of Reading, Reading.

Douthwaite, Richard. 1996. *Short Circuit.* Green Books, Totnes.

Douthwaite, Richard. 1999a. *The Ecology of Money.* Schumacher Briefings 4. Green

Books, Totnes, for The Schumacher Society in association with the New Economics Foundation.

Douthwaite, Richard. 1999b. *The Growth Illusion.* New Society Publishers, Gabriola Island, British Columbia.

Douthwaite, Richard and Dan Wagman, 1999. *Barataria: A Community Exchange Network for the Third System.* Sroham, Netherlands; Rural Forum, Scotland; Enterprise Connacht–Ulster; La Kalle, Spain.

The Economist. 1992. Obviously not: intellectual property. October 3, p.90.

The Economist. 1999. Linux loot. December 18–30, p. 131.

The Economist. 2000. Who owns the knowledge economy? (Leader) April 8, p. 17.

Egziabher, Tewolde. 1999. The WTO Seattle Conference, What Happened? The Way Ahead? Downloaded from carryon.oneworld.org/panos/WTO/workshop_addis_presentation2.htm.

Fisher, Irving. 1933. *Stamp Script.* Adelphi, New York.

Florida, Richard and Martin Kenney. 1990. *The Breakthrough Illusion,* Basic Books, New York.

Frossard, D. 1995. Asia's Green Revolution and peasant distinctions between science and authority. Downloaded from lucy.ukc.uk/Postmodern/David_Frossard_1.html.

Fujisaka, S. 1993. Were farmers wrong in rejecting a recommendation? The case of nitrogen at transplanting for irrigated rice. *Agricultural Systems* 43, pp. 271–86.

Galbraith, J. 1975. *Money: Whence it Came, Where it Went.* Pelican, Harmondsworth.

Gardner, Gary. 1996. IPM and the war on pests. *World Watch* 9, pp. 20–28.

Garfinkel S. 1993. Is Stallman stalled? *Wired.* Downloaded on 15 August 1999 from irc.bu.edu/faculty/heddaya/CS103/gnu.html.

Gates, Bill. 1976. An open letter to hobbyists. 3 February. Downloaded from www.eskimo.com/~matth/hobby.html.

Giampietro, Mario and David Pimentel. 1994. The tightening conflict: population, energy use, and the ecology of agriculture. Downloaded from www.dieoff.com/page69.htm.

Gipe, Paul. 1996. *Wind Energy Comes of Age.* John Wiley, New York. p. 421.

Gipe, Paul. 2000. Overview of worldwide wind generation. Downloaded from www.chelseagreen.com/Wind/articles/Overview.htm.

Gomes, L. 1999. Upstart Linux draws interest of a Microsoft attack team. *Wall Street Journal,* 21 May.

Hanson, Jay. 2000. Energy synopsis. Downloaded from dieoff.com/synopsis.htm.

Hardin, L.S. 1994. Whence international agricultural research. *Food Policy* 19, pp. 561–7. Downloaded from www.agrisci.unibo.it/wchr/ucf/hardin.htm.

Harlan, J.R. 1976. The plants and animals that nourish man. *Scientific American* 235, pp 89–97.

Harlow, J. and S. Toyne. 1999. British are the saddest case in Europe. *Sunday Times,* 15 August.

Harrison L. and T. Møller. 1998. Patent office warning. *Windpower Monthly,* February, p. 22.

Hayakawa, S.I. and A. R. Hayakawa. 1990. *Language in Thought and Action,* 5th edn, Harcourt Brace Jovanovich.

Hien, P.H. 1996. Application of rice harvesting, drying, and milling technologies in Vietnam – a sketch of 20-year evolution. Paper presented at the Conference on Engineering in Agriculture and Food Processing, Gatton College, Toowoomba, Queensland, Australia, 24–27 November.

Holden, John, James Peacock and Trevor Williams. 1993. *Genes, crops and the environment.* Cambridge University Press, Cambridge.

Horton, Doug and Gordon Prain. 1989. Beyond FSR: new challenges for social scientists in R&D. *Quarterly Journal of International Agriculture* 28, December.

Hume, David, 1752. Of money. In *Essays, Moral, Political and Liberal,* 1758. Downloaded from socserv2.sociosi.mcmaster.ca/~econ/ugcm/3113/hume/money.txt.

Hunt, D. 1987. *Beginning with Ourselves: In Practice, Theory and Human Affairs.* OISE Press, Toronto.

IDC (International Data Corporation). 1999. IDC study reveals companies are increasing their use of the Linux operating environment. 17 August. Downloaded from www.idcresearch.com/Data/Software/contents/SW081799PR.htm.

Ignatius, David. 2000. Firestorm in cyberspace. *Washington Post.* 19 March. Downloaded from www.washingtonpost.com/wp-srv/2000–03/19/1721–031900–idx.html.

The Irish Times. 1997. Meeting seeks to reduce greenhouse gas emissions. 24 November. Downloaded from www.ireland.com/newspaper/ireland/1997/1124/.

IRRI (International Rice Research Institute). 1970. *Semi-annual Substantive Report no. 10.* January 1 to June 30. IRRI, Los Baños, Philippines.

IRRI (International Rice Research Institute). 1993. *IRRI rice almanac.* IRRI, Los Baños, Philippines.

Jackson, M. 1997. The problem of over-accumulation: examining and theorising the structural form of LETS. *International Journal of Community Currency Research* 1, p. 1. Downloaded from www.geog.le.ac.uk/ijccr/volume1/1mj.htm.

Kaimowitz D., M. Snyder and P. Engel. 1989. A conceptual framework for studying the links between agricultural research and technology transfer in developing countries. *Linkage Theme Paper no. 1.* International Service for National Agricultural Research (ISNAR), The Hague, Netherlands.

Karnøe, Peter. 1993. Approaches to innovation in modern wind energy technology: technology policies, science, engineers and craft traditions. *Center for Economic Policy Research (CEPR) Publication No. 334.* Stanford University, Stanford, CA.

Karnøe, Peter and Raghu Garud. 1998. Path creation and dependence in the Danish wind turbine field. *Papers in Organization No. 26.* Institute of Organisation and Industrial Sociology, Copenhagen Business School.

Kesbergen, Lianne. 1999. Without political support integrated pest management will fail. *Wisp'r archive* 10. Downloaded from www.gcw.nl/wispr/w991001.htm.

Kohn, A. 1987. Creativity and intrinsic interest diminish if task is done for gain. *Boston Globe,* 19 January. Downloaded from www.gnu.org/philosophy/motivation.htm.

Kolb, D.A. 1984. *Experiential Learning: Experience as the Source of Learning and Development*. Prentice-Hall, Englewood Cliffs, NJ.

Krishnasreni, S. and T. Kiatwat. 1998. Combine harvester development in Thailand. In M.A. Bell, D. Dawe and B. Douthwaite (eds), *Increasing the Impact of Engineering in Agricultural and Rural Development. Deliberations of a Think-tank.* IRRI Discussion Paper No. 30. IRRI, Los Baños, Philippines, pp. 66–78.

Kropff, M.J., K.G. Cassman, S. Peng, R.B. Matthews and T.L. Setter. 1994. Quantitative understanding yield potential. In K.G. Cassman (ed.) *Breaking the Yield Barrier*. IRRI, Los Baños, Philippines.

Landsman Community Services Ltd. 1992. Forward to Comox LETS trading records. Downloaded from www.gmlets.u-net.com/.

Landsman Community Services Ltd. 1994. LETS design: LETSystem design manual. Version 1.2, August, 1600 Embleton Cresent, Courtenay, British Columbia.

Landsman Community Services Ltd. 1997. Community way proposal for Kitsilano Community Centre. Downloaded from www.gmlets.u-net.com/go/kitsproj. html.

Layton C. with C. Harlow and C. de Hoghton. 1972. *Ten Innovations. An International Study on Technology Development and Use of Qualified Scientists and Engineers in Ten Industries.* George Allen & Unwin, London.

Lazaroff, Cat. 1999. USA: farmers sue Monsanto over biotech seeds. Environmental News Services, 15 December. www.corpwatch.org/trac/corner/worldnews/other/523.html.

Learmonth, Michael. 1997. Giving it all away. *Metro*, 8–14 May. Downloaded from lcewww.et.tudelft.nl/~haver/linux/metroarticle.html.

Leonard, D. 1995. *Wellsprings of Knowledge: Building and Sustaining the Sources of Innovation*. Harvard Business School Press, Harvard NJ.

LetsLink UK. 1999. Following the LETS reception on the House of Commons on 14th June. Downloaded from www.letslinkuk.demon.co.uk/westmn.htm

Lianchamroon, Witoon. 1992. Escape from the Green Revolution [in Thai only].

Lindvall, B. (ed.). 1994. *National Systems of Innovation: Towards a Theory of Innovation and Interactive Learning*. Pinter, London.

Linton, Michael. 1996. *LETSgo Manchester*. Downloaded from www.gmlets.u-net. com/explore/lgm.html.

Lund, G. 1999. Denmark's clean energy future from waves. *CADDET Renewable Energy Newsletter* 3/99, www.caddet-re.org/html/body_399art3.htm.

McDonald F. 1998. Go ahead for peat-fired generating station. *The Irish Times*, 28 December. Downloaded from www.ireland.com/newspaper/ireland/1998/1228/.

McHugh J. 1998. For the love of hacking. *Forbes Magazine*, 10 August.

McKie, R. 1999. Planning protests thwart the switch to green power. *Observer*, 11 July 1999, p. 16.

McWilliams, B.E. (ed.). 1991. *Climate Change: Studies on the Implications for Ireland*, Department of the Environment, Dublin.

Manalo A.S. 1973. A low-cost grain dryer. Paper presented at the Annual Convention of the Philippine Society of Agricultural Engineers. Manila, 25–26 January 1973.

Manicad, G. and V. Lehmann. 1997. CGIAR: evaluation and new directions. *Biotechnology and Development Monitor* 33, December.

Martinson, Jane. 1999. Monsanto pressured to sell off GM assets. *Guardian*, 22 October.

Merrick, T.W. 1986. World population in transition. *Population Bulletin*, 41:2.

Mokyr J. 1990. *The Lever of Riches: Technological Creativity and Economic Progress.* Oxford University Press, Oxford.

Mongkoltanatas, J. 1986. Axial-flow threshers in Thailand. In *Small Farm Equipment for Developing Countries.* IRRI, Los Baños, Philippines.

Moody, Glyn. 1997. The greatest OS that (n)ever was. *Wired*, August. Downloaded from www.wired.com/wired/5.08/linux.html

NAPHIRE (National Postharvest Institute for Research and Extension). 1990a. *NAPHIRE Postharvest Digest* 2:3. Muñoz, Nueva Ecija, Philippines.

NAPHIRE (National Postharvest Institute for Research and Extension). 1990b. *NAPHIRE Postharvest Digest* 2:6. Muñoz, Nueva Ecija, Philippines.

NAPHIRE (National Postharvest Institute for Research and Extension). 1992. *NAPHIRE News* 9:3. Muñoz, Nueva Ecija, Philippines.

NAPHIRE (National Postharvest Institute for Research and Extension). 1994. *NAPHIRE News* 11:1. Muñoz, Nueva Ecija, Philippines.

Naughton, J. 1998. Darth Vader meets his match. *Observer*, 8 November. Downloaded from molly.open.ac.uk/Personal-pages/Pubs/981108.htm.

Neary, Michael and Graham Taylor. 1998. *Money and the Human Condition.* Macmillan, London.

Nelson R.R. 1987. Understanding technical change as an evolutionary process 8. Professor Dr F. de Vries Lectures in Economics. North Holland, Amsterdam.

Netscape. 1999. Netscape Communicator open source code white paper. Downloaded from home.netscape.com/browsers/future/whitepaper.html.

Nixon, Lance. 1999. New technology would help seed companies protect research investments. Knight Ridder News Service. Downloaded from matu1.math.auckland.ac.nz/~king/Preprints/book/upd/monsanto/pages/background/patent.htm.

Ormerod, Paul. 1998. *Butterfly Economics: A New General Theory of Social and Economic Behaviour.* Faber & Faber, London.

Paddock, W. and P. Paddock. 1967. *Famine 1975! America's Decision: Who Will Survive?* Little, Brown, Boston, MA.

Patiño, O.B., M.V. Gottret, D. Pachico and C.E.L. Cardoso. 1999. Integrated cassava research and development strategy in northeast Brazil – CIAT. In L. Sechrest, M. Stewart and T. Stickle (eds), *A Synthesis of Findings Concerning CGIAR Case Studies on the Adoption of Technological Innovations.* CGIAR–TAC Secretariat, Rome.

Peng, S. and D. Senadhira. 1998. Genetic enhancement of rice fields. In N.G. Dowling, S.M. Greenfield and K.S. Fischer (eds), *Sustainability of Rice in the Global Food System.* Pacific Basin Study Center (Davis, California) and International Rice Research Institute (Manila, Philippines), pp. 99–125.

Peters T. J. and R.H. Waterman. 1982. *In Search of Excellence: Lessons from America's Best-Run Companies.* Harper & Row, New York.

Peterson, Melody. 1999. Backlash on gene-altered exports threatens US markets. *New York Times*, 30 August.

Petreley, Nicholas. 1998. The next 10 minutes. Downloaded from www.ncworldmag.com/ncw-03–1998/ncw-03–nextten.html.

Powell, Jeff and Menno Salverda. 1998. A snapshot of community currency systems in Europe and North America. CUSO Thailand, Bangkok. Downloaded from ccdev.lets/snapshot.html.

Pretty, Jules. 1998. Strange fruit. *Red Pepper*. November, pp. 17–18.

Prindle, T. 1996. Native American history of corn. Downloaded from www.nativeweb.org/NativeTech/cornhusk/cornhusk.html.

Radosevich, Lynda. 1998. Corel backs Linux, *InfoWorld Electric*, posted 12 May. Downloaded from www.idg.net/idg_frames/english/.

Raven, Gerrard. 1993. As Pound sinks, Britons turn to alternative currencies. *Wall Street Journal*, February. Downloaded from www.letslinkuk.demon.co.uk/needtoknow/wall-st.htm.

Raymond, E.S. 1997. The cathedral and the bazaar. Downloaded from www.openresouces.com/documents/cathedral-bazaar/index.htm on 15 August 1999.

Reichard, W., A. Dobermann and T. George. 1996. Intensification of rice production systems: opportunites and limits. In K.S. Fischer (ed.), *Caring for the Biodiversity of Tropical Rice Ecosystems*, IRRI, Los Baños, Philippines. Downloaded from thecity.sfsu.edu/~sustain/chap3.html.

Renewable Energy World. 1999. Denmark restructures renewables support system. May.

Rhoades, R.E. and R.H. Booth. 1982. Farmer-back-to-farmer: A model for generating acceptable agricultural technology. *Agricultural Administration* 11, pp. 127–37.

Richards, P. 1993. Culture and community values in the selection and maintenance of African rice. Paper presented at the conference on Intellectual Property Rights and Indigenous Knowledge, Granlibakken, Lake Tahoe, 5–10 October 1993.

Rockefeller Foundation. 1999. *The Rockefeller Foundation – A History*. Downloaded from rockfound.org/rocktext/t_history/t_1940.html.

Rogers, E.M. 1995. *Diffusion of Innovations*. 3rd edition (rev. edn of *Communication of Innovations*). The Free Press, New York.

Röling, N. 1996. Towards an interactive agricultural science. *Journal of Agricultural Education and Extension* 4, pp. 35–48. Downloaded from www.agralin.nl/ejae/v2n4–5.html.

Rosenberg, N. 1982. *Inside the Black Box: Technology and Economics*. Cambridge University Press, Cambridge.

Rural Forum. 1997. Alternative economic systems report. Downloaded from www.socsystem.org.uk/aesreport/section_9_capital_barter.htm.

Ruthenberg, H. 1985. *Innovation Policy for Small Farmers in the Tropics*, ed. H.E. Jahnke. Clarendon Press, Oxford.

Ruttan, V.W. 1999. Biotechnology and agriculture: a sceptical perspective. *AgBioForum* 2:1. Downloaded from www.agbioforum.missouri.edu/agbioforum/vol2no1/ruttan.html.

Scott, James C. 1998. *Seeing Like a State: How Certain Schemes to Improve the Human Condition Have Failed.* Yale University Press, New Haven and London.

Seron, Sidonie. 1995. LETS. Downloaded from www.gmlets.u-net.com/resources/sidonie/home.html.

Seyfang, Gill. 1994. LETS: political economy and social capital. M.Sc. thesis. Leeds Metropolitan University. Available from www.cerise.org.uk.

Shand, Hope. 1998. Teminator seeds: Monsanto moves to tighten its grip on global agriculture. *Multinational Monitor*, November. Downloaded from www.thirdworldtraveler.com/Transnational-corps/TerminSeeds_Monsanto2.htm.

Shiva, Vandana. 1991. The violence of the Green Revolution: ecological degradation and political conflict in Punjab. *Ecologist* 21:2, pp. 57–60.

Shiva, Vandana. 1993. *Monocultures of the Mind: Perspectives on Biodiversity and Biotechnology.* Zed Books, London.

Shiva, Vandana. 1996. The seeds of our future. *Development Journal* 4. Downloaded from www.waw.be/sid/dev1996/shiva.html.

Software Magazine. 1998. In LINUX we... September. Downloaded from www.softwaremag.com/Sept98/sm098cv.htm.

Sperling, L. 1998. CGIAR programme promotes farmer–scientist collaboration in breeding. *Geneflow* special feature. Downloaded from www.cgiar.org/ipgri/pa/gene98/special/spec7.html

Sperling L., M.E. Loevinshohn and B. Natbormvra. 1993. Rethinking the farmers role in plantbreeding: local bean experts and on-station selection in Rwanda, *Experimental Agriculture* 29, pp. 509–19.

Spurgeon, B. 1999. Windmills are on a roll: operating costs are down while energy capacity is up. *International Herald Tribune*. 24 June.

Steele, Jonathan. 1999. The bear and the honey pot. *Guardian Weekly*, 23–29 December, p. 12.

Taylor, R. 1999. Server software: smooth operator. *Financial Times*, 13 August. Downloaded from www.ft.com/hippocampus/q137a6e.htm.

Torvalds, Linus. 1992. Linux history. Downloaded from www.li.org/li/linuxhistory.shtml.

Torvalds, Linus. 1998. Linus Torvalds on Microsoft – excerpts from an interview. Downloaded from www.tamos.net/ieee/linus.html

Tranæs, Flemming. 1997. Danish Wind Energy Co-operatives, Part 1. Downloaded June 1999 from www.windpower.dk/articles/coop1.htm.

Trident. 1999. Windows NT 4.0 history and features. Downloaded from www.flix.com/-trident/winnt/features.htm

Tripp, Robert and Wieneke van der Heide. 1996. The erosion of crop genetic diversity: challenges, strategies and uncertainties. *Overseas Development Institute (ODI) Natural Resources Perspectives*. Series editor John Farrington. Downloaded from www.oneworld.org/odi/odi_erosion.html.

UNDP (United Nations Development Program) in the Philippines and UPDAE (University of the Philippines at Los Baños Department of Agricultural Engineering). 1970. *A Rice Dryer for the Farm*. Training of technicians for grain industries SF PHI 70/534. UNDP, Manila, Philippines.

United Nations Population Division. 1996. *World Population Prospects 1950–2050 (The 1996 Revision)*. United Nations, New York.

Valloppillil, V. 1998. 'Halloween Memorandum' 11 August. Downloaded from www.opensource.org/halloween/halloween1.html

van Bueren, L., E.T., M. Hulscher, J. Jongerden, M. Haring, J. Hoogendoorn, J.D. van Mansvelt, G.T.P. Ruivenkamp. 1998. *Sustainable Organic Plant Breeding.* Louis Bolk Institute. Downloaded from www.anth.org/ifgene/breedap4.htm.

van de Fliert, E., J. Pontius and N. Röling. 1995. Searching for strategies to replicate a successful extension approach: training of IPM trainers in Indonesia. *Journal of Agricultural Education and Extension.* 1:4. Downloaded from www.bib.wau.nl/ejae/v1n4–3.html.

von Hippel, Eric. 1988. *The Sources of Innovation.* Oxford University Press, New York and Oxford.

Wilkinson R.G. 1973. *Poverty and Progress.* Methuen, London.

Weinberg, Gerald P. 1971. *The Psychology of Computer Programming.* Van Nostrand Reinhold, New York.

Windkraft Journal. 2000. Sonderausgabe – Jobs in der windenergie.

Witcombe, J.R., Arun Josi, K.D. Josi and B.R. Sthapit. 1996. Farmer participatory crop improvement I: Varietal selection and breeding methods and their impact on biodiversity. *Experimental Agriculture* 32:4, pp. 427–44.

Yacub, E. 1999. Comox Valley community currency project. Report 1 to 10 July 1999. Downloaded from www.ratical.org/communityway/ComoxValley/071099.html.

Index